Ballet

Ballet

An Illustrated History

MARY CLARKE
AND CLEMENT CRISP

HAMISH HAMILTON

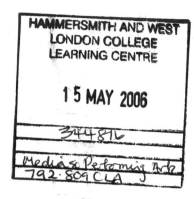
For Roland John Wiley,

with affection and admiration

HAMISH HAMILTON LTD

Published by the Penguin Group
Penguin Books Ltd, 27 Wrights Lane, London W8 5TZ, England
Penguin Books USA Inc., 375 Hudson Street, New York, New York 10014, USA
Penguin Books Australia Ltd, Ringwood, Victoria, Australia
Penguin Books Canada Ltd, 10 Alcorn Avenue, Toronto, Ontario, Canada M4V 3B2
Penguin Books (NZ) Ltd, 182–190 Wairau Road, Auckland 10, New Zealand

Penguin Books Ltd, Registered Offices: Harmondsworth, Middlesex, England

First published by A & C Black 1973
This revised edition first published in Great Britain by Hamish Hamilton Ltd 1992
1 3 5 7 9 10 8 6 4 2

Filmset in $11\frac{1}{2}$/$13\frac{1}{2}$pt Lasercomp Bembo
Printed in Great Britain by
Butler & Tanner Ltd, Frome and London

A CIP catalogue record for this book is available from the British Library

ISBN 0–241–13068–9

Frontispiece: Antoinette Sibley and Anthony Dowell in Frederick Ashton's *Daphnis and Chloe,* one of the happiest ballets of their famous partnership. They inherited the roles created for Margot Fonteyn and Michael Somes.

Contents

List of Illustrations

Illustration Acknowledgements

A large number of the photographs used in this book are owned by the authors who have now given them to the *Dancing Times*, and they are therefore credited to the magazine's collection unless they can be properly attributed to individual photographers. Every effort has been made to trace the owners of copyright and apologies and thanks are offered to those who have proved untraceable because there was no imprint on the back of the photograph.

We wish to thank: Leslie E. Spatt for the frontispiece and photographs 153, 154, 156, 160, 268; Kuntsthistorisches Museum, Vienna, for 1; the Royal Academy of Dancing for 2, 4, 7, 23, 24, 26, 27, 29, 30, 34, 38, 41, 44, 48, 52, 81, 91, 104, 105, 115, 120, 122, 129, 172; the British Museum for 3, 5, 32, 33; Bibliothèque Nationale, Paris, for 8, 17; Graphische Sammlung Albertina for 11; H. Roger Viollet for 16; Victoria & Albert Museum for 18, 19, 25, 36, 37, 40, 51, 53, 111, 130, 131, 132, 134; the *Dancing Times* for 20–22, 28, 31, 35, 39, 42, 43, 47, 49, 50, 54, 56, 58–62, 65, 66–80, 82–90, 92, 93, 96–103, 106, 108, 109, 110, 112, 113, 114, 117–19, 121–8, 135–8, 144, 145, 151, 161, 162, 164, 169, 171, 175, 179, 184, 187–93, 215–17, 223–37, 246, 251, 252, 264, 266; Ivor Guest for 45, 46, 55, 57, 64; the Joffrey Ballet for 95; *The Times* for 107; Roger Wood for 139, 148, 163, 170, 220, 259, 261; Donald Southern for 140; Zoë Dominic for 141, 143; Houston Rogers Ltd for 142, 158, 239, 241; Anthony Crickmay for 146, 147, 149, 152, 155, 165, 167, 173, 174, 176, 180, 182, 214, 239, 276, 285; Roy Round for 150; Reg Wilson for 157; Alastair Muir for 159, 263, 281; Rambert Dance Company for 166, 168; Bill Cooper for 181; London Contemporary Dance Trust for 185, 186; the Cunningham Foundation for 194, 195, 196; the Paul Taylor Company for 198, 199; Klaus Lefebre for 202; New York City Ballet for 204–7, 210, 213; American Ballet Theatre for 203; Fred Fehl for 208, 209, 211, 212, 218, 274; Andrew Cockrill for 222; Janet P. Levitt for 244, 249, 250; Axel Zeininger for 247; Lavolé, Paris, for 248; Rodolphe Torette, Paris, for 254, 256; Holger Badekow, Hamburg, for 267, 270; Mydtskov, Copenhagen, for 272, 273, 275; Nederlands Dans Theater for 278, 279.

Preface to the Revised Edition

'The history of ballet is but a fragment of the history of dancing.' The statement was made by Arnold Haskell in his *Ballet*, which was published by Penguin Books in 1938, sold more than a million copies, and helped to fire a vast new audience that came to love and understand ballet. It is an axiom on which this book is based.

We have sketched the historical background that led dancing-masters to codify the technique of classical ballet, the *danse d'école*, but we must also warn readers and students that the early years, before the publication of Carlo Blasis's *Code of Terpsichore*, really belong to a history of dancing, a mammoth task (as we know from experience) which is periodically attempted, but rarely with success. The study of early dance forms is a fascinating but highly specialized matter, and must be combined with a study of music of the same period. We would advise students of dance history to venture into the sixteenth, seventeenth and eighteenth centuries only if they are able to work with specialists, which we do not claim to be.

We have illustrated our text with pictures that help to tell the story, and since the text tells mostly of ballet-masters and choreographers, we have allowed ourselves some fairly lengthy captions on dancers and personalities who have contributed to the history of ballet.

In the vexed question of spelling Russian names we have followed the most rational transliteration, accepting some modern versions which have become usual since this book was first published in 1973. In updating the text we have tried to include material which seems to us to have cast significant new light since our first edition. Many illustrious people helped us in that first project; our debt to them remains, as to writers whose subsequent volumes have lightened and enlivened our task. As in the first edition, the length of chapters has been dictated by studies already in existence. Where a number are available, we have attempted to provide a text which draws on many sources. Where one or two books have thoroughly covered the ground – Kathrine Sorley Walker's and Jack Anderson's exhaustive studies on the post-Diaghilev Ballets Russes are a case in point – we can confidently refer readers to these volumes. For illustrations, we are grateful to the Royal Academy of Dancing in London for allowing us to draw upon a superb collection. The picture library of the *Dancing Times* yielded many treasures. Roger Wood gave us *carte blanche* to use his photographs (the negatives are now in the collection of the Library of the Performing Arts at the Lincoln Center, New York), and Anthony Crickmay, Fred Fehl, Zoë Dominic, Brenda Rogers (on behalf of her late husband, Houston Rogers), Martha Swope, Janet P. Levitt and Andrew Cockrill were most generous. To all the photographers, our thanks. And thanks, too, to Roderick Gibb for undertaking the formidable task of preparing the Index.

NOTE: At the time this text was written, Leningrad was still Leningrad and the Soviet Union still existed. We have not changed the names as they relate to the period described. In 1991, Leningrad became St Petersburg again and its great opera house reverted to the name of Mariinsky instead of Kirov.

Introduction

What a pleasure it is to have the beautiful *Ballet: An Illustrated History* revised
and brought up to date, so that a new generation can learn and enjoy from
it.

Originally published in 1973, its co-authors, Mary Clarke and Clement
Crisp, are two of our most esteemed ballet historians and critics and have
been deeply involved with the ballet world, watching, talking and writing
about it for an amazing fifty years! They have seen its development, first-
hand, since the mid-1940s.

We must feel grateful to them for having devoted so much of their lives to
informing the public, spreading the word and making people more aware and
knowledgeable about our art. This inevitably contributes to ballet's increasing
popularity and brings with it an ever-growing audience. Their writing is
eloquent and perceptive and they are able to penetrate to the heart of a
portrayal or ballet, enabling the reader to appreciate and understand more
fully the essence and meaning behind a work.

I found this book stimulating and authoritative – compelling reading – but
it doesn't achieve this by words alone. It is unusual in a history book, but
totally appropriate since ballet is a visual art, to find such a profusion of rare
illustrations and photographs. It is wonderful to see the dancers literally
dancing their way across the pages and an added bonus to have the amusing
and informative captions.

We can see history unfolding, before our eyes, taking us on a journey from
the fifteenth-century courts of Europe to the present day. We start in the

courts of the Renaissance with only the nobles taking part in the dance. We then see Catherine de'Medici bring extravagant spectacles to the French Court and then move on to Louis XIV, the Sun King, who loved to dance and whose reign saw professionals dancing in a theatre for the first time. We come to the Romantic Era, with the emergence and domination of the ballerina, and observe how the popularity of ballet shifts from one capital of Europe to another – with the arrival and departure of the choreographers and artists. Even after the demise of the Romantic Era, Bournonville remains strong in Copenhagen. We then arrive in St Petersburg, where we find three great Frenchmen working with the Imperial Russian Ballet, the greatest, of course, being Marius Petipa, whose masterpieces have become our classics.

Then to the glories of Pavlova and the Diaghilev period, who not only revived interest in ballet in Europe, but whose illustrious achievements have reverberated into my own time. Most of the important influences on my career came from people who were very much part of this period or were directly influenced by it. Diaghilev and Pavlova acted like a whirling planet, exploding and sending off sparks that ignited and inspired a whole new era of ballet in our time – not only in Europe but in the United States, South Africa, Australia, Canada, South America, indeed throughout the whole world.

Reading this history, we learn of the incredible survival of ballet through wars and revolutions, kept alive by the great teachers, choreographers and dancers passing on their heritage. In this great tradition, this book will help ensure that we never allow 'a forgetful generation' (as Arnold Haskell said) to ignore the fascinating and inspiring history of ballet.

This is the ideal book to keep on one's bedside table, to dip into and peruse. I was utterly engrossed and know that young children, ballet students, professionals and ballet devotees alike will feel as I do about it.

Antoinette Sibley
February 1992

1 How It All Began

The story of ballet as we know it today really begins in the next chapter when professional dancing-masters and professional dancers, working inside theatres, codified and perfected the classical style known as the *danse d'école*. But before we embark on our five positions, let alone reach the 90° turn-out of the feet or the rise onto the tips of the toes, we need to know a little about the dance entertainments of earlier years.

The seed of ballet is to be found in Italy, the Italy of the high Renaissance. There, in an age of richness, rivalry and the rediscovery of the arts of the ancient world, there was a great flowering of creative activity that has never been surpassed. Emerging from the restrictions of the Middle Ages and freed from the complete domination of the Church, men were intoxicated with a desire for knowledge and a wish to emulate the achievements of their ancestors who had established the supremacy of Rome and whose culture owed much to the earlier civilization of Greece.

Their endeavours were helped by the political structure of Italy at that time. The country was divided into a number of small states ruled over by powerful princes. These princes were wealthy and they sought to demonstrate their might by, among other things, the magnificence of their courts. The Medici, Sforza and d'Este families all wanted to have the finest buildings, the most beautiful paintings and the most lavish entertainments. They may at times have used their artists to help them to further their ulterior motives, but the political aspect should not be over-stressed. They adored the arts – and they had the artists. All civilized nations are proud of

1. The Emperor Maximilian I with the torchbearers in a court entertainment staged in Vienna at the beginning of the sixteenth century. The men, in costumes more elaborate than those of the women, are wearing gold-mesh masks. The musicians follow them round the dance-floor.

artistic achievement. The early spectacles in Italy and then in France were of course used to impress, but even today it is not unusual for state visits to include a gala performance of ballet if the country has a ballet company of which it is proud. (Visits to the Bolshoy Theatre in Moscow and to the Royal Opera House, Covent Garden, are almost obligatory on such occasions.)

It is known that Lorenzo de'Medici, who during his reign in Florence established that city as 'the mother of arts and the cultural capital of Italy', staged great 'triumphs' or pageants, both out of doors (the climate encouraged this) and in the palaces. Dancing played an important part because every man and woman of the nobility was a practised dancer in the simple measures of the day. They incorporated dancing, with verse and song, into their entertainments simply because they loved to dance. The greatest artists were employed to design the elaborate floats or chariots used in these displays. The floats resembled those seen nowadays in the London Lord Mayor's Show or in the St Patrick's Day Parade in New York; the difference lay in their beauty. Lorenzo employed the architect Brunelleschi, designer of the great dome of Florence Cathedral; Lodovico Sforza called in none other than Leonardo da Vinci.

Dancing-masters were publishing books by the early 1400s. The earliest known, which was produced before the invention of printing, is that by Domenico of Piacenza. The manuscript, now in the National Library of Paris, is entitled *De arte saltandi et choreas ducendi* ('On the Art of Dancing and Conducting Dances'), and in it Domenico describes not only the basic elements of dancing but also some dances he himself had arranged. In the history of dance his book is important in that for the first time a distinction is made between a *danza* and a *ballo*. This is not a question of mime or different technique, but a musical difference. A *danza* had a uniform rhythm throughout; a *ballo* had varied rhythms, of which there were four principal ones. By this time the courtiers were dancing to, as well as for, each other and dance historians point out that the *danse à deux* was by then so completely taken for granted that it was not even described.

From the works of Domenico's disciples, such as Guglielmo Ebreo of Pesaro (known as William the Jew) and Antonio Cornazano (endearingly described as a nobleman who 'could turn his hand to devotional works or obscene proverbs with equal facility'), researchers have been able to reconstruct the dances of the time and many of these early books have been re-published in recent years in paperback form, easily available to all students. They are concerned, of course, with dancing as a social grace and they give much guidance about polite behaviour. They are also illustrated with quaint and delightful drawings – but dance teachers are not necessarily good draughtsmen. For an idea of dancing, dress and deportment in the fifteenth and sixteenth centuries it is safer to study the works of the great painters: Botticelli's graceful ladies, for instance, and his angels dancing in a heavenly circle above the crib in the London National Gallery's 'Nativity'.

When the Italians of the fifteenth century staged indoor entertainments these sometimes took the form of 'dinner ballets'. They were long and lavish, for during the feasting there would be danced interludes called 'entries', often so closely linked with the banquet that the mythological characters would represent the dishes being served – Neptune and his minions to bring on the fish; Hebe, the nectar; Pomona, the fruit. The French words for these 'entries' have survived in their (and our) menus to this day. An *entrée* is the dish served between courses; *entremets*, a side dish, has come to mean sweetmeats served at the end of a meal.

France was soon to discover the splendours of the Italian Renaissance and the 'dinner ballets', and both these and its greater glories were to be copied in other courts throughout Europe. Travel, if not as rapid as today, was widespread, and travellers' tales have always been exciting.

The Italians had led the way through their dance spectacles and they also led the way in the theatre, where plays and entertainments of music and dancing took place on an elevated stage framed in a proscenium arch. Such theatres date back to 1580, and by 1594 the famous Teatro Olympico had been built in Vicenza. In the early theatres, and in the French and other court theatres of the next two centuries, the division between stage and auditorium was not so pronounced as it later became. Today we have returned to more open stages but with one very significant difference: the early ballets were performed by the courtiers because they loved dancing,

2. (Left) A figure from Cesare Negri's dance manual *Nuove Inventioni di Balli*, published in 1604, which shows a gentleman practising kicks (towards the bell-rope) for a galliard.

3. (Right) A scene from *La Liberazione di Tirrenio*, a ballet danced in Florence in 1616. This engraving by Jacques Callot shows the choreographic patterns of the period; the audience surrounds the dancers, who have come down from the platform stage and are advancing towards 'the presence'. Soft lighting by candles adds to the beauty of the scene. Other dancers were lowered from the flies in 'machines' which could be clouds, chariots or any other caprice of the designer's fancy.

but they were also performed to 'the presence', the honoured guest and the royal host. The dancers, actors and singers could move from the broad parterre to the centre of the auditorium or hall and sometimes the spectators themselves would take part. It is wrong to think that all these early court ballets were watched from above. On the contrary, the principal guests

4. A courtier and his lady pictured in Marco Fabritio Caroso's *Il Ballarino*, published in Venice in 1581. Men were far less encumbered by costume than women and were therefore able to perform more intricate steps. Despite the complexity of female dress, though, women did perform sprightly dances. Queen Elizabeth I was fond of La Volta in which there were a number of positively daring lifts, which doubtless delighted her courtiers.

5. Court social dancing: a royal marriage dance in 1612 in Germany. An illustration from *Electio et coronatio* by Jan Theodor de Bry (1561–1623), showing the 'torch dance' at the wedding of Elizabeth, daughter of James I of England, to Frederick V, Elector Palatine of the Rhine and later King of Bohemia.

usually sat facing the stage on about the same level and if galleries were built they were occupied by the less important people. The dancing might form patterns but mostly it was viewed 'head-on' – at least by the people who mattered.

Before we leave Italy, which was to lose supremacy temporarily to France although it played a vital role in ballet history until the end of the nineteenth century, we must mention two more important early textbooks. They were *Il Ballarino* by Fabritio Caroso (published in 1581) and Cesare Negri's *Nuove Inventioni di Balli* (1604). These record further advances in technique and the more complicated use of rhythms, but they are still concerned with courtly dancing. Negri, who had staged elaborate masquerades in Milan and was a favourite of the future Henri III of France, trained a number of pupils and it is estimated that about forty of them were scattered throughout the courts of Europe.

An interesting footnote to Negri's royal connections and the widespread interest in court productions throughout Europe is to be found in a copy of his book, now in the Richardson Collection of the Royal Academy of Dancing in London: it bears the arms of the Holy Roman Emperor and has a dedication to Philip III of Spain. Philip III, said to have devoted his life to court festivities, was the first cousin of Rudolf, who was Holy Roman Emperor when the book was published.

CATHERINE DE'MEDICI AND THE BALLET DE COUR

Court ballet probably arrived in France at the end of the fifteenth century but was given its biggest impetus by an Italian, Catherine de'Medici (1519–1589), great-granddaughter of Lorenzo the Magnificent and daughter of Lorenzo, Duke of Urbino. From both she inherited a love of pageantry and she was aware of how lavish entertainments could be subtly adapted for useful purposes, such as cementing an agreement or a dynastic marriage. She came from Italy to marry the Duc d'Orléans and when Francis I died in 1547 she found herself Queen of France. Catherine was a remarkable woman; she was looked on as a 'foreigner' and a 'banker's daughter' and, like Elizabeth I of England, she needed all her wits to maintain her position. Her husband died in 1559 (after a particularly nasty accident – he was pierced through the eye during a tourney) and for the next thirty years Catherine effectively ruled France as each of her three sons in turn became King. She made use of the court ballets and similar festivities to distract her sons from some affairs of state. It would be wrong, again, to give too much political importance to the entertainments, but they were lavish enough, and continued to be so over the next hundred years, to give France supremacy in this field.

6. (Above) A contemporary painting of the festivities that accompanied *Le Ballet Comique de la Reine Louise* of 1581, which marked the marriage of the Duc de Joyeuse – a favourite of the King, Henri III – to the Queen's sister. The painting suggests the importance of the dignified carriage and deportment which were part of every courtier's education; the posture of the Duc, however, is somewhat exaggerated in its sway.

7. (Right) Frontispiece to the description of *Le Ballet Comique de la Reine Louise*, published to commemorate this most celebrated *ballet de cour* in 1581. The scene shows the opening of the entertainment: a court gentleman hurries to approach the royal party (seen with their backs to us), to whom the performance was dedicated. On either side of the gentleman are two structures, one a cloud in which musicians are hidden, the other a sylvan glade for Pan. At the back of the hall is the enchantress Circe's domain, in which part of the action took place. Down either side of the hall are galleries from which the courtiers could view the five-and-a-half-hour performance.

Catherine staged a great ball in 1558 when her eldest son, Francis II, was married to Mary, Queen of Scots. Similar celebrations marked the marriages of her other sons who became, in turn, Charles IX and Henri III (the patron of Negri). Not only in Paris but in the great châteaux of the Loire and in

royal palaces throughout France court balls were held at which Catherine herself sometimes danced.

The first important court ballet in France was *Le Ballet des Polonais* ('The Polish Ballet'), given in the palace of the Tuileries on 19 August 1573. Catherine was celebrating the election of her son Henry as King of Poland and wished properly to impress the visiting Polish ambassadors. In the great hall of the palace a temporary stage was erected with steps leading down to the ballroom floor. The spectators occupied three sides and at the end of the formal entertainment they took part in 'general dancing'. The production was supervised by Balthasar de Beaujoyeulx, an Italian dancing-master in Catherine's employ and the real founder of the *ballet de cour* in France. The music, 'played by thirty viols', was by the Italian-trained Flemish composer, Orlando di Lasso, and the words of the songs, glorifying the King and especially Catherine, were by the court poet, Pierre Ronsard. A pattern of music, song and dance was thus set which was to reach its greatest achievements during the reign of Louis XIV.

BALTHASAR DE BEAUJOYEULX

Catherine's ballet-master was born Baldassarino di Belgiojoso in Italy and arrived in France in 1555, where his name was changed to the form in which it has come down to us. As well as being a gifted arranger of dances he was a skilled violinist, and it was in that capacity he first found favour at court. He made his name – and entered every history of ballet – with his staging of the famous *Ballet Comique de la Reine Louise* in the Salle Bourbon of the Louvre on 15 October 1581. The production was commissioned by Catherine de Medici to celebrate the marriage of Marguerite de Lorraine, sister of the reigning Queen Louise, wife of Henri III, to the Duc de Joyeuse. No expense was spared on this most brilliant of the several entertainments given on that occasion. The production cost a fortune to stage, and was watched by a huge assembly of guests. Starting at ten at night and lasting five and a half hours, it was acknowledged by its participants and by the audience as a performance of exceptional significance and splendour. It hymned the monarch's power; it attributed to the monarchy especial grace, and in its artistic achievements it proclaimed both the magnificence and the culture of the court that performed and watched it. Its significance was held to be so considerable that a lavishly illustrated description of the performance was printed and circulated to various European courts. Illustrations from this book are well known, and a facsimile of the original edition was published in Turin in 1962.

Beaujoyeulx was well pleased with his production. In his introduction to the book he described ballet as 'a geometric combination of several persons

8. Entry of the herald and drummers from *Les Fées des Forêts de Saint Germain*, a *ballet de cour* staged at the palace of the Louvre in Paris in February 1625. Among the performers were the King, Louis XIII (who appeared as a Spanish dancer, a guitar-player and a brave warrior in various *entrées*), and twenty others from among the noblest gentlemen. The ballet was fantastic, containing various grotesque and bizarre *entrées* – much to the taste of the time – and also involved professional performers who appeared as the drummers in the illustration. Their costumes – hats like drums, false wooden legs – convey much of the vitality of this celebrated court ballet. The design was by Daniel Rabel, and the ballet is known to have cost a considerable sum to stage.

9. A gentleman of the court of Louis XIV at a time when the King was still an active dancer and his courtiers emulated him. The position of feet and hands indicates the existence of a precise technique.

dancing together', a definition which, because of the word 'geometric', gives a slightly false impression of the patterns made on the ground by the dancers' movements. The *Ballet Comique* was still directed to 'the presence'. The dancers were still noblemen and women – the parts of the naiads who featured in the action were performed by Queen Louise and ladies of her court, including the bride – although in these early 'dinner ballets' and court ballets professional tumblers were used for grotesque or comic interludes, since it would not have been fitting for people of noble birth to appear in these roles. Louis XIII of France liked to dance in vulgar *entrées*, but he was a man of curious tastes.

THE ENGLISH COURT

Court ballet in France became somewhat debased during the reigns of Henry IV and Louis XIII, but in England dancing flourished from about 1530, when the first mention of the galliard is found in English. Henry VIII was fond of music and dancing, and his daughter, Elizabeth I, was an enthusiastic

10. (Left) Mademoiselle de Subligny (1666–?1746) first danced on stage in 1690, and was famous for her noble style. She succeeded Mademoiselle Lafontaine, the first 'ballerina', and appeared in London performing a gigue. The complexity of her costume indicates that women were still physically weighed down by their dress.

11. (Right) An engraving showing *Le Triomphe de l'Amour* of 1681, the first publicly performed ballet in which professional female dancers took part. It was a ballet of twenty *entrées* with music by Lully and costumes by Bérain. Both Pecour and Beauchamp were in the cast as well as Mademoiselle Lafontaine, who led the first group of women. Her companions were Mesdemoiselles Roland, Lepeintre and Fanon.

dancer. There are many references at this time to 'the dancing English'. Dances are often referred to in contemporary writings, notably in the plays of Shakespeare.

The English court entertainments differed from the French in that the most important role was that of the poet or playwright. They reached their finest

12. Louis XIV as the Sun in *Le Ballet de la Nuit* (a *ballet de cour* in four parts, with forty-three *entrées*). It was first performed at the Salle du Petit Bourbon in Paris on 23 February 1653. The King had first appeared in a ballet two years previously, but this is probably the first time he had danced the role of the Sun, from which he gained his title 'Le Roi Soleil'. His interest in dancing and his skill were to have a profound influence on the expansion of court ballet during his reign. His appearances had a political significance, conveying the King's supremacy.

form as the court masques performed during the reign of James I and his pleasure-loving queen, Anne of Denmark. Court patronage was lavished on these spectacles, the best of which were written by Shakespeare's friend Ben Jonson. (Shakespeare himself included a masque in *The Tempest*.) Starting with *The Masque of Blackness* (1605), Jonson wrote no fewer than thirty-seven masques for the English court and twelve of them were designed by the great architect Inigo Jones. The designs survive in the library of the Duke of Devonshire at Chatsworth House.

Jonson's masques were a combination of speech, dance and song, but the literary content was so good that dancing was relegated to a subordinate position. Milton's *Comus*, with music by Henry Lawes, was produced for Lord Bridgwater's family in 1634, and the last of the masques came in 1640 when, at the palace of Whitehall, *The Fount Salmacis* was produced for Charles I. But Charles, who was one of the few English monarchs to patronize the arts, was on the verge of his quarrel with Parliament. With the Civil War, his execution and the Puritan regime of Oliver Cromwell, the masque died, for the theatres were obliged to close. England had to wait three hundred years before she had a national ballet.

13. *Les Noces de Pelée et de Thétis* was an Italian play with music, containing ten ballet *entrées*, which was given in the Salle du Petit Bourbon in the Louvre in April 1654, with the young Louis XIV among its performers. It was noteworthy for the magnificence of its decorations by the Italian technician and designer, Giacomo Torelli. In the second act a scene was devoted to military sports: as we see from the commemorative engraving above, the magnificent Italian stage design, with its insistence upon perspective, probably included the painted figures watching from the stands surrounding the dance area in which the real dancer-warriors are seen in combat.

LOUIS XIV AND HIS TEAM OF ARTISTS

During the infancy of Louis XIV of France, when his mother Anne of Austria ruled as regent, opera had already made its way from Italy to the French court and pushed ballet slightly out of favour – thus establishing a love–hate relationship between the two arts which persists to this day. Throughout the seventeenth and eighteenth centuries they were linked together, but once they went their separate ways fashion and taste have tended to favour either the ballet or the opera.

Louis, however, loved dancing and was an accomplished practitioner. He

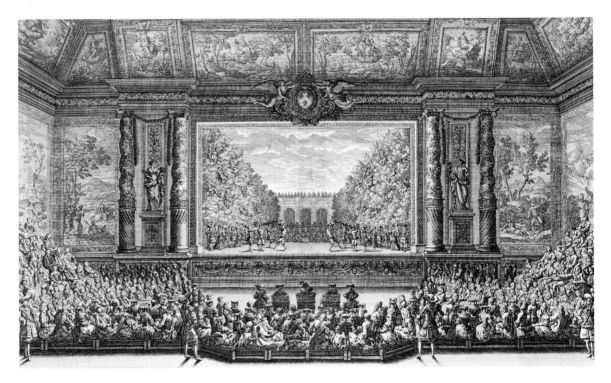

14. (Above) *Les Fêtes de l'Amour et de Bacchus* with music by Lully and dances by Beauchamp (and some of the text by Molière) was first seen in the park at Versailles in 1668. The design by the Italian decorator Vigarani made use again of the fascination of perspective: in the branching trees which line the stage, musicians are seated. Facing the stage are the monarch himself and members of the court – their relative importance indicated by the type of chairs on which they are placed.

15. (Right) In 1662 a 'horse ballet' – *Le Grand Carrousel* – was given to celebrate the birth of Louis XIV's first son, the Dauphin. The King, his brother and three other great noblemen led the *entrées* of squadrons of horsemen, the steeds as gorgeously caparisoned as their riders. The illustration shows the grooms and attendants for the Indian quadrille. Costumes were designed by Henri de Gissey.

appeared in his first court ballet at the age of twelve, in 1651, and by 1653 was dancing his favourite role, that of the Sun in *Le Ballet de la Nuit* at the Salle du Petit Bourbon in the Louvre. It was a part from which he gained his famous title, *Le Roi Soleil*, and which he was to play in real life when he assumed the role of absolute monarch. Mazarin, his First Minister, was anxious in 1653 to establish the supremacy of Louis and the monarchy, and one of the ways in which he did it was by showing the young man in public performances in roles of the utmost splendour.

Having acquired a taste for dancing, Louis continued to appear in allegorical parts for several more years. He was becoming the greatest monarch in Europe; he also happened to be the finest of noble dancers, the greatest aristocrat. His interest and influence ensured that during his reign, even when he had ceased to appear in public (at a fairly early age, when 'growing portly'), dancing was held in high regard. Moreover, he engaged some remarkable artists to take charge of the court productions.

Chief among them was the Italian musician Jean-Baptiste Lully, or Lulli (1632–1687), who had come to the French court as a young man to work for a cousin of the King, Louise d'Orléans, *La Grande Mademoiselle*. He soon became a favourite of the King and wielded extraordinary power at court until the end of his life. He profoundly influenced the development of both opera and ballet, working with the finest collaborators. Lully's ballet-master was Pierre Beauchamp (1636–1705), who was in charge of court ballets by

the 1660s and is credited (by Pierre Rameau in his book *The Dancing Master*, Paris, 1725) with the invention of the five positions of the feet. He also arranged the dances in the so-called *comédie-ballets* created for the court by the great dramatist Molière, of which the first, *Les Fâcheux* ('The Bores') was produced in 1661. Greatest of these collaborations was probably *Le Bourgeois Gentilhomme* (1670), in which Lully played the role of the Mufti.

The plots of the court ballets were usually adapted from classical legend and comprised a series of 'entries' in which the mingling of speech (usually verse), music and dance produced a work that combined elements of drama, opera and ballet. A formula had been found that satisfied the court audience. When Louis XIV stopped dancing, opera-ballets in this form moved from court to theatre. Lully's importance resides in the fact that he had established a formula that would soon have to call upon professional performers. It was to last for many years after his death, being carried on in the opera-ballets created by Jean-Philippe Rameau (1683–1764).

The year 1661 is prominent in ballet history as the date of the founding by Louis XIV of the Académie Royale de Danse, when thirteen dancing-masters were appointed to 're-establish the art in its perfection'. Their concern was with polite and courtly dancing rather than with the theatre. The Académie survived until the eve of the French Revolution but its importance to theatre dance is minimal, since its members concerned themselves only with social dance.

In 1669 Louis initiated the foundation of the Académie d'Opéra for the performance of opera in French (with dance, of course, as its essential partner). Three years later Lully gained control of this organization, which the King agreed to re-name the Académie Royale de Musique and which in time was to become the Paris Opéra. Lully's works dominated the repertory, and a shortage of professional dancers now needed to perform in what was a professional theatre led to the recruiting of new dancers from the classes of teachers in Paris (the nobility and gentry naturally finding it unacceptable to appear in a theatre with professional singers). Female roles were taken by young boys *en travesti*. Under Pierre Beauchamp's direction, the standard of

---

16. The *Ballet de la Délivrance de Renaud* was staged at the Louvre in 1617. Its purpose, politically speaking, was to indicate to his court that the young King Louis XIII was determined to stand upon his own authority and be rid of the constraints imposed by his mother and his ministers. In the first *entrée* the King appeared as a fire demon (No. 1); his favourite, Monsieur de Luynes, was the hero, Renaud (No. 2); the Chevalier de Vendôme was a water demon (No. 3); Monsieur de Monpoullan was a spirit of the air. The identity of each character was clear from the costume: fire was suggested by the fabric, cut out like flames; water by the bullrush decoration; air by the wings and feathers in the hat; Renaud's noble status by an elaboration of court dress.

dancing was improved and more dancers were recruited for the *corps de ballet* of the Académie.

Thus 1672 becomes a most significant date for ballet. In effect, King Louis was accepting the real need for professional dancers, allowing them to perform noble dances as well as character parts. In 1681 the first 'ballerinas', women who were to make dancing their career, took the stage in performances by the Académie. They still had the example of the nobility from which to learn. They were dancing parts 'above their station', but they danced them correctly. They were also starting to codify technique. It was the beginning of the end of the old regime of noble amateurs, which was finally extinguished by the Revolution. We see the beginning of ballet as we know it today.

2 The Age of Reason and Technique

When that royal balletomane Louis XIV died in 1715 after seventy-two years as King of France, a great change had already overtaken ballet, altering it from a court entertainment in which the young (and slim) Louis had delighted to appear to an art that was now completely part of the theatre of its day.

It was also – and this is sad – already showing signs of having lost its originality. But as so often happens when an art begins to be set in its ways, there are people who react against the established artistic forms; they think along different lines, and in the ballet of the eighteenth century these innovators (Weaver in England; Noverre in France and Germany; Marie Sallé in England and France; Hilferding and Angiolini in Vienna) sought new ways of using dance, of making it more expressive, of widening its horizons. At the same time ballet was extending its technical range, steps were becoming more difficult, and a technique was evolving which shaped the future development of ballet. Thus throughout the century there is a parallel and inter-reacting activity between ballet itself and dancing that was largely centred on France, although Italy remained a vital force, notably in extending technical expertise.

THE PARIS OPÉRA

Jean-Baptiste Lully had ruled the opera-ballet world in Paris until his death in 1687. When he died, Pierre Beauchamp decided to retire as first ballet-

17. Claude Balon. So privileged was he that he could greet the king by shaking his hand.

master, to be succeeded by Louis Pecour (*c.* 1655–1729), and there flourished such famous dancers as Blondi, a nephew and pupil of Beauchamp, and Claude Balon, who was famous for his lightness. But they were outshone by Louis Dupré (1697–1774), who was known as *Le Grand Dupré* and was the first dancer to win the nickname 'The God of the Dance'. Casanova's memoirs contain a touching picture of him: 'I can still see this fine figure, advancing with measured steps, and having reached the footlights slowly raising his rounded arms, moving them gracefully, stretching them, moving his feet lightly and precisely, taking small steps, *battements* on the calf, a pirouette, and then disappearing like a zephyr. All this had lasted half a minute.'

As the dancers became more proficient, so ballet – reflecting the growing powers of its interpreters – found an increasingly important place in the opera house; a hybrid entertainment, the opera-ballet, evolved which soon gave equal place to dancing and singing. The opera-ballet comprised a series of *entrées*. One of the earliest and most famous of these was *L'Europe Galante* of 1697 with music by Campra, which started with a prologue called *Les Forges de l'Amour* and continued with four 'entries': France, Spain, Italy and Turkey. The loose structure of this type of production allowed 'entries' to be altered, added to and amended at will, and opera-ballet became a thoroughly frivolous entertainment – so much so that on some evenings a programme was shown under the title *Fragments*, which contained the most popular excerpts from several works. The opera-ballet retained its popularity for many years, and it reached a high point of magnificence in *Les Indes Galantes* of 1735, with a superb score by Jean-Philippe Rameau; this was a work so notable that in 1952 the Paris Opéra revived a version of it, although, of course, only the original music had survived.

The design of these opera-ballets was always opulent and many of the finest artists of the time were called upon to create costumes and settings. The most famous of the early designers was Jean Bérain (1638–1711) and he was succeeded by Claude Gillot. Costumes followed the style of contemporary court dress, beautiful but cumbersome (hence there were no opportunities for steps of elevation from women dancers), and the symbolism of a character was indicated by decoration on the costume: Spring might be dressed in green, scattered with flowers; a wind would be covered in feathers and wear a hat shaped like a windmill. It was Gillot who later stylized costumes and introduced panniers for female dancers, and for men the classical Roman costume with the *tonnelet*, a form of scalloped skirt that came just above the knee.

The increased importance of dancing in the opera-ballet implied an advance in both technique and training. In 1713 a new, fully professional school of dance was established at the Paris Opéra. Steps had by this time already assumed a recognized form and style, and names that we know today in the classroom were current even then: *entrechat, cabriole, coupé, chassé*. Although male dancers dominated the scene (not least because their clothes permitted a greater freedom of movement), the first female stars were to make their names at this time.

THE BIRTH OF THE BALLERINA

Ladies of the court had appeared in *ballets de cour* during the reigns of Louis XIII and Louis XIV, just as their predecessors had joined in the court dances that led to the birth of the *ballet de cour*. On certain occasions professional female dancers might make an appearance in a court ballet, but when professional male dancers arrived it was considered unsuitable for high-born ladies to appear with them. For a time female roles were taken by men *en travesti*; then in 1681 professional female dancers made their theatrical appearance, when four women, led by Mademoiselle Lafontaine, took the stage in Lully's *Le Triomphe de l'Amour*. The successor to this first 'ballerina'

18. Marie-Anne de Cupis de Camargo (1710–1770), after Lancret.

was Mademoiselle Subligny (1666–1736), and she in turn was succeeded by Françoise Prévost (1680–1741), who excelled in that gay dance the *passepied*. Françoise Prévost also took part, with Claude Balon, in a version of part of Act IV of Corneille's play *Les Horaces* at the Duchesse du Maine's château at Sceaux in 1715 – a significant occasion in that the action was mimed to music. In this we see the germs of the *ballet d'action* (a ballet that tells its story through linked dance and gesture), which was to be so important as the century progressed.

Mademoiselle Prévost, though, is remembered more for her two most celebrated pupils: Marie-Anne de Cupis de Camargo (1710–1770) and Marie Sallé (1707–1756). La Camargo was a brilliant dancer, too brilliant indeed for Françoise Prévost, who did her best to keep the dazzling young artist

19. Marie Sallé (1707–1756), after Lancret.

in the ranks of the *corps de ballet*; but one evening in 1730 a male soloist forgot to appear for a variation and Camargo immediately danced it in his place, so triumphantly that Prévost soon felt impelled to retire. Camargo's style, said Jean-Georges Noverre, was 'quick and active. She only danced to lively music, and such quick movements do not lend themselves to a display of grace, but instead she substituted ease, brilliance and gaiety.' It was her dazzling footwork that led to one of the first real reforms in costume for the ballerina. Camargo had mastered the *entrechat quatre*, and in order to show off her twinkling feet she shortened her skirts from floor-length to something a discreet inch or two above the ankle – thus realizing an earlier opinion expressed by Campra, composer of *L'Europe Galante*, that the only way to make opera-ballet more popular was to lengthen the dances and shorten the *danseuses'* skirts!

No greater contrast could be imagined than Marie Sallé: comparing her with Camargo, Noverre said, 'Mademoiselle Sallé replaced the tinsel with as much finesse as lightness; it was not by leaps and frolics that she went to your heart.' Sallé's way to her audience's heart was by dancing more expressively than any previous ballerina. She had trained first with her uncle, a famous mime, and these early dramatic studies made her intolerant of the formal, repetitious work of the opera-ballets in Paris. She left the Opéra on two occasions for London, the second time fleeing to escape imprisonment, the punishment that awaited any artist who broke a contract with the Opéra.

It was in London in 1734, at the Covent Garden theatre then being run as an opera house by G. F. Handel, that Sallé staged and danced in a ballet that has been famous ever since: *Pygmalion*. In it she introduced reforms far more important than Camargo's shortened skirt. Wearing simple draperies instead of the traditional panniers, her hair loosely dressed instead of piled high on her head, she created an expressive mime-ballet about the sculptor who models a perfect female statue, to which the gods grant life. *Pygmalion* was sensationally successful, and its triumph was repeated in another of Sallé's works, *Bacchus and Ariadne*. On her return to the Paris Opéra she appeared in *Les Indes Galantes*, and although she could not introduce her ideas about the dramatic possibilities of pantomime-ballet, she is generally considered to have made her dances more expressive than the original choreography suggested.

JOHN WEAVER (1673–1760)

It was in London too, some years before Sallé's arrival, that an English dancing-master was to invent a style of entertainment that was a notable forerunner of the *ballet d'action*. John Weaver was born in Shrewsbury, but it was at Drury Lane Theatre in 1717 that he staged *The Loves of Mars and Venus*, which told its story through music, mime and dance without speech, singing or declamation. In this, and in his *Orpheus and Eurydice* (1718), *Perseus and Andromeda* (1726) and *The Judgement of Paris* (1732), Weaver evolved a form of *ballet d'action* in which the dancers expressed in mime gestures the emotions that were the mainspring of the action. He said of an early piece, *The Tavern Bilkers*, that it was 'the first entertainment in which the tale was carried forward with movement rather than words'.

Not content with these innovations, Weaver taught, wrote books on dancing, and translated an important French textbook on the art. It is a tragedy for ballet in England that there were no later ballet-masters to carry on and extend his innovations. It was on the Continent that ballet-masters

20. An engraving from the famous English dance manual, Kellom Tomlinson's *The Art of Dancing*, published in London in 1735. The picture shows the minuet, and the two dancers' movements are explained by the notation set out at their feet. This notation was adapted by a French ballet-master, Raoul Feuillet (*c*.1675–*c*.1730), from a system devised by Pierre Beauchamp. It was published in his *Chorégraphie* in 1700. Ballet-masters have tried to make systems of notation almost from the beginnings of ballet. Feuillet's is one of the most famous of the early systems and can still be deciphered today. Whether Tomlinson's readers, as distinct from his fellow dancing-masters, could make much sense of it is open to question, but *The Art of Dancing* said: 'The Manner of Performing the Steps is made easy by a New and Familiar Method.'

were to come to many of the same conclusions as Weaver, and put them into practice.

THE BALLET D'ACTION

The mimed version of *Les Horaces* in 1715, Weaver's pantomimes, Sallé's *Pygmalion*, all contained a basic idea about the relationship of movement to drama that was to flower during the latter part of the eighteenth century. In Paris a French dancer, Jean François de Hesse (or Deshayes), made use of the lively dramatic mime traditions of the Italian *commedia dell'arte* to help him in staging dramas which were described as genuine tragedy pantomimes, while in Vienna Franz Hilferding (1710–1768) mounted versions in mime of Racine's *Britannicus*, Voltaire's *Azire* and other classic tragedies. Hilferding's pupil Gasparo Angiolini (1731–1803) took charge of the Vienna ballet when his master went to Russia to teach (Angiolini himself later worked long and influentially in Russia) and there collaborated with Gluck, a composer who was as concerned with extending the expressive range of opera as Angiolini and Hilferding were with ballet. All this activity indicated that thinking men were now occupied with a more serious view of ballet than that represented by the opera-ballet, and one man in particular, by his writings and his choreography, crystallizes for us the whole movement towards the *ballet d'action*.

This was Jean-Georges Noverre (1727–1810). If Noverre did not invent the *ballet d'action* (and this was, as we have seen, a spontaneous creation in various ballet centres), his *Letters on Dancing and Ballet*, published in 1760, are the most powerful and celebrated illustrations of the new serious approach to ballet as an art which was capable of great depth.

Born of a Swiss father and a French mother, Noverre had been a pupil of Dupré (although his father had intended him to be a soldier), and as a young dancer he had gone to Berlin, where he is said to have made Frederick the Great laugh by impersonating the leading ballerinas of the day. From there he embarked on a career that was to take him through the French provinces: he staged ballets in Marseille and Lyon, and then in Paris where he hoped, perhaps through the influence of Madame de Pompadour, mistress of Louis XV and a great patroness of the arts, to be appointed *maître de ballet* to the Opéra. But even La Pompadour's influence could not win him this position, and he had to content himself with joining the secondary opera house, the Opéra Comique.

Here in 1754 he gained his first great success with the *Ballet Chinois*, a lavish and opulent staging which echoed the then fashionable interest in Chinese decoration. Noverre wanted to create a ballet that suggested something authentically Chinese in its dancing and design, and by the novelty as well as the richness of the staging he evidently succeeded. Paris flocked to see the work, in whose finale 'thirty-two vases rose up and hid thirty-two dancers so that the stage seemed transformed into a china cabinet'. In the following year the great English actor-manager David Garrick invited Noverre to stage the *Chinese Ballet* at Drury Lane.

Alas, by November 1755 England and France were on the brink of war; audiences in London hated the idea of French ballet. Despite the presence of King George III at the first performance, and Garrick's protestations that Noverre was Swiss (which he was) and that forty of the sixty dancers were English, the audience – rather more prone to rioting than audiences today – at the fifth and sixth performances rioted, tore up the benches, broke looking-glasses and chandeliers in the theatre, tried to destroy the scenery, and threw dried peas and iron nails onto the stage to make life difficult for the dancers. They then set out to attack Garrick's private house, and as one witness of the troubles wrote, 'finally for the preservation of the inhabitants of London the ballet was withdrawn'. It had received six performances. Despite all this excitement, Noverre and Garrick became fast friends and very perceptively Garrick called Noverre 'the Shakespeare of the Dance'.

In 1757 Noverre was back in Lyon, where he wrote and later published his *Letters on Dancing and Ballet* (1760), in which he set out his theories on all the aspects of his art. In brief, he advanced the idea that ballet should be a dramatic spectacle – a play without words – in which action was developed through

21. Jean-Georges Noverre (1727–1810).

22. 'La Barbarina'. Barbara Campanini (1721–1799), known as 'La Barbarina', had a technique so dazzling that she quickly outshone Camargo when she arrived in Paris from her native Italy. She was adored by the public, and numbered Frederick the Great, King of Prussia, among her conquests. He admired her 'boyish' legs.

an expressive dance where virtuosity merely for the sake of display had no place. The dance would be made more dramatic by working in harmony with the music, and movement should be natural and clearly appropriate to the theme. He discussed the relationship of dance to music, advocating scores 'written to fit each phrase and thought', and he urged a greater use of ensemble dances rather than solos and variations that concentrated upon one or two principal dancers, to give variety to the ballet. He also insisted that ballet should study the other arts, notably painting, and observe and draw upon natural forms of movement so that 'all of these elements should be combined with poetry and imagination'.

These ideas, which seem entirely right and even obvious to us, were to have a profound influence upon later choreographers. They suggested for the first time that the choreographer was to be the chief architect and influence upon ballet, an idea we understand today as basic to our ballet but which was not to be accepted and put into practice for many years after Noverre.

In 1760, the year that he published his *Letters*, Noverre moved to Stuttgart

23. Costume for a shepherd, attributed to P. Lior. The elegant design, from ostrich-feathered hat to the wide-spreading *tonnelet*, was conventional dress for a male dancer in the noble style. The *tonnelet* was a survival from the undergarments worn by men in armour, and at this time reached its most extravagant form; it was almost the width of the outstretched arms of the dancer.

to become ballet-master to the Grand Duke of Württemberg, a great lover of the theatre. In Stuttgart Noverre had a beautiful theatre, ample funds with which to extend the company, and distinguished associates as composers and designers, and during the next seven years he created ballets that were widely acclaimed. In his company were dancers who were to be much influenced by his theories, notably Jean Dauberval (later the choreographer of *La Fille mal gardée*), while the great Gaëtan Vestris came as guest artist each year, appearing in such celebrated ballets by Noverre as *Medée et Jason*.

After seven years in Stuttgart Noverre moved on to Vienna, where he laboured to create a fine company. During his time there he was involved in a literary quarrel with another choreographer, Gasparo Angiolini. The latter believed that Noverre's *Letters* plagiarized ideas about the dramatic power of ballet and the *ballet d'action* that had been first formulated by Franz Hilferding, who had been ballet-master in Vienna for many years and was Angiolini's master and teacher. Eventually Noverre left Vienna for Paris, where his former pupil, the Austrian Archduchess Marie Antoinette, was now Queen of France, and through her influence he was given the post he had so long desired and

24. Madeleine Guimard (1743–1816) visiting the sick. A succession of wealthy lovers allowed La Guimard to indulge such fantasies as having private theatres in two of her residences and in employing the best architects and furnishers to build and enhance her little palace in the Chaussée d'Antin in Paris, for which Fragonard provided some of the decoration. But she was a woman of great grace of spirit (when not plotting against Noverre as director of the Opéra) and parish priests in the poorer parts of Paris knew of her generosity to the poor. This contemporary engraving shows her distributing food and money to the needy: she once received 6,000 crowns from a lover and immediately gave it to the deserving poor. Loss of her fortune after the Revolution of 1789 did not dim her wit or her charm: she settled into happy domesticity, married to the dancer and writer Jean-Étienne Despréaux.

---

which Madame de Pompadour had been unable to gain for him. In 1776 he was nominated *maître de ballet* at the Opéra.

The post had just been relinquished by Gaëtan Vestris, and his assistants, Maximilien Gardel and Jean Dauberval, had assumed that the post would fall to one or other of them, as was the rule. The imposition of Noverre, an outsider, caused intense anger. Noverre's sojourn at the Opéra was

25. Gaëtan Vestris as the Prince in *Ninette à la Cour* (1781). This engraving admirably illustrates the nobility and distinction of style that made him the supreme male dancer of his time: 'Le Dieu de la Danse'.

clouded by the enmity of Gardel, Dauberval and the leading ballerina, Madeleine Guimard (whom he admired and who danced with great success in his works). Despite his successes at the Opéra Noverre was forced to resign in 1781 and retired to his house at Saint-Germain-en-Laye, just outside Paris. From there he went to London to stage ballets. With the outbreak of the French Revolution in 1789 he lost his money and his state pension, and his later years were spent in retirement at Saint-Germain, revising and editing his writings, watching ballet at the Opéra and looking after his garden. He died in October 1810. His writings afford a telling summary of his life's ambitions: 'Dancers must speak and express their thoughts through the medium of gestures and facial expression; all their movements, their every action, their repose even, must have a meaning and be eloquent.' 'Poetry, painting and dancing are, or should be, no more than a faithful likeness of beautiful Nature.'

26. Engraving after a watercolour sketch by Carmontelle showing Marie Allard (the mother of Auguste Vestris) and Jean Dauberval in the duet of the Scythians from the opera-ballet *Sylvie*, first produced at the Paris Opéra in 1766. The two characters are describing their mutual affection.

THE GOD OF THE DANCE:
GAËTAN VESTRIS (1729–1808) AND HIS FAMILY

Any account of dancing in the eighteenth century must accord a place to a man whose conceit and vanity (he declared that his century had produced only three great men: Frederick the Great of Prussia, Voltaire and himself) were rivalled by his genius for dancing – a gift that earned him the only half-mocking title *Le Dieu de la Danse*. Noble in manner, light, precise, Gaëtan Vestris was Italian, born into a family of dancers and singers. Like many theatrical families of the time, this brood wandered through Europe, eventually arriving in Paris, where Gaëtan studied with Dupré and entered the Opéra's ballet troupe in 1749. His superb style and technique – he excelled in jumps and the newly developed pirouette – soon earned him recognition as the leading dancer in Europe in the 'noble style' which still reflected the dignity and grace associated with the aristocratic performers of the court ballet. A contemporary wrote: 'When Vestris appeared at the Opéra one really believed that it was Apollo who had come down to earth to give lessons in grace. He perfected the art of dancing, gave more freedom to the positions already known, and created new ones.'

Proud, quarrelsome and insufferably vain, Vestris was imprisoned for trying to provoke a duel and was expelled from the Opéra; his career was a series of triumphant appearances in the theatres of Europe and a sequence of liaisons with female dancers, by one of whom, Marie Allard, he had a son, Auguste, born in 1760. He also had a son by the German ballerina Anne Heinel, a beautiful, very tall woman credited with perfecting the pirouette for female dancers. She and Vestris had been rivals for years, but eventually in 1782 they retired together in the greatest amicability and married in 1792, a year after their son Apollon was born.

It was, however, Auguste Vestris who was destined to become his father's

Mademoiselle Heinel the celebrated Opera Dancer

27. (Left) Anne Heinel (1753–1808) was a German dancer who made her début in Stuttgart during Noverre's time there. She was a celebrated technician.

28. (Right) Auguste Vestris, caricatured in the year his father was illustrated as the Prince in *Ninette à la Cour*. The vitality and exuberant technique of the young Vestris is mockingly conveyed, while the couplet below the picture suggests the eagerness for money and the arrogance of the youthful virtuoso. The phrase 'Oh qui Goose-toe' under his feet reminds us of his Italian father's pronunciation of 'Augusto'.

successor. He made his stage début at the age of twelve in 1772, and his father's teaching ensured that by the age of twenty-one he would achieve the rank of *premier danseur* at the Paris Opéra. Of slighter build than his father, he was destined to the *demi-caractère* style at a time when physique and temperament dictated a dancer's employment and theatrical identity. (A fact sometimes true today: the tall, elegant *danseur* is still an ideal for princely and cavalier roles in the classic repertory.) Auguste benefited immensely from his father's teaching, and extended the range and vocabulary of his dance style to notable effect. He danced at the Opéra for thirty-five years, retiring in 1816 to take on the task of teaching the best pupils in the ballet school. Thus he passed on the great traditions of the *danse noble* of the eighteenth century – traditions that he and his father had done so much to enhance and advance – to a new generation that numbered in its ranks such vital figures of nineteenth-century ballet as Jules Perrot, August

He Danc'd like a Monkey, his Pockets well cram'd,
Caper'd off with a Grin, Kiss my A—— & be D——d.

Bournonville, Fanny Elssler and the Petipa brothers. Auguste Vestris, a crucial figure in the shaping of nineteenth-century dance style, made his last appearance on stage in 1835 at the age of seventy-five, partnering Marie Taglioni, that divinity of the Romantic age, in a minuet. On this extraordinary occasion the audience could see the very spirit of eighteenth-century dance partnering the incarnation of the new Romantic image of the ballerina. Born in the year that Noverre's *Letters on Dancing* was published, Auguste Vestris died in 1842, the year after *Giselle* was first staged.

BETWEEN CLASSICAL AND ROMANTIC: VIGANÒ; DAUBERVAL; DIDELOT; GARDEL; BLASIS

These five choreographers form a bridge between the world of Auguste Vestris and that of Marie Taglioni, between the classical heroes of eighteenth-century ballet and the mystery and imagination of the Romantic age. Salvatore Viganò (1769–1821) was born in Naples and became interested in Noverre's theories on ballet, which were passed on to him by his friend Jean Dauberval (1742–1806), a pupil and disciple of Noverre. Dauberval, remembered today especially as the first choreographer of *La Fille mal gardée*, which he staged in Bordeaux in 1789, believed in the power of

29. (Left) Madeleine Guimard, Jean Dauberval and Marie Allard in a *pas de trois* at the Paris Opéra in 1779. Guimard was one of the stars of the Opéra, despite the fact that she was too thin for contemporary tastes, and off-stage was noted for the extravagance of her life-style which was paid for by a series of wealthy protectors. Although Noverre admired her as a dancer, she became a bitter opponent of his appointment as ballet-master to the Paris Opéra. Marie Allard, the mother of Auguste Vestris, retired three years after this engraving was made because she had become very fat.

30. (Above) The burial of Salvatore Viganò in Milan in August 1821. Viganò was greatly honoured in Milan – commemorative medals had been struck to celebrate the creation of some of his ballets – and this print suggests the depth of public feeling at his passing.

---

pantomime and gesture which 'explains with rapidity the movements of the soul; it is a universal language, common to all times, and better than words it expresses extreme sorrow and extreme joy... I do not want just to please the eyes, I must interest the heart.' In his choreography Dauberval put these ideals into practice, with notable success in *La Fille mal gardée*, and in a celebrated *pas de deux* in *Sylvie* in which a nymph and a faun mimed

31. Salvatore Viganò and his wife Maria Medina, whom he met in Spain. Their extensive tours throughout Europe earned them great renown; clothes, sweets, cigars and hairstyles were named after them. This engraving by Gottfried Schadow shows the great advance that was made in stage costumes at the turn of the nineteenth century. It reflects, of course, social dress – notably in the gauzy draperies that were to become fashionable for women in the early 1800s.

an amorous intrigue while dancing. At a time when the French court could play at shepherds and shepherdesses amid the artificialities of Versailles, Dauberval's ballets suggested the dance possibilities of ordinary people and, on the eve of the French Revolution, implied a further break with the sterile manner of eighteenth-century ballet.

Viganò was born into a dancing family: his father was a ballet-master, his mother – a sister of the composer Luigi Boccherini, who gave young Salvatore music lessons – a ballerina. Viganò danced in Italy, Spain (where he met and married the dancer Maria Medina, and first knew Dauberval), and Vienna, where he created a ballet, *The Creatures of Prometheus* (1801), for which Beethoven provided the score. In his earliest ballets Viganò stressed the use of mimed action on a basis of danced steps, and in his first ballet based on Shakespeare, *Coriolanus*, a contemporary account speaks of 'dance ... so explicit that the audience could follow it without a libretto'. In later ballets – *The Titans, Otello, La Vestale, Gli Strelizzi* – he elaborated his theories of clearly expressive gesture still further, and his grandiose mime-dramas were a final display of neo-classical formulae before the

32. Thomas Rowlandson's cartoon shows Didelot dancing with Madame Théodore in the ballet *Amphion and Thalia* at the Pantheon Theatre, London, in 1791. The drawing records a celebrated incident in London when the rivalry of two theatrical managers was complicated by the burning down of their respective theatres; the subject provided a theme for a delightful work by Dame Ninette de Valois for the Sadler's Wells Ballet in 1940, which took its title from the caption for this cartoon, *The Prospect Before Us*.

onslaught of Romanticism (which he foreshadowed) swept the old ballet away.

Charles-Louis Didelot (1767–1837) was a pupil of Dauberval, Noverre and Auguste Vestris. In 1796 he created a sensation in London with his staging of *Flore et Zéphire*, in which the use of stage machinery allowed the dancers to fly and made the air the domain of the dancer. Didelot's greatest influence, though, was in Russia, where he worked from 1801 to 1811, and from 1816 to 1830. He set about amplifying and improving the training of pupils at the Imperial Ballet School in St Petersburg, developed a notably fine ballet troupe, and created many ballets that explored the possibilities of mimetic dancing, laying the foundations for Russian ballet's later excellence.

When Noverre was finally forced to leave the Paris Opéra in 1781, he was

33. A cartoon by Woodward mocking the concern of the House of Lords at the pernicious moral influence of the French dancers in London in 1798. Lord Salisbury, the Lord Chamberlain, and the Bishop of Durham are suitably shocked: the Bishop opined in the House that the French government had sent the dancers expressly to 'taint and undermine the morals of our ingenuous youth'.

succeeded by Maximilien Gardel (1747–1787) and by Jean Dauberval. Gardel was soon to disembarrass himself of Dauberval, who left to work in Bordeaux, and installed his brother Pierre as his assistant. Maximilien Gardel's ballet stagings bore the influence of Noverre's theories in the form of ballet pantomimes, often inspired by the comic operas of the time. But an injury sustained while dancing turned gangrenous, and Maximilien died. He was succeeded as chief ballet-master by his brother Pierre, whose reign at the Opéra lasted for over thirty years. Through periods of Revolution, Republic, Napoleonic Empire and Bourbon Restoration, Gardel remained at his post. He believed in the absolute supremacy of the Opéra's style of dancing, and in his creations for the troupe he produced a repertory which included such

34. Pierre Gardel (1758–1840) was appointed chief ballet-master at the Paris Opéra on the death of his brother Maximilien in 1787. He remained a vital influence as choreographer and as guardian of dance style until the 1820s. He is seen here in a pose which reveals his elegance in the 'noble style' of which he was a notable exponent.

lasting successes as *Télémaque*, *Psyché* and *The Judgement of Paris*, starring his wife, the ballerina Marie Miller Gardel, with Auguste Vestris in many roles. Pierre Gardel has been reproached for failing to invite many outside choreographers to work at the Opéra during the long years of his reign, but it could be argued that he felt that his own works were the best means of maintaining those artistic and technical standards which he believed were the hallmark of Opéra style. He was as concerned with standards of instruction in the Opéra's school as he was with the level of performance in the company at a time when brilliant dancers abounded. Certain other choreographers – Louis-Jacques Milon, Louis Henry, Louis Duport (though more celebrated as a dancer) – contributed to the repertory, but Gardel's was the dominant, and conservative, influence. It was not until 1820, when Jean Aumer (1774–1833) was invited to become choreographer, that fresh choreographic impulses were felt. Aumer was a pupil and disciple of Dauberval, and his ballets – notably *Alfred le Grand*, *La Somnambule* and *Manon Lescaut* – were deservedly popular and served as portents of changes that were to come with the flowering of Romanticism.

Carlo Blasis (1797–1878) is celebrated as one of the great theorists and codifiers of dance technique. Born in Naples, he lived much of his early life in France, working in Bordeaux with Dauberval (where he must have come in contact with Noverre's theories and with Dauberval's practice of them),

35. James D'Egville (born in London *c.* 1770) and Monsieur A. J. J. Deshayes. D'Egville was choreographer at the King's Theatre, Haymarket, from 1799 to 1809, and again in 1826 and 1827. He was also famous as a teacher. Deshayes's career stretched from the 1790s to the years when he collaborated with Perrot in the first London staging of *Giselle* in 1842.

36. A scene from Jean Aumer's ballet *Cleopatra in Tarso*, staged at the Teatro alla Scala in Milan in 1822. The design is by the great master of neo-classical decoration, Alessandro Sanquirico (1777–1849), and it conveys the grandiose scale of Milanese theatre design of the period.

37. Ciceri's design for the second act of Jean Aumer's *Alfred le Grand* at the Paris Opéra in 1822. Based on the story of the Saxon King Alfred the Great, it was – as Ivor Guest points out in his masterly *Romantic Ballet in Paris* – 'the last ballet produced at the Opéra for more than a hundred years in which the principal character was a male hero played by a male dancer'. Serge Lifar restored the male dancer as star when he became *premier danseur* and choreographer at the Opéra in 1930.

and in Paris with Pierre Gardel. By 1817 he was back in his native Italy, dancing with Viganò at La Scala, Milan, and in 1820 he wrote his first technical primer, *The Elementary Treatise*. In London, as dancer and choreographer at the King's Theatre between 1826 and 1830, he wrote *The Code of Terpsichore*, invaluable both as a manual for dancers and as a guide to dance technique of the time.

The good sense and clarity of Blasis's writings are as important today as when he set pen to paper, and he put them into practice as a teacher in 1837 when, following an injury that curtailed his dancing career, he became head of the ballet school at La Scala. Soon, the excellence of the instruction to be

38. A page from Carlo Blasis's first book, *The Elementary Treatise,* published in 1820. We see here Blasis's adaptation of the *attitude* of the Renaissance statue of Mercury by Giovanni da Bologna.

had there attracted dancers from all over Italy, and from further afield. Blasis's teachings produced dozens of virtuoso dancers; his system of training, developed by his pupils Borri and Lepri, continued this output of superbly accomplished performers, and their pupils in turn (notably Enrico Cecchetti and that galaxy of ballerinas who dazzled Russia in the later years of the century, headed by Pierina Legnani) helped to shape the future of ballet world-wide.

Blasis was a man of wide knowledge and talents. His father had given him a liberal artistic education, and throughout his life he demonstrated a multiplicity of talents. He could compose music as well as dances; he was a keen student of sculpture, of anatomy and geometry; he was a poet, and author of works on music, on singing and on politics. One of his contemporaries called him a universal genius. It is singularly fortunate, then, that he should have devoted himself primarily to teaching and thinking about dancing – he even invented that position we call an *attitude*, inspired by Giovanni da Bologna's statue of Mercury. Blasis gave a stronger technique to the dancers of the nineteenth century,

39. Émilie Bigottini (1784–1858) in *Le Ballet du Carnaval de Venise.* She entered the Paris Opéra in 1801. Napoleon admired her and had a present of books sent to her; she replied that she would rather be loved with money than with books. She did in fact marry a millionaire in 1816 and retired in 1823. The costume she wears here is for a Folly.

a technique which was to be seen from Italy to Russia and was to influence the rebirth of ballet in the West. Ballet would have been incalculably poorer without his work.

 # 3 The Romantic Movement

By the end of the eighteenth century the political, social and artistic world of Europe was undergoing the extreme stresses and changes that were to alter the way of life and thought of the next generation. The French Revolution and the Napoleonic wars, the spread of the Industrial Revolution, the blossoming of intellectual ideas that had been sown during the latter part of the eighteenth century, all brought profound changes to life and art. In ballet we have seen how the innovators of the time – Noverre, Viganò, Dauberval, Blasis – were, in a sense, preparing the way for a new form of dance.

In all the arts there was a reaction against the cold, formal classical manner: feeling and sensibility seemed more important than reason; art became subjective rather than objective, and what the creator felt, his emotional reactions to the world around him, provided the new inspiration. In music, the portrayal of nature in Beethoven's Pastoral Symphony led on to the richer dramatic content of Weber, to the music of Chopin and Mendelssohn, the operas of Meyerbeer. The publication of Lamartine's *Les Contemplations* in 1820 brought a new voice into poetry; by 1819 Géricault had exhibited his great canvas of *The Raft of the 'Medusa'*, an emotionally stirring painting of the survivors of a drama at sea. In France, the fervour of artistic experiment led painters, musicians and writers to seek fresh inspiration, a freer and more expressive style, as they turned to the poetry of Germany, the plays of Shakespeare, the novels of Walter Scott. The paintings of Delacroix, Berlioz's Symphonie Fantastique, and the plays and poetry of Victor Hugo were central to the new

40. The *Pas de Quatre*. Marie Taglioni stands surrounded by Fanny Cerrito, Carlotta Grisi and Lucile Grahn.

movement. Ballet, no less than the other arts, felt this great gust of change, and from 1830 onwards, during twenty years of the high Romantic movement, dancing became enormously popular and reflected the new feelings and the new themes.

A picture can sometimes evoke a whole age for us. A pose, a grouping of people, will reveal a great deal about a society or way of life, and few images tell us so much about the Romantic movement in ballet as the lithograph of the *Pas de Quatre*, in which Brandard, a favourite artist of the time, immortalized one of the most extraordinary ballet performances ever given. Compare the view of the ballerinas in this picture – infinitely delicate, lightly poised, sweetly gracious, charmingly clothed in clouds of soft tulle – with pictures of the dancers of the eighteenth century, and you will see how vast a change has taken place. Significantly, there is no male dancer. We have entered a period when men took a subsidiary place in ballet: this is the era of the ballerina's dominance. The use of point-work and the impression of ethereal lightness are indicative of a change which altered both the outward aspect of dancing and its themes. Ballet, like the other arts, had found new inspiration, new stories to tell. In literature, painting and music, creators sought an escape from their everyday world. An interest in the exotic, the supernatural, in distant scenes – distant both in place and time – took them and their audience away from a newly industrialized world of grime and

41. Fanny Bias (1789–1825) dancing in a version of *Flore et Zéphire*. Uncomfortable as she looks, Mademoiselle Bias *is* on point, and the date is 1821. Unblocked shoes may account for her expression, but this portrait of a charming *demi-caractère* artist is one of the earliest records of a dancer having risen onto full point. Thomas Moore wrote of her:

Fanny Bias in *Flora* – dear creature – you'd swear
When her delicate feet in the dance twinkle round
That her steps are of light, that her home is the air
And she only *par complaisance* touches the ground.

smoke. Ghosts and sprites, far-off lands and far-off times, the local colour of Italy or Spain or the Middle East, provided a vivid stimulus to choreographers and dancers. And this new view of ballet was reflected in a new view of dancing, epitomized by the first ballerina of the age, the central figure of the *Pas de Quatre*, Marie Taglioni.

MARIE TAGLIONI AND *La Sylphide*

It must have seemed unlikely that the thin, round-shouldered and by no means pretty daughter of Filippo Taglioni, himself a member of a famous Italian dancing family, could become a great ballerina. Her father decided she was destined for a dancing career, and her childhood was spent in one European city after another in the wake of her father's engagements as ballet-master. But by the end of the Napoleonic wars Marie and her mother were resident in Paris, where the young girl was sent to learn dancing with Jean-François Coulon, her father's former teacher. Coulon realized that Marie had talent, and her father arranged her first professional engagement, in Vienna in 1822. When she joined him there some time before her performances, he was far from satisfied with her capabilities. There ensued a five-month period of exhausting daily labour with her father, during which Filippo was determined to polish and develop his daughter's natural abilities so that her innate grace of manner should be enhanced by a formidable ease of technique and an imponderable style. Lightness was sought; decorum, as opposed to the bolder manner usual in many *danseuses* of the age; an ineffable charm of pose and position that would disguise the length of her arms and enhance the delicacy of her features. After days during which she sometimes worked for six hours, then would be bathed and given a change of clothes by her mother before fresh labours started, Filippo saw that his daughter was ready for her début, shortly after her eighteenth birthday.

The occasion was a triumph, but it was not until five years later that Marie Taglioni (with her brother Paul as partner, and her father as choreographer) reached the Mecca for dancers of this time: the Paris Opéra. Marie's style had by now been further polished by her father. Its lightness, grace and modesty, beauty in elevation and feathery softness in landing, were totally novel to the Opéra stage. Here was an entirely fresh image of the female dancer, decorous, ethereal, gracious. Taglioni's success was absolute, despite considerable enmity from the Opéra's *danseuses*, whose jealousy was quickly aroused by an amazingly different artistry which served to make them seem old-fashioned and somewhat coarse. Yet Taglioni had to wait for some years before a work was created that did justice to her unique talent.

In 1831 Meyerbeer's opera *Robert le Diable* was given at the Opéra. It was a fine example of Romanticism, telling how Duke Robert of Normandy loved a princess and encountered the Devil and the supernatural. In the third act he enters the cloister of a ruined abbey and the ghosts of nuns appear, dancing a wild bacchanal. Leading them was Marie Taglioni, a spectral figure in white. Adolphe Nourrit, singing Duke Robert, had already been inspired to devise a libretto for a ballet, based on a contemporary novel dealing with a Scottish elf, in which the combination of moonlight, white draperies and an other-worldly atmosphere might be made to serve Taglioni's prodigious gifts and the translucent grace of her style.

With some alterations to the narrative, the libretto became *La Sylphide*, which was staged at the Opéra on 12 March 1832 with Marie Taglioni in the leading role. This is the first true Romantic ballet, and in it we see elements that made for the success of *Robert le Diable* (the use of gas-lighting to simulate moonlight on stage; the extinguishing of the lamps in the auditorium; the appeal of the supernatural) brought to the ballet. The plot introduced ideas dear to Romanticism: an exotic setting (Scotland was a distant and curious spot for the good bourgeois of Paris) and ghostly incidents, and a theme which portrayed the impossible love of a human for a supernatural being. All these now found their expression in the ballet. The role of the Sylphide enshrined the novelty and grace of Marie Taglioni's dancing, so that the creature seemed unbelievably light and delicate, a thread of mist drifting over the stage, and helped to fly by various ingenious pieces of stage machinery.

The ballet tells of a young crofter, James, on the eve of his marriage to Effie, a charming neighbour. But a sylphide, a spirit of the air, has fallen in love with him, and so beguiles him that he deserts home and fiancée in order to follow her to the forest. In the second act James unwittingly causes the Sylphide's death when he seeks to possess her; as she drifts away to some

42 and 43. Marie Taglioni in two contrasting roles: as the Sylphide, poised at the window of James's croft and as Angela, the heroine of *L'Ombre*, which her father created for her in St Petersburg in 1839. She is seen here in a London staging at Her Majesty's Theatre, partnered by Antonio Guerra. The persistent image is, of course, of Taglioni's incomparable lightness as she poses upon a flower. Even in the time of Adeline Genée, in the first years of this century, ballerinas still made use of strong metal structures in the shape of flowers to enable them to seem weightlessly graceful.

sylphide heaven and James is left disconsolate and alone, his former fiancée, Effie, passes with a new lover on the way to her wedding.

The success of *La Sylphide* and of Taglioni, the visible expression of the Romantic idea, was absolute. The ballet and its star were the heralds of a golden age, a period of supernatural and exotic creations that starred not only Taglioni but a galaxy of ballerinas during the next twenty years. *La Sylphide* altered the nature of ballet in theme and decoration (Ciceri's forest set for Act II was indicative of a new style of Romantic décor) throughout Europe.

Taglioni's greatness imposed a new vision on dancing. Her successors

44. Another of the earliest exponents of point-work was the Italian ballerina Amalia Brugnoli, seen here partnered by her husband Paolo Samengo. Brugnoli astonished audiences in Vienna in 1823 by her use of points: Filippo Taglioni, working with his daughter in Vienna at the time, realized that this physical trick could be made a part of Marie's armoury of skills and be transformed into something graceful and theatrically vivid.

45. Arnout's lithograph of the interior of the old Paris Opéra in the rue le Peletier (destroyed by fire in 1873) shows a performance of Meyerbeer's opera, *Robert le Diable*, with its celebrated 'Ballet of the Nuns'. Moonlight and white draperies were portents of the Romantic dance. This illustration is of the opera house during the time of the Second Empire under Napoleon III, when ballet was already in decline after its great days of a quarter-century before.

46. Emma Livry (1842–1863) was one of the bright-est hopes of the Paris Opéra Ballet at the end of the Romantic era. The illegitimate daughter of a member of the Jockey Club and a sixteen-year-old dancer at the Opéra, she had a marvellous talent. Marie Taglioni, seeing her dance in *La Sylphide* said, 'I must have danced rather like that', and created her only ballet, *Le Papillon*, for her. During a rehearsal of *The Dumb Girl of Portici* Livry's dress caught fire, a tragically commonplace accident at a time when dancers refused to wear fire-proofed muslin despite the naked gas-lights on stage. She was severely burned and died after eight months of great suffering.

might differ in style – and none could match the ethereal and poetic delicacy or the modest grace she brought to her roles – but Taglioni remained the first, in every sense, of the ballerinas of the age; even today her image is for us the essential picture of the Romantic dancer. For seven years after *La Sylphide* she reigned at the Opéra, until the arrival of such brilliant rivals as Fanny Elssler, in every way the opposite of Taglioni, induced her to tour extensively for a decade. She triumphed wherever she went, not least in London (where she appeared in the *Pas de Quatre*) and most notably in Russia where balletomanes acquired a pair of her shoes, had them cooked and served in a sauce, and solemnly ate them.

After her retirement from the stage in 1847, Taglioni settled down to what should have been a happy middle age, staging her only ballet, *Le Papillon*, at the Paris Opéra for the tragic Emma Livry. Taglioni's early marriage to the feckless and ungrateful Count Gilbert de Voisins had been dissolved after three years; her later years were darkened by financial uncertainties, and she was obliged to give social dancing lessons to well-born children in London. She died in Marseille in 1884. Yet whatever clouds overshadowed her years of retirement, Taglioni is immortal. Her technical authority and the ineffable lightness which is associated with her name live on in the ideals of grace and elevation that are still the goal of dancers today – ideals we can see in Fokine's tribute to the Romantic manner, *Les Sylphides*.

FANNY ELSSLER

In 1834, when Fanny Elssler arrived in Paris at the age of twenty-four, she was already celebrated as a dancer in her native Vienna, and in Berlin and London. She was accompanied by her sister Thérèse: taller than Fanny, she served as her partner as well as her business manager. It was the director of the Paris Opéra, the astute Dr Véron, who sensed that Fanny's style would make a fascinating contrast with Taglioni's. Elssler was a brilliant dancer, excelling in the most difficult technical feats, in fast and dazzling steps, making very skilful use of point-work. The Romantic age saw the recognition of dancing on point as an essential feature of the ballerina's arts. The use of the very tips of the toes had been known for twenty years, but Taglioni had, characteristically, been the first to use her points to enhance the impression of lightness. She rose onto her toes as if maintaining the briefest contact with the earth before flying into the air. With Elssler, point-work was yet another aspect of her virtuosity.

An instant rivalry broke out among the Parisian public between supporters of Taglioni and adherents of the new star, which reached fresh heights with Elssler's triumph in *Le Diable boîteux* in 1836. In this Spanish ballet Fanny danced for the first time her most celebrated solo, the *cachucha*, a display of fiery temperament and voluptuous movement which, although it represents the other side of the artistic coin from Taglioni's style, also serves as a true image of the Romantic ballet.

Another of Elssler's gifts was to prove of real significance to the ballet of that era: she was a superb actress. In ballets both good and (more often) indifferent, she revealed a dramatic power that could sustain the feeblest plot. In 1839 *La Gypsy* was staged at the Paris Opéra, where she was now the reigning ballerina, and provided her with a triumph, as did *La Tarentule* later that year. But rumours were already circulating that Fanny was to embark upon an American tour – no mean adventure at this time – and in the spring of 1840 she set out for the New World. Fanny spent two years in the Americas. She visited not only the United States but also Havana, where she coped with an unenviable supporting *corps de ballet* in *La Sylphide*: she wrote of 'plump and swarthy ladies ... incapable of activity as a superannuated cow', whom

47. Adèle Dumilâtre and Eugène Coralli in *La Gypsy*, a highly dramatic ballet – as this Deveria drawing suggests – choreographed by Joseph Mazilier and set in Edinburgh during the reign of Charles II. Created for Fanny Elssler, the role of Sarah was that of a gypsy girl who is revealed as the long-lost daughter of Lord Campbell; the part was later successfully taken by the beautiful Dumilâtre, who first danced the role of the Queen of the Wilis in *Giselle*. *La Gypsy* also contains a character irresistibly named Narcisse de Crakentorp.

48. Fanny Elssler as Esmeralda, with her pet goat. In Perrot's ballet *La Esmeralda*, Elssler had one of her greatest triumphs as a dance actress. The drawing is by Paul Burde and admirably conveys that seriousness and dramatic intensity which contemporary writers so admired in Elssler's performance.

the manager daubed with wet-white to try and make them look more sylph-like. She created a sensation everywhere, dancing amid scenes of unprecedented enthusiasm.

On her return to London (as a result of breaking her contract with the Opéra she could no longer appear in Paris), Elssler reached a new pinnacle of success. In *Giselle*, which had been staged two years before at the Opéra, she offered a far more dramatic and moving interpretation of the title role than had its creator, Carlotta Grisi (see below). Fanny spent much of the next four years dancing in Italy; the final glorious period of her active career was passed in Russia, where she journeyed in 1848. Here she was shortly joined by Jules Perrot (see below), and it was in his ballets – *La Esmeralda, Catarina* – and in his staging of *Giselle* that she knew successes which rivalled anything she had attained before. Her official farewell performance in Moscow in 1851 occasioned a rain of three hundred bouquets, forty-two curtain calls, and gifts of jewels. She returned to Vienna to give a brief farewell season, then retired from the stage to devote herself to her family. Her last years were spent quietly, and she died in Vienna in 1884, leaving those fortunate enough to have seen her with an indelible memory of a supreme dance actress.

JULES PERROT AND CARLOTTA GRISI

The Romantic age established the dominance of the ballerina in the public's affections. Such performers as Taglioni and Elssler, the novelty of dancing on point, the attitude of Romantic artists towards women as either ethereal or passionate creatures (typified by the contrasting styles of the 'Christian' Taglioni and the 'pagan' Elssler – to borrow a comment made by Théophile Gautier, poet and dance critic), were factors that helped relegate male dancers to the position of a necessary evil. They were needed to partner and support the ballerina, but were not otherwise worthy of serious consideration. This reversal of the state of affairs that existed in the eighteenth century, the age of Gaëtan Vestris, *Le Dieu de la Danse*, was an element fatal to Romantic ballet. An essential and harmonious theatrical balance between

49. Jules Perrot (1810–1892) in *Nathalie*.

male and female was being destroyed, and amid the galaxy of female stars at this time only a few male names survive. They include Lucien Petipa (the first Albrecht in *Giselle*), Paul Taglioni (Marie's brother), and Arthur Saint-Léon and Jules Perrot, both remembered now as choreographers rather than dancers. Jules Perrot was born in 1810 and started his career in his native Lyon as a child acrobat. He also learnt to dance, and his earliest successes were as a grotesque mime and dancer; his style emulated that of Mazurier, a celebrated acrobatic dancer. By the age of thirteen, Perrot was in Paris, and it was here that he first thought seriously of classic ballet as a career. He took lessons with Auguste Vestris, and the illustrious teacher was sufficiently impressed with Perrot's talent to promise that, with hard work, he might overcome his natural disabilities: a thick and rather stocky body, and a face less than conventionally handsome. These might have been an advantage in those 'monkey roles' in which Perrot had first known success as a child performer, but they were hardly the requisites for a classical *premier danseur*.

Auguste Vestris had himself been destined by nature to be a *demi-caractère* dancer, for he lacked the elegance of proportion that had blessed his father in his career as the greatest dancer of his time in the 'noble' style, which demanded just such harmony of physique and grace of bearing. Nevertheless, as his father's pupil, Auguste had been given the polish and distinction of presence needed for the 'noble' style, and allied with his own prodigious technical aptitude it resulted in dancing both brilliant and distinguished. *Demi-caractère* virtuosity was given the elegant utterance of the grand manner. Steps were enhanced and embellished in execution (August Bournonville wrote to his family of 'many new things' when he was studying with Auguste Vestris), and in shaping these technical developments – which in due course he passed on to his pupils, Bournonville and Perrot – Auguste Vestris stands as one of the crucial influences upon the dance technique that flowered as the nineteenth century progressed.

Under Vestris's tuition, Perrot worked hard. Vestris advised him to use his natural lightness and *ballon* to keep in constant motion, with the result that his audience would never have time to consider his physical defects. Perrot understood the merits of what Vestris said ('Turn, spin, fly, but never give the public time to examine your person closely'), and developed a mercurial style that was to earn him theatrical success. He was described as 'a restless being of indescribable lightness and suppleness, with an almost phosphorescent brightness'.

Perrot thus combined the felicities of his master's technique with his own dramatic skills as a clown, and these elements were to unite later in his own choreographic output. By 1830 Perrot's dancing had received a rare accolade: he was invited to appear at the Opéra, and was soon dancing with

50. The death of Giselle. This engraving from *Les Beautés de l'Opéra* depicts the original Paris production. The group is similar to that seen in stagings of *Giselle* today, but the Duke of Courland and Bathilde nowadays usually leave the stage in distress at the onset of Giselle's madness.

Taglioni, who was at the outset of her Paris career. For five years they appeared together, Perrot's bounding lightness providing an admirable foil for Taglioni's ethereal grace – so much so that he was called Taglioni's 'dancing brother'. But the ballerina was jealous of sharing public acclaim, and in 1835 Perrot quit the Opéra after a disagreement about salary and embarked on a European tour. This eventually brought him to Naples, where he discovered a talented sixteen-year-old girl in the ballet company. She was Carlotta Grisi. Sensing her rare potential, Perrot decided to teach her and shape a talent that he believed might rival those of Taglioni and Elssler. For four years he guided Grisi, partnered her, staged his first ballets for her and gave her his name. After well-received performances in Milan, Munich and London, Perrot brought Carlotta to Paris. He hoped that through her talent he might make his own return to the Opéra, but this proved impossible. The couple appeared in a boulevard theatre in the ballet-opera *Le Zingaro*, in which Carlotta, possessed of a pretty soprano voice (her family were distinguished as singers), not only danced but sang. Her success was such that, early in the following year, the Opéra's directorate approached Perrot with an offer for Carlotta. The theatre was without a star dancer; Taglioni was in Russia, Elssler in America, and the rising Danish ballerina, Lucile Grahn, had sustained an injury. Carlotta Grisi's gifts were promising enough for the Opéra, and in February 1841 she made a successful début, though there was no invitation for Perrot to appear. Yet it was Perrot who largely contributed to Carlotta's triumph later that summer, when *Giselle* was staged at the Opéra.

The inspiration for this most celebrated ballet of the Romantic era came from a book by Heinrich Heine about Germany, in which Théophile Gautier

51. (Left) Carlotta Grisi and Jules Perrot in *La Esmeralda*.

52. (Above) Fanny Cerrito in the *pas de l'ombre* from *Ondine*.

discovered the Slav legend of Wilis, ghosts of young women who danced to death any man they came upon at night. Gautier was already struck by Carlotta's beauty and, with the assistance of the dramatist Vernoy de Saint-Georges, he devised a scenario that was accepted by the Opéra. The composer Adolphe Adam, a friend of Perrot and Grisi, was entrusted with the score, which he drafted in record time. The choreography was to be created by Jean Coralli, chief ballet-master at the Opéra, and not by Perrot; nevertheless, though Coralli was credited with the staging, it was common knowledge that Perrot composed all the dances for Grisi, and in them lay the heart of the

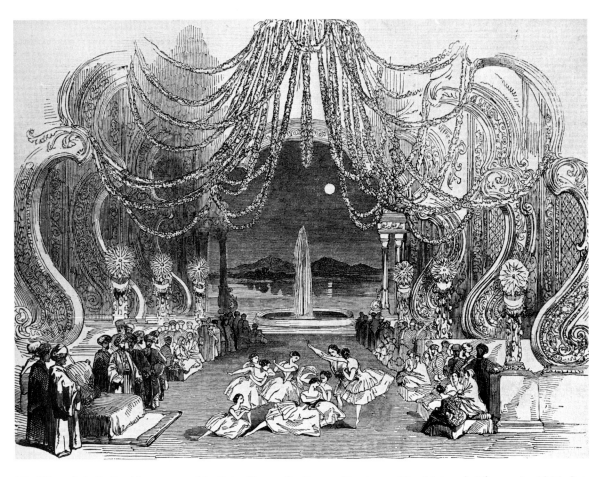

53. (Above) *Lalla Rookh* was staged by Jules Perrot for Fanny Cerrito at Her Majesty's Theatre in 1846. Set in India, it was inspired by a section from Thomas Moore's poem of the same name. It was the last of the major ballets that Perrot created in London.

54. (Right) Left to right: Fanny Cerrito, Arthur Saint-Léon, Marie Taglioni and Lucile Grahn in Jules Perrot's *Pas des déesses*. This formed part of Perrot's *divertissement The Judgement of Paris*, which featured these artists with Perrot himself as Mercury and seven other dancers in subsidiary roles. It was first produced in London at Her Majesty's Theatre in 1846.

---

ballet. *Giselle* was a tremendous success, and it marked the beginning of the most important period of Perrot's career, not as a dancer but as one of the master choreographers of the century.

Carlotta's triumph, and that of *Giselle* to which Perrot had contributed so much, did not open the doors of the Opéra to him. In the next year, 1842, he was invited to London to work at Her Majesty's Theatre, then under the management of an inspired impresario, Benjamin Lumley. After helping to stage *Giselle* for Grisi and devising a *pas* for Fanny Cerrito (see below) in *Alma*, Perrot was entrusted with most of the ballet productions at the theatre for the next six years. It was a time when his genius reached an extraordinary flowering, and he produced some of the finest ballets of this Romantic heyday. *La Esmeralda, Éoline, Catarina, Ondine* and *Lalla Rookh* were ballets in which the themes and ideas of Romanticism, the delight in the exotic and the supernatural, the love of local colour and vivid drama, were given superb expression. They were true *ballets d'action*. The choreography carried the action forward without relying on extraneous display or *divertissement*; the interpreters were called upon to be expressive at all times; crowd scenes or intimate duets were equally informed with lively dramatic interest. Perrot's daring in achieving such effects was wholly successful. The characters in his

ballets were real and sympathetic. Mime and dance were fused in a convincing style that emphasized naturalism rather than empty posturing or worn-out balletic traditions. Here, it seems, Noverre's theories were brought to bold theatrical life.

Perrot also created a series of *divertissements* that served as showpieces for the finest dancers of the day. In 1843, Queen Victoria had expressed a wish to see Elssler and Fanny Cerrito (then the darling of London's ballet audience) dance together. This undreamed-of partnership at Her Majesty's Theatre was brought off with consummate skill by Perrot, who balanced with the nicest exactitude the steps and effects that each ballerina could best display. In 1845 Benjamin Lumley conceived a plan that must have seemed wildly unlikely of success: a *pas de quatre* for the divinities Taglioni, Cerrito, Grisi and Lucile Grahn. By dint of Lumley's diplomacy and Perrot's choreographic skills the plan was realized, though not without dramas concerning precedence. Taglioni would, of course, take pride of place, and Grahn, as the junior of the quartet, would come last. But to choose between Grisi and Cerrito when each lady was inordinately jealous of her position might have taxed a Solomon. Yet Lumley was equal even to this, announcing quite simply that the elder of the two goddesses should take precedence; smiling sweetly, both drew back and proved amenable to the place Perrot wished to give them. The *Pas de Quatre* was a thunderous success, and in the next three years similar displays were devised to include whatever stars happened to be available. *The Judgement of Paris* in 1846 featured Taglioni, Cerrito and Grahn, with Perrot himself and Arthur Saint-Léon (who privately referred to these affairs as 'steeplechases'); in 1847, *The Elements* united Cerrito, Grisi and Carolina Rosati; and in 1848, *The Four Seasons* starred Grisi, Cerrito, Rosati and the younger Marie Taglioni (the great Marie's niece).

By this time London's interest in ballet was waning, due in no small part to an upsurge in the popularity of opera occasioned by the arrival of Jenny Lind, 'the Swedish Nightingale'. In December 1848 Perrot made his first visit to Russia, where he was to work with little interruption for the next decade, re-staging his ballets, creating some new works and participating in the renaissance of ballet there. His assistant in these productions, and interpreter of several leading roles, was Marius Petipa, who maintained and edited the Perrot repertory in Russia for the rest of his long career there. Perrot left Russia in 1860 and returned to Paris, where he lived quietly, visiting the ballet and teaching; in the paintings of Degas he can be seen as an old gentleman giving classes at the Paris Opéra. He died in 1892.

Carlotta Grisi's career, launched so splendidly in *Giselle*, continued to undiminished acclaim for her roles in *La Jolie Fille de Gand* (1842), *La Péri* (1843), *Le Diable à Quatre* (1845) and *Paquita* (1846). She visited Russia, where

55. Carlotta Grisi and Lucien Petipa in *La Péri*. First seen at the Paris Opéra in 1843, *La Péri* had a scenario by Théophile Gautier, choreography by Coralli and a score by Burgmüller. It told of a pasha (Lucien Petipa, elder brother of Marius) who takes opium and dreams of a realm of Péris whose queen (Grisi) he loves. The most famous scene in the ballet was one in which Grisi had to drop six feet from a platform into Petipa's arms – a moment whose danger never failed to thrill the public. (Ivor Guest records that audiences in Paris insisted that the leap be repeated three times if it did not come off perfectly, otherwise they would not applaud Carlotta; in London they besought her not to attempt it again after it had once failed.)

her success was considerable, assisted by the presence of Perrot. But in Europe the interest in ballet was declining and in 1854 she left the stage, still at the height of her powers. She retired to live quietly and serenely near Geneva for the next forty-five years, dying in 1899.

FANNY CERRITO AND ARTHUR SAINT-LÉON

Of all the divinities of the Romantic era, one in particular became the darling of London. Fanny Cerrito (who appears in Barham's *Ingoldsby Legends* as Ma'mselle Cherrytoes) was born in Naples in 1817, and her early successes as a dancer were at La Scala, Milan, where she enthralled audiences by her brilliant technique. But it was her first London season in 1840 which set the seal on her claim to be considered one of the brightest stars of this heyday of ballet. Bounding, sparkling with life and speed, turning and, it seemed, flying in the air, the diminutive Cerrito won London's heart more completely than any other dancer since Taglioni's début ten years earlier.

It was in London that she first worked with Perrot, in the *pas* in *Alma* that earned him his engagement at Her Majesty's Theatre, and their artistic association over the following years was to draw fine things from them both. *Ondine* (1843) remains one of the key works of the period; its *pas de*

56. Fanny Cerrito and Arthur Saint-Léon dancing the *pas de fascination* in *La Fille de marbre* in Paris, 1847.

l'ombre, in which Fanny, as the water-sprite, sported with her own shadow, is famous still, and inspired Frederick Ashton's shadow-dance for Fonteyn when he staged his *Ondine* for the Royal Ballet. Between her London seasons Cerrito returned to Italy to receptions no less enthusiastic than those she had experienced in England, and though Perrot's next piece for her, *Zélia* (1844), was a failure, the *Pas de Quatre* and the subsequent *divertissements*, as rich in ballerinas as a pudding in plums, were works that displayed her bounding qualities superbly, as did *Lalla Rookh* in 1846. Three years earlier she had met Arthur Saint-Léon (born 1821), a dancer of impressive gifts (he was also an accomplished violinist) whose virile brilliance set off Carlotta's style to perfection in *pas de deux*. Saint-Léon undertook his first choreography for her, and in 1845 the couple were married, much to the chagrin of the wealthy English aristocrats who had for years been laying siege to Fanny's heart.

Despite her fame in London and Italy, and in a number of European cities, Cerrito had still to dance at the Paris Opéra, that magnet for dancers. In 1847, however, the Opéra made overtures to Cerrito and Saint-Léon, and in October that year Saint-Léon concocted a version of Fanny's early triumph *Alma*, editing and re-naming it *La Fille de marbre*. The piece proved much to Parisian taste, and during the next three years Cerrito starred with Saint-Léon in several of his ballets, outstandingly in *La Vivandière* and in an extraordinary confection, *Le Violon du Diable*, for which Saint-Léon was choreographer as well as dancer, playing the violin to accompany Fanny's dancing.

In 1851, during Fanny's visit to Spain, a rift opened between the pair, which ended in separation. Fanny formed a liaison with a Spanish aristocrat by whom she had a daughter in 1853, but this did not end her career. Although her technique was suffering with advancing years, she returned for a time to Paris, visited London for some performances, and then – although the Crimean War was raging – travelled to St Petersburg, where she found Perrot as ballet-master. Her success there was by no means as complete as she had enjoyed throughout the rest of Europe, for the Russians were beginning to realize that their own ballerinas – Marfa Muravieva, for instance – were as gifted as foreign stars. By 1857 Cerrito was back in Europe, but it was clear to her that her career was near its end. The Paris Opéra seemed closed to her, and her farewell to the stage took place in London, a city which had given her such generous and loving acclaim for so

57. Giuseppina Bozzacchi (1853–1870), like Livry, a tragic young star of French ballet. She was born into an impoverished Italian family in Paris, and at an early age her talent was so evident that the director of the Opéra and generous friends secured her training at the Opéra school. When still only sixteen years old she was chosen to create the role of Swanilda in *Coppélia*, the only part she was ever to dance on stage. The outbreak of the Franco-Prussian War in 1870 closed the Opéra and, during the famine brought on by the Siege of Paris in the same year, she contracted smallpox and died on her seventeenth birthday.

58. An engraving by Gavarni, showing a characteristic scene in the wings of a Paris theatre in the middle of the nineteenth century. The dashing gentleman's interest is not solely in the dancer's technique; the Foyer de la Danse (the Green Room at the Paris Opéra) was a meeting-place for dancers and their admirers and proved a happy hunting-ground where the *danseuses* were given every sort of jewellery except a wedding ring.

many years. Without fuss or special announcement, Fanny Cerrito appeared for the last time in public on 18 June 1857, dancing a minuet in a staging of Mozart's *Don Giovanni*. She lived on in Paris for another fifty-two years, devoting herself to the education and marriage of her beloved daughter Mathilde, and to the joys of her grandchildren. Her death in May 1909 coincided almost exactly with the arrival in Paris of the Russian dancers for the first prodigious ballet season under the command of Serge Diaghilev. It is extraordinary to think that as Karsavina and Nijinsky rehearsed for *Les Sylphides* a ballerina died who had danced *La Sylphide* sixty-eight years before.

Saint-Léon had left the Paris Opéra in 1852, and following the break-up of his marriage with Cerrito he went to Portugal in the next year. He staged ballets there, and in various European capitals, before being invited to succeed Jules Perrot as first ballet-master in St Petersburg. For ten years Saint-Léon commuted between Paris and Russia, spending winters in St Petersburg and the summer months in Paris when the Russian ballet season was over. In Russia he was responsible for a considerable number of additions to the repertory, works which combined sparkling *divertissements* with national dances, which he adapted with great skill to the forms of ballet. His *Little Humpbacked Horse* was notably successful because of its Russian theme, and it remained for many years a favourite with audiences.

But it was in Paris, after his final departure from Russia, that Saint-Léon created his last and most famous work, *Coppélia* (1870). Into it he seems to have poured the best of himself. The charming solos, the clever use of national dance and the *divertissements* of the last act were enhanced by the irresistible delights of Léo Delibes's score, one of the supreme masterpieces of ballet music. Yet, curiously for this happiest of ballets, its creation was attended by great sadness. In the summer following its first production the Franco-Prussian War broke out, sweeping away the elaborate elegance of the Second Empire. Saint-Léon died of a heart attack in September of the same year, and two months later the delightful Giuseppina Bozzacchi, who had created the role of Swanilda, died of smallpox on her seventeenth birthday. During the fierce winter of the Siege of Paris, Dauty, the first Dr Coppélius, also died. But *Coppélia* lives on in its immortal score and in the recollections of those who knew the one-time Paris Opéra version with all the charm that Saint-Léon had given this beguiling work.

59. The Danish ballerina Lucile Grahn in Perrot's *Éoline*. Éoline was half mortal and half wood-sprite (hence the costume); she met a tragic death when the Prince of the Gnomes set fire to a tree on which her safety depended.

LUCILE GRAHN AND AUGUST BOURNONVILLE

The junior member of the *Pas de Quatre* was the Danish ballerina Lucile Grahn, who was born in Copenhagen in 1819. Her career, though less well known than that of her companions in the quartet, followed much the same pattern of triumphant performances throughout Europe, with exultant débuts in Paris, London and St Petersburg. It ended, intriguingly, with a position as ballet-mistress in Munich, helping in the staging of Wagner's *Die Meistersinger* and *Rheingold* (Wagner 'thought highly' of her). It is through her that we make contact with one of the greatest choreographers of the Romantic age, and one whose ballets are still treasured today: August Bournonville.

Born in Copenhagen in 1805, son of Antoine Bournonville, a French dancer, and his Swedish wife, the young Bournonville made his début as a child in a ballet by Vincenzo Galeotti, who was then ballet-master in Copenhagen.

60. (Left) Valdemar Price (1836–1908) as Gennaro in Bournonville's *Napoli*. Price was a member of a famous family of dancers (of English extraction) who danced in Copenhagen. His sister Juliette and his cousin Amalie were also dancers in the Royal Danish Ballet. It is interesting to note that Gennaro's costume has changed but little since the ballet was created in Copenhagen in 1842.

61. (Right) Emilie Walbom in Bournonville's *Valdemar*. This photograph shows a production of 1875. The weighty gentlemen on either side show how the Danish Ballet stressed the importance of character parts and realistic mime, a tradition that still survives in Copenhagen today.

Galeotti's ballets reflected the influence of Noverre and Angiolini; for forty years he directed the Royal Danish Ballet, but in his later years (and after his death, when Antoine Bournonville directed the troupe) the Royal Danish Ballet fell upon sad times. Antoine, meanwhile, had sent his son to study dancing in Paris, where August worked for several years during the 1820s with Vestris, absorbing from him the finesse and nobility, as well as the technical virtuosity and mimetic traditions, of the French school of dancing. He was to maintain this style throughout the rest of his life, and it formed the basis of the training system he initiated when, in 1829, he returned to Copenhagen and in the following year took charge of the Royal Danish Ballet.

He came to power as a brilliant dancer and excellent dramatic mime, filled with ambitions to improve the status of the company and of dancing as a profession. His task was a difficult one. He had to dance, train his company and provide a repertory, but fortunately his gifts were equal to these demands. During the next forty-seven years, with brief interludes when he worked in Stockholm and Vienna or travelled in Europe, Bournonville created a fine company and a superb repertory. He saw the social and moral standards of his dancers rise, and demonstrated to his Copenhagen public that dancing was, as he believed, a noble and inspiring art. His surviving ballets and his training system, lovingly preserved in Copenhagen,

offer valuable insights into the nature of ballet in the middle of the last century.

In 1834 Bournonville visited Paris, bringing with him his gifted pupil, the fifteen-year-old Lucile Grahn. They saw Marie Taglioni (Bournonville's 'ideal' as a dancer) in *La Sylphide*, and two years later Bournonville staged his own version of the ballet for Grahn. Although the score was different and Bournonville provided new choreography, this *Sylphide* was faithful in plot and style to Filippo Taglioni's original, with one significant exception that is characteristic of Bournonville's work. With male dancing declining in importance elsewhere in European ballet, Bournonville – himself a superior technician – insisted on maintaining the prestige of the male dancer in his creations. His system of training produced, and continues to produce, elegant, bounding and virile male stars. Bournonville's *Sylphide* has survived in unbroken Danish performance since 1836, but it is far from characteristic of his work, for in its Romantic fever there are elements which the choreographer sought to expunge from ballet. His own passion for Grahn was to oblige her to leave Copenhagen and find her greatest successes in France and England.

When ballet was losing its popular appeal in the rest of Europe, the relative artistic remoteness of Denmark meant that fashion did not alter the Danes' affection for their ballet and the masterpieces that Bournonville was creating. (In an even more remote centre, St Petersburg, the ballet also

62. (Left) Anna Regina Tychsen and Hans Beck in the second act of Bournonville's *La Sylphide*, when the Sylphide is begging James to give her the fateful scarf. Beck's kilt may not seem very Scottish in shape, nor yet his ribboned shoes, but it is to him that we owe the preservation of the Bournonville repertory.

63. (Right) Rosita Mauri (1849–1923) was of Spanish birth and made her début at the Paris Opéra in 1878. She was to remain one of the greatest stars of that theatre for the next twenty years, dazzling audiences with her technique. This portrait by Debat-Ponsan shows her in the ballet *La Maladetta*, choreographed by Joseph Hansen, at the Opéra in 1893.

64. The Italian-born Carlotta Zambelli (1875–1968) succeeded Mauri as the leading ballerina at the Paris Opéra. She did not retire from the stage until 1934, forty years after her début, and thereafter continued to serve the Opéra as a celebrated teacher. She was also much admired in St Petersburg, where she danced in 1901. In her dancing and that of Mauri we witness the final supremacy of Italianate virtuosity over the older French style. Zambelli is seen here in Hansen's ballet *Bacchus* in 1902.

survived untouched by changes in public taste at this time.) More than fifty ballets of all types flowed from Bournonville, each illuminated by his poetic imagination and fertile creativity, each proposing that proper balance between male and female dancing, each offering wonderful opportunities for drama and for a style of dancing that was firmly rooted in the grand traditions of the Vestris school – which Bournonville enhanced and developed. Bournonville could create brilliantly joyous *enchaînements*; his travels (he especially loved Italy) enabled him to adapt folk-dance, and in his finest works he produced a picture of the world he knew, showing real people – like the townsfolk of Naples in *Napoli*. He composed true Romantic *ballets d'action* that found their place among the great achievements of nineteenth-century choreography. He drew on legendary themes in *A Folk Tale*; on historical subjects for *Cort Adeler*, *Valdemar* and *The King's Lifeguards on Amager*; he chose topical events for *Zulma, or The Crystal Palace in London*; scenes of travel inspired *Kermesse in Bruges*, *Far from Denmark* and *La Ventana*; even his own student days in Paris with Vestris were used to form the basis of his *Conservatoriet*. Through these and many other fine works Denmark gained a vital ballet tradition, and, through Bournonville's teaching, a great

65. The Grand March from *The White Fawn*, the ballet extravaganza which followed *The Black Crook* at Niblo's Garden, New York, in January 1868. It did not enjoy the same success as *The Black Crook* (which lasted in various forms for nearly forty years) but the ballet interludes and the delightful ladies helped to sustain an interest in dancing. Ballet in America, like ballet in England, was degenerating into an item in the music hall.

performing history. These remain the foundation for the identity of the Royal Danish Ballet today.

Bournonville's interests encompassed music. He encouraged native composers to provide his scores, he produced plays and operas – especially by his beloved Mozart – and he even introduced Wagner to Denmark by staging *Lohengrin* in Copenhagen. In 1877 he retired from the ballet and died two years later, but on the day before he died he saw the début of a young dancer, Hans Beck, who was to prove a guardian of the traditions of Bournonville's ballets and dance teaching until his own death in 1952.

# 4 Marius Petipa and the Imperial Russian Ballet

As we trace the history of ballet, we can observe how the centres of dance activity change, how interest seems to shift from country to country. Romantic ballet, born in France, found new life in England when Jules Perrot moved to Her Majesty's Theatre in London. When Perrot was invited to St Petersburg in 1848, we might suppose that the centre of balletic activity would be transferred to that distant and beautiful city. So in fact it proved, though in rather different fashion than had been anticipated. By 1848 the Romantic ballet was in decline. The impulse that had given it such momentum in Paris and London was almost lost. The great ballerinas were reaching the end of their careers: Taglioni retired in 1847, Elssler in 1852, Grisi in 1854. In Copenhagen, Bournonville was in the full flood of creativity, but elsewhere in Europe ballet fell on hard times. It was not until the twentieth century that it was to revive, when the Ballets Russes under Diaghilev, with Russian dancers and choreographers, renewed Western balletic values.

There had been ballet in Russia since the eighteenth century; the first professional performance is generally considered to have taken place on 29 January 1736, when dancing had been included in a performance of Araja's opera *The Power of Love and Hate*, with the participation of a hundred pupils from a military school for the sons of noble families. They had been trained by a French dancing-master, Jean-Baptiste Landé. Two years later he was given permission by the Empress Anna to open a ballet school in the Winter Palace for twelve boys and twelve girls, children of palace servants.

This was the birth of the Russian school, and henceforth the Russians were to work under the guidance of a succession of foreign teachers and visiting dancers, a tradition that did not end until the Revolution of 1917. By the time Perrot was invited to Russia, the Imperial Ballet was a healthy, well-established organization working at theatres in St Petersburg and Moscow, with schools designed to provide fully trained dancers for two companies. It is important to stress, though, that from its inception the ballet was dependent upon the Tsar: it was his ballet, under the direct supervision and guidance of a court minister appointed by the Tsar and answerable to him.

The most important figure in Russian ballet in the first decades of the nineteenth century was Charles-Louis Didelot (1767–1837). As a pupil of Dauberval, Noverre and Auguste Vestris, he was a fine dancer and his early ballet *Flore et Zéphyre* (first given in London in 1796) is remembered for the fact that by the skilful use of wires the dancers were enabled to fly. This invasion of the air presages the image of flight that would haunt the Romantic imagination and inspire the dance of Taglioni. As choreographer and teacher in Russia (1801–1811; 1816–1830), he laid the firm technical foundations upon which the later excellence of Russian dancing was built, and in his many stagings displayed a mastery of the *ballet d'action* which delighted public and connoisseurs alike. The poet Alexander Pushkin said that there was 'more poetry in his ballets than in all the French literature of his time'. An added impetus to ballet-going came with the first visit to Russia of Marie Taglioni in 1837 – she 'stirred up a stagnating pool', said one Soviet critic. For five years she made annual visits and knew astonishing success and adulation.

66. Marius Petipa (1818–1910), principal architect of the Imperial Russian Ballet.

67. The temple set for the original production of Petipa's *La Bayadère* (1877) at the Bolshoy Theatre, St Petersburg. The Bolshoy (Grand) Theatre was the home of the Imperial Ballet until the company moved to the refurbished Mariinsky Theatre in 1886. This beautiful theatre, later known as the Kirov Theatre, has been the ballet's home ever since. This design of an Indian temple is characteristic of the opulently literal stage settings found in the great opera houses during the latter half of the nineteenth century. Settings were generally provided by the resident designers working in the theatre. Scenery was sometimes, for reasons of economy, made to serve for several ballets, and at a performance of Petipa's *Daughter of the Snows* in 1879 some old scenery was brought out, which collapsed. So upset was the stage manager that, as Petipa observed, 'he lost his reason right there on stage'. The St Petersburg Ballet still uses the magnificent scenery that was designed for the important revival of *La Bayadère* in 1901: it is a masterpiece of stage décor of its period.

In 1847, the year before Perrot's appointment as ballet-master in St Petersburg, another Frenchman was invited to the capital. This was Marius Petipa, who became the most potent influence on ballet in Russia during the latter years of the century and was the chief architect of its greatness. Petipa was a member of a family of dancers, one of several such families who travelled throughout Europe, staging ballets, dancing, then moving on. His father Jean was a ballet-master and choreographer, and at the time of Marius's birth in 1818 the family were in Marseille. By 1822 a move had been made to Brussels, and there Marius started dancing lessons at the age of seven. Family fortunes took them to Antwerp, whence they fled after revolution in Brussels, moving to Bordeaux, and at the age of sixteen the young Marius had obtained an engagement in Nantes. He joined his family for a tour to America, which proved a financial disaster thanks to a theatre manager who absconded with the box-office takings. Back in Paris, where his elder brother Lucien was *premier danseur* at the Opéra and later became the first Albrecht in *Giselle*, Marius took lessons from Auguste Vestris. He then moved to Bordeaux, and southward to Madrid, where he had a four-year engagement as dancer and choreographer. After he left Madrid − because of an affair of the heart and the threat of a duel − Marius was offered a post as *premier danseur* in St Petersburg, where his father was teaching.

Marius Petipa arrived in St Petersburg in 1847; he was to spend the remaining sixty-three years of his life in Russia. He worked as a dancer and staged revivals of ballets; he might have hoped to pursue his career as a

68. Ekaterina Vazem (1848–1937) in Petipa's *The Bandits* (1875). Vazem, with her impeccable technique and cool style, was Petipa's favoured artist during the twenty years (1864–1884) of her reign with the St Petersburg Ballet. She retired, wisely, with her powers undiminished, and thereafter taught several generations of St Petersburg ballerinas, notably Agrippina Vaganova (see Chapter 9). As a very old lady she dictated a fascinating volume of memoirs to her son, a vivid account of ballet in the middle of the nineteenth century, part of which was translated into English and appeared in the journal *Dance Research*.

69. Virginia Zucchi (1849–1930) in *Esmeralda* (1886). The divine Virginia inspired all who saw her, from the artist Alexandre Benois to the ballerina M. F. Kshessinska.

choreographer were it not for the fact that Perrot arrived in St Petersburg and was installed as principal ballet-master. Petipa worked with Perrot during the latter's Petersburg years, dancing in many of his productions, and although he had little opportunity to work as a choreographer he was able to learn a great deal from assisting Perrot, great master of the *ballet d'action*.

In 1860 Perrot was dismissed – he was unpopular with the administration of the Imperial Theatres – and Petipa may have hoped for an appointment as first ballet-master in his place. He had composed a few short ballets, chiefly for his wife Marie, but the director of the Imperial Theatres had already installed another Frenchman, Arthur Saint-Léon, and Petipa's career continued to be that of dancer and assistant ballet-master. During the ten years he stayed in Russia, Saint-Léon produced many ballets that confirmed his skill in the confection of brilliant *divertissements*, and his taste for national dances gave them increased popularity on the ballet stage. He was a man jealous of his position, reluctant to allow Petipa much opportunity to create choreography. However, in 1861 Petipa was given the chance to compose a

70. Nicholas Legat (1869–1937) as he appeared in Petipa's *Raymonda* in 1898. One of the leading *danseurs* at the Mariinsky Theatre, he was also a choreographer, succeeding Petipa as ballet-master in 1903, and a very influential teacher, numbering many of the most illustrious dancers at the Mariinsky among his pupils. He left Russia in 1923 and eventually settled in London where he continued to pass on to his pupils the greatest traditions of his art.

ballet; this was no easy task since the ballet was to be full-length and designed to feature the dramatic abilities of Carolina Rosati, a guest ballerina no longer in her first youth.

Petipa was aware, nevertheless, that this was an important opening, and one to be seized. He had already been back to Paris and had consulted with Vernoy de Saint-Georges, a well-known librettist who was skilled in the construction of balletic drama, and who had devised the first act of *Giselle*. Together they concocted the action of *The Pharaoh's Daughter*, a massive piece inspired by Théophile Gautier's story, *The Mummy's Tale*. Petipa was – and remained throughout his career – astute in the choice of theme: archaeological excavations in Egypt were exciting public interest, and the tale provided ample opportunity for dramatic scenes and *divertissements*. To read the plot of *The Pharaoh's Daughter* in C. W. Beaumont's *Complete Book of Ballets* is to be amazed by its ramifications as well as by its quaintnesses.

Petipa had only six weeks in which to complete the staging, but he came to the task well armed, since his work with Perrot and Saint-Léon had taught him much about ballet-making and about the tastes of his audience. He was

71. Lev Ivanov (1834–1901) in the role of Conrad in *Le Corsaire.*

an amazingly fluent creator of dances, and as we shall see later, he was a choreographer who came fully prepared to the rehearsal room. It is not surprising that *The Pharaoh's Daughter*, a complicated, spectacular ballet, should have met with such great success, or that it should have initiated a kind of entertainment – filled with a profusion of dramatic effects, processions, *divertissements*, solos and well-made ensembles – that Petipa was to continue to devise throughout the rest of his career. Yet despite the welcome given to *The Pharaoh's Daughter* at its first performance at the Bolshoy Theatre in St Petersburg in 1862, Petipa's fortunes did not run smoothly. Saint-Léon was not to be dislodged from his position as first ballet-master, and Petipa's ballets during the next few years were not all to the public's liking. However, in 1870 Saint-Léon left Russia and Petipa was named, at last, as chief ballet-master. His task, he was told, was to 'produce a new ballet at the beginning of every season', and this obligation Petipa more than handsomely met. During the next thirty years he staged no fewer than forty ballets, many of them full-length, as well as reviving and revising works already in the repertory, and providing the ballets for operas. It is, on any terms, an immense achievement, but it was not without problems.

Petipa had accustomed his audiences to expect vast and complicated spectacles, filled with that profusion of effects that he had first given them in

The Pharaoh's Daughter. His apprentice years with Perrot and Saint-Léon had taught him much, and his particular genius enabled him to continue making the hollow but magnificent display-pieces that his St Petersburg audiences wanted, even though he privately said that he was not happy to turn out the same type of ballet time after time. His audiences also gave evidence of not being happy since, in the 1870s, the number of ballet performances during the season dropped from three each week to one. Petipa sought to maintain the element of novelty by seizing upon events of current interest to suggest themes for his ballets: when in 1877 Russia declared war upon the Turks over the re-partition of the Balkans, Petipa staged *Roxana, the Beauty of Montenegro*; two years later a polar explorer lost his life in the Arctic wastes, and Petipa created *The Daughter of the Snows*.

It was during these years that Petipa also composed two major ballets that survive to this day, *La Bayadère* and *Don Quixote*. The latter was first produced in Moscow in 1869, then mounted in St Petersburg, rather differently, in 1871, since there existed a gulf between Muscovite affection for comedy and strong dramatic effects and St Petersburg's more aristocratic taste. In Moscow, *Don Quixote* was a vivid *ballet d'action*; St Petersburg

72. Pelageia Karpakova (1845–1920) in *La Fille mal gardée*. Karpakova, a Moscow dancer, was Odette in the first staging of Tchaikovsky's ballet *Swan Lake* in 1877. *La Fille mal gardée* had been known in both St Petersburg and Moscow since Didelot's time in Russia and had been altered by various ballet-masters and dancers.

420.

73. Mathilde Felixovna Kshessinska (1872–1971). Born into a family of dancers – her father, brother and sister were all artists in the Imperial Ballet – Kshessinska became *prima ballerina assoluta* of the Imperial Ballet at the Mariinsky Theatre. This title was clear and specific and Kshessinska, because of her relationship with members of the Imperial family, wielded very great power in the ballet during her twenty-five years as ballerina. She was a pupil of Ivanov, and one of the first dancers to be inspired by Virginia Zucchi's dramatic gifts. Her career lay largely inside Russia, although she did dance in Paris at the Opéra and appeared with the Diaghilev ballet for a few performances, dancing in London in 1911 and returning to Covent Garden for a charity gala in 1936 to perform her *Russian Dance* at the age of sixty-four! Kshessinska's jewels, as the necklaces she is wearing indicate, were real and prodigious, tributes from her admirers in the Imperial family. When she came to dance for Diaghilev in London in 1911 her jewels excited quite as much press attention (perhaps more) as her artistry as a ballerina.

demanded classicism above all else, and when Petipa re-worked the piece for his court audience it lost much of its comic and dramatic effects and its Spanish national character, these elements being replaced by more formal classical inventions. *Don Quixote* was later revised in Moscow by Alexander Gorsky when he took charge of the troupe there in 1900; his more lively dramatic staging was preserved in Moscow at the Bolshoy Theatre and adopted by the St Petersburg/Leningrad Ballet, who still perform it at the Kirov Theatre.

St Petersburg's pre-eminence as the capital city and seat of the Tsar's court, and the artistic and social differences between Moscow and St Petersburg, meant that ballet there was more aristocratic in style and better funded than in Moscow, the ancient first city as well as the mercantile heart of the nation. This state of affairs was to last for many years, and the difference that exists between the classical ideals of Leningrad's Kirov Ballet and the more exuberant style of Moscow's Bolshoy Ballet can still be discerned. It is significant that Leningrad (now again known as St Petersburg) remains the home of much creative activity: the great pedagogue Agrippina Vaganova, whose teaching

74. Julia Siedova (1880–1970) was much admired as a ballerina at the Mariinsky Theatre and, in her later years, as a teacher in Nice, where she settled after leaving Russia at the time of the October Revolution. She is seen here as Aspicia, the heroine of *The Pharaoh's Daughter* by Petipa, in the first decade of this century.

system provides the basis for Russian excellence in dancing, worked there, and it has also furnished major choreographers for both the Kirov and Bolshoy Ballets.

La Bayadère had its first performance in 1877. The score, and that of *Don Quixote*, was by Ludwig Minkus (1826–1917), holder of the official post of composer of ballet music to the Imperial Theatres. *La Bayadère* is preserved in a somewhat edited version in Leningrad, and one passage – the famous 'Shades' scene from the fourth act – was a revelation to audiences when the Kirov Ballet first visited the West in 1961. Petipa introduces the ghosts of *bayadères* (Indian temple dancers) in a celebrated sequence of choreography in which thirty-two members of the *corps de ballet* pour down a ramp in *arabesques penchées*. Full-length versions of *La Bayadère* have now been presented in the West, but the ballet's most persistent image, and a sure indication of Petipa's genius, still comes with the entry of the Shades and the succeeding variations for the heroine and a trio of female soloists.

The decline in public interest in ballet was halted in the summer of 1885 when a group of Italian dancers arrived in St Petersburg to perform in one

75. Ekaterina Geltzer (1876–1962) was the great Moscow ballerina almost from the time of her début in 1894 until the late 1920s. She was the star of many of Alexander Gorsky's important stagings in Moscow from 1901, and her career continued in importance after the Revolution because she was one of the few *prima ballerinas* to stay in Russia. At the age of fifty-one she created the ballerina role in the first successful Soviet ballet, *The Red Poppy*. And, indeed, she continued dancing in character roles until 1935. Famous also as a teacher, she married Vasily Tikhomirov, a dancer, choreographer and teacher who had an equally distinguished career in Moscow. He too was one of the first generation of Soviet dancers.

of the rustic theatres that used to spring into life during the summer months. Leading the troupe was Virginia Zucchi (1847–1930), and it is no exaggeration to say that her artistry brought back the audiences to ballet. Zucchi was a fine technical dancer – Italy was still the home of training for virtuosi, and the teaching system codified and elaborated by Carlo Blasis continued to produce artists capable of feats impossible for dancers elsewhere. But more important than Zucchi's physical skill was her dramatic power. In the extravaganza, *A Flight to the Moon*, which brought her to Russia, and in other more challenging dramatic pieces, Zucchi's profoundly moving interpretation and her vivid dramatic presence caught the hearts of the St Petersburg public, who flocked to see her. The Directorate of the Imperial Theatres determined that this unique performer should be seen within the more fitting framework of the Imperial Ballet, and for three years Zucchi danced in St Petersburg, winning back an audience which, it seemed, had deserted the ballet. A succession of Italian virtuosi came in her wake: Pierina Legnani, Carlotta Brianza, Antonietta dell'Era, and the bounding Enrico Cecchetti, who was to stay in Russia to become a teacher with the Imperial Ballet and later to return to Europe to give classes

76. Olga Preobrazhenska (1871–1962). *Prima ballerina* at the Mariinsky Theatre, a darling of the gallery and famous for the gaiety which infused her personality both on and off the stage, she was much loved throughout her career. She taught in St Petersburg until 1921, when she – like so many others – arrived in Paris and opened a ballet school. It was famous to all dancers as 'Madame Préo's' and her pupils included Baronova, Toumanova and nearly every dancer worth his or her salt. A small but adorable figure, armed with a tiny watering-can with which she would sprinkle the studio floor, she was still giving exhilarating classes when over ninety years old.

to the Diaghilev company and, later still, to many creators of today's ballet.

These Italian artists offered a real challenge to the Russian dancers, who struggled to emulate their virtuosity and who learnt much from them. The Russian school of dancing became an amalgamation of many schools: the French school of such men as Perrot, Saint-Léon, Petipa; the Italian manner of Blasis; the Franco-Danish school of Bournonville. This last element was the result of the presence in St Petersburg of Per Christian Johansson (1817–1903). Elegant and distinguished in technique, he had studied with Bournonville and was recognized as a rising star of the Swedish ballet. On a private visit to St Petersburg in 1841 he asked for an opportunity to show his paces as a dancer, and was soon engaged as a *premier danseur*. He partnered Marie Taglioni on her visits to Russia in 1841 and 1842, and remained in that country for the rest of his life, adopting Russian nationality and proving himself one of the most admired artists on the stage. From 1860 he was also invited to start teaching. In 1869, when he retired from dancing, he was appointed a leading instructor at the Imperial Ballet School, where he moulded several generations of dancers. He was notably important as a teacher for men, on whom he impressed the virtues of Bournonville training. He observed to

Nicholas Legat (1869–1937), his finest male pupil, 'The Russian school is the French school, only the French have forgotten it.' Legat records that the highest praise Johansson ever gave to a dancer was to say, 'Now you may do that in public.' Marius Petipa – almost Johansson's contemporary, although the slightly older Swede always called him 'Old 'un' – had little facility in composing male variations; it is reported that Petipa would sit through Johansson's classes for men with notebook and pencil, and when he left, Johansson would wink and say, 'The old man's pinched some more.' Johansson's daughter, Anna Johansson (1860–1917), became a ballerina in St Petersburg, her style not dissimilar to Taglioni's. She was later to become a celebrated teacher, heading the *classe de perfectionnement* (the ballerinas' class) until her untimely death.

The arrival of Zucchi, and the renewed interest in ballet she inspired, came at a time when important changes were already taking place in ballet. These followed the appointment of Ivan Alexandrovich Vsevolozhsky as director of the Imperial Theatres. During the sixteen years of his service, from 1883 to 1899, this highly cultured and charming man set about reorganizing the ballet, initiating new rehearsal rooms, instigating a new ballet teaching syllabus, abolishing the post of official composer to the ballet (Minkus was the last to hold that position) and offering support to Marius Petipa. His patronage also extended to Tchaikovsky, for whose music he had a great admiration, and after a preliminary attempt to persuade Tchaikovsky to compose a ballet, he succeeded in interesting him in *The Sleeping Beauty*. The creation of this ballet is well documented in Roland John Wiley's essential study, *Tchaikovsky's Ballets*, and offers a good example of Petipa's methods of work. It was the choreographer's habit to prepare the stage action with great care at home, planning a scenario, using small figures like chess-men with which to sketch groupings and important scenes. He provided his composer with a detailed working scenario, containing the action fully explained, even with details

77. (Left) Marie Mariusovna Petipa and Pavel Gerdt (1844–1917) in the bacchanal from Petipa's *The Seasons*, first produced in St Petersburg in 1900. Gerdt was the principal male dancer of the St Petersburg Ballet from 1866 until his jubilee in the year before his death. He created many of the chief roles in the Petipa–Ivanov repertory and was famous for the nobility of his style. He taught many of the finest dancers of the Imperial Ballet in its heyday.

78. (Right) Anna Pavlova (1881–1931) and Vaslav Nijinsky (1889–1950) in Fokine's *Le Pavillon d'Armide* as first staged at the Mariinsky Theatre in 1907 (see Chapter 5).

79. Tamara Karsavina (1885–1978) in *La Fille mal gardée* at the Mariinsky Theatre. Adored for her beauty and her intelligence and for the grace – physical as well as spiritual – of her performances, Karsavina contributed enormously to the success of the early Diaghilev seasons. She left Russia with her second husband, the English diplomat H. J. Bruce, in 1918, and after her retirement from the stage continued as a guide to and beneficent influence on British ballet.

of length and type of music required, and sometimes with indications of orchestration.

The success of *The Sleeping Beauty*, after an initial coolness (the Tsar did not much like it at the official dress rehearsal in January 1890), was assured. The Italian guest ballerina Carlotta Brianza was the first Aurora, and Pavel Gerdt, the Imperial Ballet's favourite (albeit ageing) *premier danseur* was the Prince, while the roles of Carabosse and the Blue Bird afforded Enrico Cecchetti the chance to show off both his skill as a mime and the brilliance of his dance technique. The success of *Beauty* led Vsevolozhsky to think that another score should be commissioned from Tchaikovsky for Petipa, but this second piece, *The Nutcracker*, first given on 7 December 1892, was far less of a triumph. The great disadvantage of the work is its weak libretto. Its two acts are lacking in urgent dramatic action, and the role for the ballerina is reduced to one *pas de deux* in the second act. Tchaikovsky liked his task little, and Petipa had difficulty in devising a viable scenario. Ill-health prevented him from creating the choreography, and the task was entrusted to the second ballet-master, Lev Ivanov (1834–1901).

80. Sophie Fedorova (1879–1963) was one of the most admired character dancers of the Moscow ballet. She is seen here in Alexander Gorsky's celebrated staging of *Don Quixote* at the Bolshoy Theatre.

Ivanov's career was spent in the shadow of Petipa, and outstanding though his qualities as a choreographer seem to have been, he did not have much chance to compose those romantic and emotional ballets for which he was temperamentally fitted. Constrained by Petipa's detailed plotting of the action of *The Nutcracker*, whose indications he had to follow, Ivanov's greatness can yet be seen in the snowflake sequence at the end of the first act, where he was freed from Petipa's minutiae, and in the *grand pas de deux*, in both of which he could respond directly to the music. The first production of *The Nutcracker* was a failure, and despite the myriad versions that exist by later hands it must be accounted a most difficult work to produce satisfactorily, although the lure of Tchaikovsky's miraculous score is such that choreographers cannot resist trying to make something of it. Most fail completely. George Balanchine's staging for the New York City Ballet, and the Royal Ballet's recension, which restores much of the Ivanov choreography from the notation of the original, seem to us the most valid productions of recent years.

81. (Left) Anna Pavlova as Aspicia and Mikhail Mordkin (1880–1944) as Lord Wilson in *The Pharaoh's Daughter*, staged at the Bolshoy Theatre in Moscow in 1905. Mordkin, a celebrated *danseur* of the Moscow ballet, later partnered Pavlova for some years when she started touring the world with her own company, but their temperaments clashed, and Pavlova slapped Mordkin's face at a curtain call after a particularly unhappy *pas de deux*. Mordkin, through his school and company, was eventually to become a significant influence on ballet in America.

82. (Right) Anna Pavlova in *Paquita* at the Mariinsky Theatre in 1908. The ballet was first staged by Petipa (after Mazilier's original) in Russia when he arrived there in 1847. He later revised it considerably and today the *grand pas* from this old ballet – which Petipa inserted into the staging in 1881 – is well known as a classical display piece. Pavlova's charm, and her impeccable feet, are evident in this photograph which dates from the first decade of this century.

Ivanov's bid for immortality came two years after *Nutcracker* when, on 17 February 1894, the second act of *Swan Lake* was chosen to form part of a performance dedicated to Tchaikovsky's memory. Tchaikovsky had died in the previous year, and there had already been some discussion in the Mariinsky Theatre about the possibility of Petipa staging *Swan Lake*. The ballet had originally been produced at the Bolshoy Theatre, Moscow, in 1877 – it was Tchaikovsky's first ballet score – but an inadequate choreographer, Wenzel Reisinger, plus a conductor who found the score 'too difficult' and a leading ballerina of no great quality, had all ensured that the staging would be a failure. Two later attempts to produce the ballet at the Bolshoy Theatre had little more success, and the music had finally been laid aside. Tchaikovsky's death now brought the decision to present the second act of *Swan Lake* which, because of Petipa's illness, was entrusted to Ivanov. Freed from any requirements other than his own understanding of the score, Ivanov created a choreographic masterpiece, which featured the visiting Italian ballerina Pierina Legnani as Odette. On 15 January 1895 the entire ballet was brought to the stage of the Mariinsky Theatre, with Ivanov's second act

83. Mikhail Fokine in *La Halte de Cavalerie* (Petipa, 1896). This picture gives a very good idea of the elegance and virility of the young Fokine; no wonder that nearly all the girls in the ballet school were in love with him!

84. Agrippina Vaganova (1879–1951) as Odette in *Swan Lake* at the Mariinsky Theatre. No beauty, and lacking influential friends, she did not achieve official ballerina ranking until 1915, the year before her retirement from the stage. She was, however, known as 'The Queen of Variations', and she was later to be recognized as one of the greatest teachers in the history of ballet and founder of the Soviet school (see Chapter 9).

Я. ВАГАНОВА

retained, and his version of Act IV added. Petipa was responsible for supervising the staging and the editing of the action, and for the choreography of Acts I and III.

Ivanov's career – he died six years later – produced nothing of comparable importance, but Petipa went on to create several more ballets, including the splendid *Raymonda* of 1898; despite a foolish libretto, the magnificence of Glazunov's music (a true extension of Tchaikovsky's scores) inspired the old ballet-master to produce what was his last major success, a work still performed and loved today. Petipa's declining years were embittered by his dislike of the new director of the Imperial Theatres, Colonel Telyakovsky, and by the terrible failure of his last full-length ballet, *The Magic Mirror*, in

ГЕРДТЪ.

85. Elizaveta Gerdt (1891–1975) as the Lilac Fairy in *The Sleeping Beauty.* The daughter of Pavel Gerdt, she was a ballerina at the Mariinsky Theatre and was noted for the purity of her classical style. She stayed in Russia after the October Revolution to dance and teach, moving to Moscow in 1934. Among her pupils were many of the leading artists of the Bolshoy Ballet, including Maya Plisetskaya and Raissa Struchkova.

1903, when he was eighty-four. The remaining seven years of his life were spent in retirement, and the Imperial Ballet, without a great guiding spirit, lived off the wealth of Petipa's repertory until the convulsive changes brought about by the Revolution of 1917. It is significant, though, that Petipa should have seen and welcomed the choreographic début of Mikhail Fokine, and the artists formed by Petipa's schooling were in part the inspiration for the first sensational Diaghilev ballet seasons in Paris in 1909 and 1910, which were to bring ballet out of Russia to the West. It is even ironic that it is the Petipa heritage rather than the Fokine works which have been so vital to the continued life of the classical ballet in the West and in Soviet Russia.

86. Vasily Tikhomirov (1876–1956) was a leading dancer at the Bolshoy Theatre who became an influential teacher and choreographer, succeeding Gorsky as director of the Moscow ballet in 1924, and sharing the choreography of *The Red Poppy*, the first successful Soviet ballet. He is seen here in Gorsky's *The Dance Dream*, which was staged in London for the coronation celebrations of 1911.

5 Émigrés:
Diaghilev and Pavlova

Virginia Zucchi, who by the soul and fire of her dancing helped to renew interest in ballet in Russia at the end of the nineteenth century, also helped to change the whole concept of ballet in the twentieth century. Had the painter Alexandre Benois and his friends, among them Léon Bakst, not been captivated by her artistry they might never have introduced Serge Diaghilev to ballet. And without Diaghilev the art of ballet as we know it today would be different indeed. He is the key figure, not only to this chapter but to nearly all that follows.

SERGE DIAGHILEV AND HIS BALLETS RUSSES

Until Diaghilev arrived on the scene the destiny of ballet had been guided by ballet-masters and choreographers. Their role will always be a vitally important one, but during the years he was presenting ballet, from 1909 until his death in 1929, Diaghilev played a greater part than that of any of his choreographers although they included Fokine, Nijinsky, Massine, Nijinska and Balanchine. Before discussing their work it is necessary to sketch the background of this man of genius whose productions were to influence all the arts, not only in the first part of this century but up to the present day.

Diaghilev was born in 1872 in the Selistchev Barracks in the province of Novgorod. His father was a colonel in the Imperial Guard and his mother, who died soon after his birth, was also well born. In 1874 his father remarried and his stepmother, Elena Valerianovna Panaeva, was to be the greatest influence during the early years of his life. She came of a distinguished and exceptionally musical family. Her father had built a private theatre where fine singers performed Italian opera, and her sister was a pupil of the singer Pauline Viardot.

The young Diaghilev grew up in Perm, where the family settled when he was ten years old, in a happy home among cultured relations and friends. The Diaghilevs were among the first families in Perm, owning a large house and entertaining freely. Young Serge even in his schooldays was full of self-confidence, adept at getting his own way and clever at persuading friends to help him out if he fell behind with his school work. For his real interests were in the music, paintings and books at home. Another mentor was his paternal aunt, Anna Pavlovna Filosofova, liberal and artistic and influential in the town. Her son Dima became a close friend, and with this cousin Diaghilev went on his first European tour.

When he arrived in St Petersburg in 1890, to study law, Dima introduced him to Alexandre Benois, Walter Nouvel, Léon Bakst and other artists who received him cautiously at first, thinking him a gauche provincial. Soon they recognized his gifts and intelligence and accepted him as one of their circle. (This period of early friendship is warmly described in Benois's *Reminiscences*.) The group of friends shared an interest in all the arts, although Diaghilev at that time was not especially interested in ballet. His enthusiasm for music was such that he went to Rimsky-Korsakov for lessons (the composer discouraged him from attempting a career in music) and he was also passionately fond of fine painting. Not surprisingly, it took him six years, instead of the customary four, to get his law degree.

In 1898 the friends launched a new magazine, *Mir Iskustva* ('The World of Art'). The name *Mir Iskustva* was also attached to the group who worked on it; it was to last until 1904. Diaghilev was the editor, and now demonstrated the unique gift which was to make possible the whole of his subsequent, enormous enterprise. Benois put it thus: 'It is impossible to believe that the painters, musicians and choreographers who gave birth to the movement known as *Mir Iskustva* ... would have worked to such good effect had not Diaghilev placed himself at their head and taken command of them.' He was to command creative artists until the end of his life. If he did not himself create, he created through others. Our debt to him is incalculable.

Between 1899 and 1901 Diaghilev had a brief association with the Imperial Theatres, then under the direction of Prince Serge Volkonsky, a friend who was sympathetic to the liberal ideals of the *Mir Iskustva* group. Diaghilev was appointed as a special assistant to edit the *Annual of the Theatres* for 1899/1900 and he produced a volume far more artistic and lively than the drier documents of former years (characteristically, it was also vastly more expensive). There was at the time a plan for a new production of Delibes's *Sylvia*, with Benois, Bakst, Korovin and Serov all participating. But the authorities frowned on such an ambitious production being entrusted to young men; there was a row, and Diaghilev was dismissed. Soon afterwards Volkonsky himself was forced to resign, having incurred the displeasure of Kshessinska; he retained his interest in ballet, travelled widely, studied the Dalcroze system of eurythmics and died in Hot Springs, Virginia, in 1937.

Temporarily abandoning ballet (temperamentally he was not suited to the role of assistant), Diaghilev returned to his first loves of painting and music. He arranged exhibitions of contemporary paintings nearly every year from 1897 onwards and in 1905 achieved his greatest success with the exhibition of Historic Russian Paintings 1705–1905, at the Taurida Palace. He had scoured Russia to assemble his pictures from the great country houses and he hung them, in the romantic setting of the old palace, in a novel and imaginative way. So successful was the Taurida exhibition that Diaghilev determined to show Russian art to the West.

In 1906 he put on an exhibition of Russian art at the Salon d'Automne in Paris and tried out a concert of Russian music as well. He met the Comtesse de Greffulhe, the greatest patron of the arts in Paris as well as one of the most influential women in society, and she introduced him to the impresario Gabriel Astruc. Like Diaghilev, Astruc was a man of artistic vision not always associated with the word impresario.

It was arranged that the following year a series of concerts entitled 'Russian Music Through the Ages' should be given in Paris. In 1908, Diaghilev took Russian opera to Paris and Chaliapin sang and acted – breathtakingly – the role of Boris Godunov. Astruc had heard much from Diaghilev about the dancers of the Russian ballet – Pavlova, Karsavina, Nijinsky – and the choreography of Fokine. For the *Saison Russe* in 1909 he wanted Russian ballet as well as Russian opera. Diaghilev had by now met not only most of the young artists in Paris, among them Jean Cocteau, but also the all-important society hostesses, and they set to work that winter to prepare the way for the first visit of the Russian ballet.

Because of his friendship with people like the Comtesse de Greffulhe, the Princesse de Polignac and Misia Sert in Paris, and with Lady Ripon in London, some writers have accused Diaghilev of being a snob. There is no doubt that he enjoyed the social world, but it was also absolutely essential for his enterprise that he should have the friendship and support of these people. His company had no direct subsidy. The Imperial Theatres at first loaned him artists and some sets and costumes, but the money had always to be raised by Diaghilev. As long ago as 1895 he had written to his stepmother: '... I think I have found my true vocation – being a Maecenas.

87. Tamara Karsavina with Adolph Bolm in *Le Pavillon d'Armide*.

88. The Diaghilev ballet in *Les Sylphides*, Paris, 1909, with Tamara Karsavina in the centre.

I have all that is necessary save the money – *mais ça viendra.*' It was a statement of complete confidence in himself and he maintained this confident attitude in public to the end of his life, but there were many times when the money did not come and when he was rescued, sometimes from near-bankruptcy and starvation, by these fashionable friends. The glorious Diaghilev ballet existed during a period when royal patronage was dying and before state aid or grants from philanthropic foundations had begun. Private patronage was still possible.

MIKHAIL FOKINE

Back in St Petersburg, Mikhail Fokine had already established himself as a choreographer of originality with an approach to ballet quite different from the stereotyped, evening-long spectaculars that Petipa had staged for so many

89. Adolph Bolm (1884–1951) as the chief Polovt-sian warrior in Fokine's *Dances from Prince Igor*. The virility and passion of Bolm and his warriors in this ballet created a great sensation during the first Diaghilev season in Paris, and did much to change the faded image of the male dancer. Bolm stayed with the company until 1914 and in 1918 went to America, where he did much valuable work in pioneering ballet as dancer, choreographer and teacher, working not only in the theatre but also in Hollywood.

years. He believed that ballet should have artistic unity, that costumes and settings as well as music should blend harmoniously with dancing that was appropriate to the theme and subject of the production. It was a time of change and unrest. The 1905 political insurrection had been brutally quelled, but in the ballet schools as well as outside the desire for reform was strong. A group of dancers, of whom Fokine was the leader, used to meet and discuss their ideals for the new ballet. Tamara Karsavina, who was to help realize so many of Fokine's ambitions, was his devoted disciple and wrote about their work together in her immortal book, *Theatre Street*. Anna Pavlova had the wit to ask him to arrange for her, in 1907, a solo for a charity performance. It was *The Dying Swan*, to music by Saint-Saëns, which was always to be associated with her name.

Isadora Duncan visited St Petersburg in 1904 and caused great controversy among the old-school balletomanes and the reformers, yet Fokine felt that her barefoot, deeply emotional dancing, to music of the great composers, confirmed his beliefs.

More important from Diaghilev's point of view was the fact that Fokine

90. A group from *Carnaval*, a picture taken from the French magazine of the period, *Comoedia Illustré*, which illustrated and described very fully the early Diaghilev seasons. Papillon is on the extreme right and Chiarina on her left. The parts were created by, respectively, Nijinsky's sister Bronislava Nijinska and Fokine's wife Vera Fokina.

had already staged a number of short ballets which might form the basis of a repertory he could take to Paris. *Chopiniana*, which was to be renamed *Les Sylphides*, had been arranged for a charity performance at the Mariinsky in 1907. *Le Pavillon d'Armide*, a ballet devised and designed by Benois with music by Nicholas Tcherepnin, was produced in 1907, and *Une Nuit d'Égypte* (which became *Cléopâtre*) in 1908. In 1908 another event took place which was to give Diaghilev a greater incentive to show Russian ballet and Russian dancers to the West: he met Vaslav Nijinsky, one of the most gifted of the galaxy of dancers then appearing with the Imperial Russian Ballet, and he fell in love with him.

The preparations for the first Paris season have been described by nearly every one of the people involved. Their various accounts, and full descriptions of the financial crises, withdrawal of backing and rescue by influential friends, have been carefully assessed and set out in Richard Buckle's books *Nijinsky* and *Diaghilev.*

The Paris Opéra was not available, so Diaghilev had the big Théâtre du Châtelet entirely refurbished for his season. While carpenters and decorators worked on the building, Fokine rehearsed the company recruited from both the St Petersburg and Moscow Imperial Theatres, and Diaghilev (much to Fokine's annoyance) brought his fashionable friends to watch and to marvel at his dancers.

The dress rehearsal augured well and the first night, 19 May 1909, was a triumph. It was the height of the season, all Paris was there and the Russian ballet did not disappoint them. The programme began with the revised version of *Le Pavillon d'Armide*, danced by Karalli, Karsavina, Mordkin and Nijinsky, which received an ovation; this was followed by the 'Polovtsian' act of Borodin's opera *Prince Igor*, designed by Roerich, with Adolph Bolm leading the dancers in Fokine's marvellous barbaric choreography for the warriors; finally, *Le Festin*, a *divertissement* to music by Russian composers with a borrowed set by Korovin and with costumes by Korovin, Bakst, Benois and Bilibin.

The press next morning was ecstatic, and Karsavina, Nijinsky and Bolm were the first great stars of the Diaghilev ballet. Later Anna Pavlova arrived to dance in *Les Sylphides* and *Cléopâtre*, as well as appearing as Armida, and she was at once recognized as an incomparable artist. Only a small part of her career was with Diaghilev, but she cemented the triumph of that first season and everything she did for him was touched with her genius. Karsavina was the ballerina who best understood Diaghilev's and Fokine's new concept of ballet (although she was not too happy with some of the modernistic ballets of the 1920s), but Pavlova's contribution at the beginning of the enterprise is important.

The Russian dancers having proved their artistic merit (for ballet had been a debased and suspect entertainment in Paris before their arrival), the doors of the Paris Opéra were opened to them for their return visit in 1910.

For this season Fokine had re-worked his ballet *Carnaval*, to Schumann's music, enchantingly decorated by Bakst; he had created the exotic *Schéhérazade* (Bakst at his most opulent and oriental), and had also arranged the dances for *The Firebird*.

The Firebird was the first ballet that Diaghilev commissioned from the young Igor Stravinsky. He had wanted something Russian and the story was drawn from various Russian fairy-tales. The choreography was not entirely successful, as the best of the dancing came in the first scene, but the ballet is of historic importance in that it introduced Stravinsky to the ballet theatre. Stravinsky was to become the most distinguished composer to write

91. A rehearsal of *The Firebird* in Paris in 1910. Fokine leans against the piano at which Stravinsky is seated, and Karsavina is the ballerina in the centre.

for ballet since Tchaikovsky, whose music he understood and loved. He wrote ballets, in addition to all his other music, until shortly before his death in 1971, finding in George Balanchine, the last of Diaghilev's choreographers, a friend and colleague with whom he could collaborate. Their collaboration helped to give the New York City Ballet of today its high musical reputation.

Fokine's choreography dominated the repertory of the Diaghilev ballet until 1912. He was to follow *The Firebird* with an exquisite *pas de deux* for Karsavina and Nijinsky, *Le Spectre de la rose* (suggested by the poet Jean-Louis Vaudoyer, from Gautier's poem '*Je suis le spectre d'une rose, Que tu portais hier au bal*'), which was first performed in Monte Carlo on 19 April 1911; with *Narcisse*, in a Grecian setting designed by Bakst; and with *Petrushka* (first produced in Paris on 13 June 1911), in which the collaboration of Benois, Stravinsky and Fokine resulted in the greatest ballet of this period. Benois's loving recreation of the Butterweek Fairs of St Petersburg in his childhood, Stravinsky's superb score, Fokine's masterly manipulation of the fairground scenes, the episodes in the puppets' booths and the inspired performances by Nijinsky, Karsavina, Orlov and Cecchetti (principal mime and ballet-master to the troupe) fused into a masterpiece that lives to this day – although no dancers have recaptured the magic of the first interpretation. The ballet, like *The Firebird*, has survived primarily because of the music.

Fokine made two more exotic ballets in 1912, *Le Dieu bleu* and *Thamar*, and another Grecian one, *Daphnis and Chloe*, to music by Ravel, which Diaghilev had commissioned in 1909 but which was not staged until 8 June 1912. Already, however, there were jealousies and rivalries among the collaborators. Benois had taken offence because he thought he had been given insufficient credit for ballets he had devised. Fokine was jealous of the way in which Diaghilev was encouraging Nijinsky to experiment with new choreography. By the end of 1912 Benois and Fokine had left the enterprise.

Looking back on those early Paris seasons (Paris counted most in those days, although Berlin, Rome, London, Monte Carlo, Vienna and Budapest had all been conquered by the Russian ballet before the First World War), the Russian critic Valerian Svetlov (who married the great classical ballerina Vera Trefilova) wrote in the *Dancing Times* in December 1929 that the Fokine period was really 'a transition between the old classical ballet and the new modernism'. He explained that the great revelation of the Diaghilev

92. Nijinsky as Petrushka. The marvel of his interpretation is clear from this photograph which admirably conveys that glimmer of a soul which inhabits Petrushka's body.

93. Vaslav Nijinsky and a frieze of nymphs from his revolutionary *L'Après-midi d'un faune* (Paris, 1912).

ballet was the impact of the male dancers, the suitability and rightness of the costumes and the tremendous difference from the productions to which Paris audiences were accustomed. There, before Diaghilev, they were used to seeing the ballerina as the centre of all the action, and the dancing of the *corps de ballet* as a sort of padding, contrived for the moments of the ballerina's rest. The same would have been true in London, where ballet had become a music-hall item; although great dancers had been seen there before the advent of Diaghilev, the works in which they appeared had little artistic value.

VASLAV NIJINSKY

Several of Fokine's ballets have survived – he staged them for companies in many different countries, until his death in New York in 1942 – but the choreography of Nijinsky has been almost entirely lost. What remains is a version of *L'Après-midi d'un faune* and a fascinating reconstruction of his *Sacre du printemps*.

Fokine had rejected the obligatory *tutu*, point shoes and variation for the ballerina. Nijinsky went much further. In *L'Après-midi*, danced to Debussy's music and decorated by Bakst in the style of Greek friezes, he made the dancers perform barefoot (except that he as the faun and Nelidova as the chief nymph wore sandals) and they moved in profile to the audience along a narrow path at the front of the stage. For the Faun, Nijinsky invented a curious walk. Gone was the soaring Spirit of the Rose, the abandoned leaps of the Golden Slave in *Schéhérazade*. Instead, a primitive animal moved on flat feet in a jerky rhythm. The ballet, which is only eleven minutes long, concerns the confrontation of some nymphs by a lazy, then lecherous, faun. The nymphs take fright, the principal one drops a veil, and in the final pose the Faun returns to his rock, where he had been sunning himself when the ballet began, and lowers his body upon the veil. The ending, which was considered by

94. Nijinsky in his own ballet *Jeux* (1913). Here was modern dress and modern man on stage in a ballet of which Diaghilev said, 'We date it 1930' as a comment on its unprecedented modernity.

95. Dancers of the Joffrey Ballet in the reconstruction of Nijinsky's *Le Sacre du printemps* which was the fruit of lengthy research by Millicent Hodson. From an extraordinary variety of sources, Dr Hodson was able to recreate a choreographic text which evoked (if it did not exactly reproduce) the Nijinsky original, with a scrupulous revival by Kenneth Archer of Roerich's designs. The result was fascinating and cast a new light on a highly significant work in the history of twentieth-century ballet. It was first staged by the Joffrey Ballet in New York in 1988.

some to be obscene, caused a typically Parisian furore (London later took it quite calmly) and Diaghilev used the scandal to obtain the maximum of publicity. Nijinsky had certainly made an impression.

His next ballet, *Jeux*, first produced in Paris on 15 May 1913 with Karsavina, Ludmilla Schollar and Nijinsky as the three dancers, has been described as the first ballet on a contemporary theme. It dealt with shifting relationships between three tennis players and the costumes were a stylized version of everyday sportswear.

Both these ballets, however, were entirely overshadowed by Nijinsky's next undertaking. He was to make a ballet to Stravinsky's great composition *Le Sacre du printemps*. To help Nijinsky with the difficult music, Diaghilev engaged from the Dalcroze School of Eurythmics one of its brightest student teachers, to be known in ballet history as Marie Rambert. The ballet had a quite extraordinary number of rehearsals and only eight performances, five in Paris and three in London. Then it was lost. Diaghilev staged a new version by

Léonide Massine in Paris in 1920 (in which the English dancer, best known by her stage name of Lydia Sokolova, was to become famous), but the choreography was entirely new.

The setting by Roerich suggested ancient Russia, but Nijinsky seemed to be attempting to go back into pre-history. He talked of stones and the earth and he invented new turned-in positions of the feet. The ballet – because of the music as much as the strange dancing – caused the expected uproar in Paris but, like *L'Après-midi d'un faune*, was seriously received in London. The critic Svetlov who, though reared on the ballets of Petipa and Ivanov, followed the fortunes of the Diaghilev ballet from the beginning, stated that *Le Sacre* was 'the masterpiece of the young artist'. Of the Massine version he wrote: 'It gained nothing in the new edition, and it is quite incomprehensible why this remarkable work was ever remodelled.'

Nijinsky was to make one more ballet, *Tyl Eulenspiegel*, which was first produced at the Metropolitan Opera House, New York, on 23 October 1916, to the music of Richard Strauss and with designs by the American artist Robert Edmond Jones. By this time Nijinsky was already showing signs of the mental illness that was to end his dancing career so tragically in the following year. He was without the guiding hand of Diaghilev and, although the ballet obviously contained some original notions, it must have reached the stage in a fairly haphazard state.

The rift with Diaghilev had occurred when the ballet company sailed for its first tour of South America in 1913. A young Hungarian socialite and balletomane, Romola de Pulszky, who particularly admired the genius of Nijinsky, was on board the SS *Avon* and Diaghilev was not. (He was terrified of the sea; a fortune-teller had said that he would meet his death by water.) In the course of the voyage Nijinsky announced that he was going to marry Romola, and marry her he did, in Buenos Aires on 10 September 1913. The company were suitably intrigued and excited by the event. Not so Diaghilev. He was deeply hurt, indeed distraught, when he heard the news. When the company returned to Europe, Diaghilev summoned Serge Grigoriev, his faithful *régisseur*, and gave him the unpleasant task of sending a telegram to Nijinsky dismissing him from the company. Nijinsky was to return to the company, after wartime internment, for the American tours of 1916 and 1916/17, but his career was virtually at an end. He danced in public for the last time with the Diaghilev ballet in Buenos Aires on 26 September 1917. Soon afterwards he succumbed to mental illness, but lived on, cared for by Romola, until 1950 when he died in London.

Diaghilev, having alienated one choreographer and lost another, continued to plan new productions. Fokine was coaxed back in 1914 to produce *Papillons* (a kind of companion piece to *Carnaval*), *La Légende de Joseph* and

Le Coq d'or, and Boris Romanov staged *Le Rossignol*. But despite the collaboration of many distinguished artists it was not a very rewarding year. In *La Légende de Joseph*, however, a new discovery of Diaghilev had made his début. Léonide Massine had been engaged by the great man during his last visit to Moscow, early in 1914. He was to become the next distinguished choreographer.

LÉONIDE MASSINE

Massine has described in his autobiography how Diaghilev had educated him, by taking him to look at paintings and sculpture, playing him music and introducing him to the artist friends who would later help in the creation of his ballets. The first to be performed in public was *Le Soleil de Nuit*, a collection of Russian scenes and dances, to music by Rimsky-Korsakov from *The Snow Maiden*. The painter Michel Larionov (with his wife, Natalia Gontcharova, by now a close friend of Diaghilev) designed the ballet and gave Massine much assistance. It was first produced at the Grand Theatre, Geneva – in neutral Switzerland – on 20 December 1915.

96. (Left) Léonide Massine as Joseph in *La Légende de Joseph* (1914). First produced in Paris, this ballet marked Massine's début with the Diaghilev company. Marie Rambert spoke of Massine's extraordinarily expressive 'Byzantine' eyes.

97. (Above) Diaghilev with his entourage, a photograph said by Vera Stravinsky to have been taken in Paris in January 1920 at the house of Rouché after *Le Chant du Rossignol*. The group includes, from left to right: the conductor Ansermet and his wife, Léonide Massine, Diaghilev holding a nosegay of flowers, Misia Sert (Diaghilev's greatest woman friend), Igor Stravinsky and Pavel Korebut-Kubatovich (Diaghilev's cousin, who acted as an assistant in administrative matters).

The war years were cruel ones for Diaghilev, but somehow he kept a company together and a nucleus of creative artists always with him. He made his headquarters in Lausanne and from there recruited new dancers (many were trapped in Russia) and, by superhuman effort and the intervention of crowned heads, secured the release of the Nijinskys so that a contract with Otto Kahn to present the company at the Metropolitan Opera House, New

York, early in 1916 could be honoured. Diaghilev braved the Atlantic crossing for that first North American tour but did not travel with the company when they returned later in the year or when they went to South America in 1917. He was busy in Spain and Italy, planning new works that would be choreographed by Massine.

It should be noted here that America saw the Diaghilev ballet at a time when it was beset by wartime problems in Europe and torn by internal conflicts as Nijinsky's illness became worse. Consequently, except for a few perceptive writers and artists, especially those who had seen the company in Europe, it made little impact. The name of Anna Pavlova, even of Adeline Genée, meant more to Americans than that of Serge Diaghilev.

Massine had danced a great number of roles, including many of Nijinsky's, during the Diaghilev ballet's first American tour in 1916. He had experienced for the first time the rigours of one-night stands, to which he would return in the 1930s, and he had been enchanted by the skyscrapers. But he shared Diaghilev's relief at their safe arrival back in Europe (they landed at Cadiz) and did not go on the subsequent American tours. The Diaghilev ballet had been invited by King Alfonso of Spain, an ardent balletomane, to give summer seasons in Madrid and San Sebastian in 1916 and for them Massine devised two new ballets. *Las Meniñas*, inspired by the painting by Velasquez he had seen in the Prado, was danced to Fauré's *Pavane*. *Kikimora*, a Russian folk tale, was done in collaboration with Larionov and Gontcharova, using music by Liadov. In September the company sailed for America but Diaghilev kept a small group of dancers in Europe with him, including Massine. He realized (as other companies were to realize later) that heavy touring makes the creation of new works impossible, and he wanted to plan for the seasons in Rome and Paris that lay ahead.

Diaghilev took his group of artists to Italy, where the studio in the Piazza Venezia, Rome, became a workshop from which new ballets quickly emerged. In the winter of 1916/1917, a period of amazing creativity, Massine was occupied with three entirely different ballets, ballets which were to establish him firmly as a choreographer of immense versatility and originality, one of which, *Parade*, was to launch a new period in the company's work. Cut off for ever from Russia, Diaghilev leaned more and more towards the composers and painters of the school of Paris.

In chronological order, the first to be staged was *Les Femmes de bonne humeur*, at the Costanzi Theatre, Rome, on 12 April 1917. The subject, a comedy by Goldoni, and the music, selected from Scarlatti, had been suggested by Diaghilev, and the beautiful décor and costumes were designed by Bakst. It was a neat compliment to the Italian audiences (who adored it) and it was the first of Massine's charming comedy ballets in which, with his unique gift for creating characters through dance and gesture, he told a

98. Léonide Massine as the Chinese Conjuror in his own *Parade*, first produced in 1917.

highly complex story clearly and with wit. He had a fantastic cast to carry out his ideas. Enrico Cecchetti, then sixty-seven years old, and his wife Giuseppina played the old couple; the brilliant Polish dancers, Idzikowski and Woizikowski, and Massine himself, had important roles; lovely Tchernicheva was the sorrowing Constanza; and Lydia Lopokova returned to the company to create the role of Mariuccia, ever to be identified with her performance. (Lopokova, an enchanting, capricious ballerina, flitted in and out of the Diaghilev company from 1910, when she danced Columbine in *Carnaval*, until 1925, when she married John Maynard Keynes and settled in England.)

At the same time Massine was preparing (for Paris) *Les Contes Russes*, a development of the earlier *Kikimora*, and working with Picasso on the first Cubist ballet, *Parade*. Jean Cocteau and Picasso had arrived in Rome with the outline of the ballet already planned and the music written by Erik Satie.

99. The American Manager in *Parade*, revived by Léonide Massine for London Festival Ballet in 1974. The costume is a 'constructed' Cubist shape.

It was to be a burlesque of the circus and music-hall with costumes executed in Cubist style. The idea had immediately appealed to Diaghilev, for controversy over the Cubist painters was at its height and he saw the possibility of another *succès de scandale*. His whole career was a balancing act, weighing his artistic vision against box-office and publicity potential. Significantly, on the only occasion when he ignored fashion and backed his own deep-rooted Russian taste in his revival of *The Sleeping Princess*, he met disaster.

The title of the ballet is explained by Massine as having been taken from Picasso's visualization of French and American managers as animated billboards: 'For the American he [Picasso] devised a montage of a skyscraper with fragmentary faces and a gaudy sign reading "PARADE", which eventually became the name of the ballet.' The fashionable Erik Satie had produced just the right witty score the collaborators wanted. Cocteau's demands for the incorporation of the spoken voice were refused by Diaghilev, but megaphones were allowed and also the sound of typewriters and ships' sirens. To *Parade* can be traced a number of today's so-called innovations in music, design and choreography.

The ballet was intended to be fun. Massine and Picasso worked happily together in Italy and then in Paris, where the final rehearsals took place. The first performance was at the Théâtre du Châtelet on 18 May 1917, only a month after the première of *Les Femmes de bonne humeur*. It provoked the expected furore but was genuinely popular with audiences. A long review by Guillaume Apollinaire said that the collaborators had 'sought to reveal the fantasy, beauty and reality of our daily life'. The painter Juan Gris, who was later to design for ballet, described it as 'unpretentious, gay and distinctly comic'.

Parade was a landmark not only in the history of the Diaghilev ballet but also in the career of Picasso. While drawing dancers at work in the studio, fascinated by their movements and by the groups devised by Massine, he met his first wife Olga Kokhlova, and they married in 1918. He designed more ballets and curtains for ballets and never lost his interest in the form. As late as 1962 he did a lively curtain for *L'Après-midi d'un faune* which was rejected by the Paris Opéra but used later for a performance in Toulouse. A full account of Picasso's work for ballet and ballet's influence upon him is given in Douglas Cooper's *Picasso Theatre* (English edition, 1968).

After the Paris season the company went to Madrid, where *Parade* was given at the request of King Alfonso, once more to great acclaim. But it was becoming more and more difficult for Diaghilev to obtain engagements, and the year 1918 saw no new productions. Spain offered a refuge, with seasons at Madrid and Barcelona and some touring, but a visit to Lisbon was disastrous and Diaghilev was almost penniless. His plight, and that of the dancers who remained so loyal to him, is movingly described in Lydia Sokolova's memoirs. Typically, however, he would not allow any pause in the planning of future productions. He was urging Massine to use some little-known Rossini music for a ballet which eventually became *La Boutique fantasque* and he had introduced him to Spanish dancing in the hope that they might make a Spanish ballet. The latter was to have a score written by Manuel de Falla, and a Flamenco dancer called Felix★ was invited to join the company to help Massine with the national dances. The four of them, Diaghilev, Massine, de Falla and Felix, travelled throughout Spain, devouring national art and music. It was all distilled in an incomparable evocation of Spain, *The Three-Cornered Hat*.

With these two ballets, *The Three-Cornered Hat* and *La Boutique fantasque*, Diaghilev re-conquered London in 1919. They had their premières at the old Alhambra Theatre in Leicester Square on 5 and 22 July. *La Boutique fantasque* was eventually designed by the painter André Derain, after a row with Bakst, who did the preliminary designs which were rejected by Diaghilev. With Lopokova and Massine as the Can-Can Dancers leading a brilliant cast, it was an immediate and enduring success. For *The Three-Cornered Hat* Karsavina had rejoined the company to create the part of the Miller's Wife. Massine himself was the Miller, and he was to return triumphantly to London after another World War when in 1947 he revived the ballet and danced the Miller at Covent Garden with the Sadler's Wells Ballet. Based on a novel by Pedro Antonio de Alarcón, the ballet was a comedy, with serious undertones, about the attempted seduction of a virtuous wife by a lecherous old town governor. The score is one of the most marvellous written for ballet in this century. The obvious designer was the Spaniard, Picasso. The result – a masterpiece.

Massine made three more ballets for Diaghilev in 1920: *Le Chant du Rossignol*, *Pulcinella* (décor by Picasso) and the opera-ballet, *Le Astuzie Femminili* (later to be known as a one-act ballet, *Cimarosiana*). He also made a new version of *Le Sacre du printemps* which was first performed at the Théâtre des Champs-Élysées in Paris on 15 December. By the spring of 1921, however, Massine in his turn had married (the English dancer Vera Clark, known as Savina) and incurred Diaghilev's displeasure. In any case he was restless and wanted to work elsewhere. He returned intermittently to Diaghilev during the rest of the company's existence.

★ He came to a tragic end. Just before the première of *The Three-Cornered Hat* he was found in the middle of the night dancing frenetically before the altar of St Martin-in-the-Fields church in London. He was taken to a mental hospital at Epsom where he lived until 1941, never regaining his sanity. Massine later wondered 'if the seed of his mental illness was not inherent in his genius'. Could the same have been true of Nijinsky and Spessivtseva?

100. Design by Léon Bakst for a Neighbouring Prince, one of Aurora's suitors in *The Sleeping Princess* (London, 1921). The magnificence of this costume, for a relatively minor character, gives an indication of the splendour – and the cost – of the production.

The Sleeping Princess AND LA NIJINSKA

In 1921 Diaghilev was without a choreographer and a bleak year lay ahead. For his Paris season he presented *Chout*, a Russian legend devised by the painter Michel Larionov and the dancer Tadeusz Slavinski, and brought some Spanish dancers and musicians, the Cuadro Flamenco, to appear in a suite of Andalusian dances. For the important London season he decided to revive one of the great Petipa classics from the old Imperial Russian repertory, *La Belle au bois dormant*, called in English *The Sleeping Princess*.

The designs were entrusted to Léon Bakst, who set the ballet in the periods of Henry IV and Louis XIV of France, for the original fairy-tale on which the ballet had been based was French, by Charles Perrault, and Petipa had been a Frenchman. The designs were of surpassing grandeur and magnificence

101. Olga Spessivtseva (1895–1991) as the Princess Aurora in the last act of the Diaghilev *Sleeping Princess*. Graduating from the Imperial School in 1913, Spessivtseva's immense talent swiftly caught the attention of all the St Petersburg balletomanes. Within five years she was named ballerina. She had already visited America with Diaghilev's troupe in 1916, and returned to his company in 1921 to dance Aurora. She danced with the Paris Opéra Ballet in 1924 in *Giselle*, of which role she is acknowledged as the supreme interpreter of this century. She danced in London with the Camargo Society in 1932 but her later years were darkened by ill-health. Her dancing was recognized as being one of the most poetic expressions of the pure St Petersburg style. A priceless record of her outstanding talent exists in a brief film originally owned by Dame Marie Rambert; the master copy is now in the British Film Archive.

and no expense was spared in having them perfectly executed. Indeed, so rich were some of the fabrics that the dancers complained of the weight of the costumes. The choreography was revived by Nicholas Sergueyev, a former *régisseur* at the Mariinsky, from his notebooks in the Stepanov notation. Additional choreography was provided by Bronislava Nijinska, Nijinsky's sister, who had rejoined the company after a spell in Russia – she had had her own school for a while in Kiev.

A galaxy of ballerinas was engaged. Aurora was danced by Liubov Egorova, Vera Trefilova, Lydia Lopokova and, supremely, by Olga Spessivtseva. Prince Florimund was danced in turn by Vilzak and Vladimirov. Carlotta Brianza, the first Aurora, came out of retirement to mime Carabosse. The first pair to dance the Blue Bird *pas de deux* was Lydia Lopokova and Stanislas Idzikowski. Anton Dolin (disguised under his first Russian name, Patrikeeff) was one of the royal pages. The cast list (given in Beaumont's *Complete Book of Ballets*, in which he describes this version of the ballet, not the original one, in his chapter on Petipa) is breathtaking.

The ballet was danced nightly at the Alhambra Theatre for some three months, from 2 November 1921. It was at first an enormous success and it made an undying impression on all who saw it, but the London public was not then accustomed to a long run of a single ballet and to recover the tremendous financial outlay – the money had been put up by Sir Oswald Stoll – it would have had to run to packed houses for six months.

102. *Les Noces*, first produced in Paris in 1923. Scene ii: the blessing of the Bridegroom.

When Stoll began to press for some triple bills, with two other ballets to alternate with *The Sleeping Princess* in an attempt to improve box-office takings, Diaghilev was faced with a terrible decision. If the triple bills also failed, Stoll would have been entitled to confiscate all the scenery and costumes to settle the debts. If Diaghilev cut his losses and closed the season, Stoll would hold all the *Sleeping Princess* sets and costumes, but the rest of the repertory would be safe. Sadly, he took off the ballet on 4 February 1922. During its run there had been another historic occasion when, on 5 January, Cecchetti returned to mime Carabosse in celebration of his fifty years on stage as a dancer.

Diaghilev salvaged only a one-act ballet from Petipa's masterpiece, which he called *Aurora's Wedding*. Ironically, it proved very popular. It remained in the Diaghilev repertory until the end and lived on in the Ballets Russes companies of the 1930s and 1940s until it was supplanted by the English revival of the full-length work.

103. *Le Train bleu* was one of Diaghilev's ephemeral ballets of the 1920s, a 'danced operetta' concerned with fashionable life on the Côte d'Azur. The Blue Train used to bring the *beau monde* down to the south from Paris – it has of course departed by the time the ballet begins – and the action, devised by Jean Cocteau, took place on a beach, where pleasure-seekers disported themselves. The ballet had been inspired by the sight of the beautiful young Anton Dolin performing acrobatic stunts – the sort of showing-off that the young indulged in on the beach. Dolin played Le Beau Gosse ('The Handsome Kid'), Lydia Sokolova played a bathing belle, Leon Woizikowski a golfer modelled on the Prince of Wales and Bronislava Nijinska (who choreographed the ballet) a tennis-player not too far removed from Suzanne Lenglen. The clothes are by Chanel, the year is 1924, and frivolity is *de rigueur*. The ballet was re-staged by the Oakland (California) Ballet in 1989 as a significant example of Nijinska's choreography.

Out of the fiasco, however, emerged Diaghilev's next choreographer. Bronislava Nijinska's new arrangements of some of the dances showed her potential. She was entrusted first with Stravinsky's *Le Renard* and then with his *Les Noces*, with which she established herself as a very great artist indeed.

Les Noces, which has words and music by Stravinsky, is a deeply moving evocation of a Russian peasant wedding. The ballet was designed in earthy colours of brown, black and white by Natalia Gontcharova, and Nijinska devised architectural groupings mingled with strong peasant dances and passages of eloquent mime. The first performance was at the Gaîté-Lyrique in Paris on 13 July 1923. Nijinska revived it for Britain's Royal Ballet in 1966, and so faithful was the reconstruction that even the old Russian dancers who had been with Diaghilev described it as authentic. This revival gave the closest insight into a Diaghilev production ever vouchsafed to audiences too young to have seen his company.

Les Noces was the last Diaghilev ballet to look back to Holy Russia. With the young Boris Kochno as his new secretary and Jean Cocteau ever present to amaze, Diaghilev turned more and more towards the fashionable world, the avant-garde in painting and design. Nineteen twenty-four was a vintage year. Nijinska made the charming *Les Tentations de la bergère*, designed by Juan Gris, the sophisticated *Les Biches* (Poulenc–Marie Laurencin) with its naughty undertones, and the elegant *Les Fâcheux*, based on Molière's comedy ballet and designed by Georges Braque. On 20 June, at the Théâtre des Champs-Élysées in Paris, came the first performance of *Le Train bleu*. The scenario – it was neatly summed up by Diaghilev: 'The first point about *Le Train bleu* is that there is no Blue Train in it' – was devised by Cocteau to show off the acrobatic skill of young Anton Dolin, who was later to play an important role in the formative years of British ballet, and to gain world renown as a superb partner and *danseur noble*. The clothes were bathing costumes of the period and the ballet was a very smart piece about a fashionable *plage* (the Blue Train ran from Paris to Monte Carlo).

The following year Massine returned to choreograph *Zéphyre et Flore* (which introduced the composer Vladimir Dukelsky, later called Vernon Dukes), danced by Alice Nikitina, Dolin and the young Serge Lifar who had been a pupil of Nijinska in Kiev and who was to become Diaghilev's last great male dancer. *Les Matelots* was a cheerful ballet about port life, designed by Pedro Pruna to music by Auric. Then came *Barabau*, which introduced a new choreographer, George Balanchine. It was first performed at the London Coliseum on 11 December 1925.

GEORGE BALANCHINE

Born in St Petersburg on 22 January 1904, George Balanchine, as he is known in ballet history, was christened Georgi Melitonovitch Balanchivadze. He was of Georgian descent, the son and brother of composers and himself a skilled musician. His entry to the ballet school in St Petersburg was almost accidental. He had failed to get into the Naval Academy and went along to a ballet audition with his sister, who wanted to be a dancer. It was the great ballerina, Olga Preobrazhenska, who decided that the boy, not the girl, should be accepted. Balanchine, uninterested in ballet, promptly ran away from school but was persuaded to return and was eventually captivated by ballet when he appeared as a cupid in *The Sleeping Beauty*. (A fascinating study could be written of the influence of this ballet on dancers and companies alike.)

His schooling took place during the war years when the school somehow succeeded in continuing to train a new generation of dancers. His favourite teacher was Andreyanov and his favourite ballerinas Karsavina and Elizaveta Gerdt (wife of Andreyanov). The 'crystalline purity' of Elizaveta Gerdt's dancing made an indelible impression on the young man and it was a quality he was to demand from his ballerinas throughout his career as a choreographer.

Surviving the terrible privations that followed the Revolution, Balanchine returned to the school when it reopened and in 1921 graduated with honours, but at the same time he was studying at the Conservatory of Music. He would have liked a career in music but chance led him to choreography, where his musical training gave him an almost unique advantage over all others. As Stravinsky remarked, there are plenty of good pianists 'but a choreographer such as Balanchine is, after all, the rarest of beings'.

Balanchine was one of the daring and experimental young choreographers of the early years of Soviet ballet, before official disapproval checked all innovation. He was greatly impressed with Fokine's *Les Sylphides* (*Chopiniana* in Russia) and with the classical choreography of Petipa. Notably, it was 'pure dance' rather than 'story ballets' which enraptured him as a young man and, although he was to make some remarkable dramatic ballets after he left Russia, the most important aspect of his work was always to be the marriage of dancing and music, as we shall see in Chapter 8. Balanchine was also influenced in Russia by the work of Kasyan Goleizovsky, who in the early 1920s was the leader of the young idealists but later fell from favour as a choreographer.

By 1923 Balanchine had a taste for choreography, but opportunities in Leningrad were denied him and he therefore welcomed the invitation of the singer, Vladimir Dimitriev, to join a small group of singers and dancers to tour Europe as the Soviet State Dancers. They left Russia in 1924. Among the dancers were Balanchine's first wife, Tamara Gevergeva, the young soloist Alexandra Danilova, and Nicholas Efimov — all of whom defected when ordered to return to Russia, and joined Diaghilev.

Bernard Taper, in his biography of Balanchine, gives an entertaining

104. *Le Bal*, first produced in Monte Carlo in 1929. The choreography was by Balanchine; the setting and costumes were by the Italian painter Giorgio de Chirico.

account of how the young man, who had never made an opera-ballet in his life, assured Diaghilev that he could produce one very quickly. He got the job. Nijinska had fallen out with Diaghilev, or vice versa, and for the remaining years of the company's life the choreography was dominated by Balanchine and Massine.

Balanchine's first production was in fact a re-working of a Massine ballet, *Le Chant du Rossignol*, which was charmingly decorated by Matisse and introduced the very young English dancer, Alicia Markova, as the Nightingale. *Barabau* was in distinct contrast. Bawdy comedy (with a beautiful backcloth by Utrillo), it was well received on the Continent but met with some disapproval in London. Nijinska returned briefly to make the surrealist *Roméo et Juliette*, which had a score by the young English composer Constant Lambert and in which Karsavina danced with Serge Lifar. Balanchine's burlesque *La Pastorale* (Kochno–Auric–Pruna) followed, then *Jack-in-the-Box* (Satie–Derain), and then the Diaghilev ballet's one attempt at an English production, *The Triumph of Neptune*.

105. (Above) *La Chatte* (Monte Carlo, 1927). The Constructivist décor was by Naum Gabo and Antoine Pevsner and typifies Diaghilev's interest in the avant-garde. Constructivism, which dates from as early as 1911, offered the idea of built, 'constructed', sets as opposed to traditional painted scenery.

106. (Right) *Le Pas d'acier*, first produced in Paris in 1927. Left to right: Tchernicheva, Lifar, Danilova and Massine. Marvellous dancers, less than marvellous costumes.

This was suggested by the Sitwell brothers, ardent balletomanes who both wrote eloquently of the Russian ballet, and thought that the 'tuppence coloured' Victorian theatrical prints would make good material for a ballet. They took Diaghilev to Pollock's shop in Hoxton, in the East End of London, where the coloured sheets of characters and the toy theatres were still being published (the shop survived the air raids of the Second World War). The music was written by Lord Berners, another devotee of the ballet (whose biggest success in the English repertory was *A Wedding Bouquet*). *The Triumph of Neptune* came at the end of the London season, being produced first on 3 December 1926 at the Lyceum Theatre. Although a success, it did not last.

From Victoriana, Balanchine turned next to the height of modernity. *La Chatte*, based on Aesop's fable, was decorated by Naum Gabo and Antoine Pevsner in the then fashionable Constructivist style of gleaming, transparent sets and costumes, made of talc and thrown into relief by the dark backcloth and clever lighting. Olga Spessivtseva danced the role of the Cat at the first performance (it was later danced by Nikitina and Markova) and Serge Lifar had one of his first successes in this ballet, making a spectacular entrance borne aloft by five handsome young men.

Massine had returned in 1926 to re-stage *Mercure*, which had been made originally for the *Soirées de Paris* organized by the rich dilettante designer Comte Étienne de Beaumont. He then made *Le Pas d'acier*, the nearest to a Soviet ballet attempted by Diaghilev. The music was by the young Serge

107. *Apollo*, first produced in Paris in 1928 under the title *Apollon Musagète*. Lifar is the Apollo in this final moment of the ballet when the young god leads the muses (Danilova as Terpsichore just behind him, with Tchernicheva and Doubrovska as her companions), to the summit of Mount Olympus. In the first production a setting by André Bauchant was used. Balanchine's ballet is today danced in simple practice costume with only a minimal setting.

Prokofiev, the constructions and designs by the Soviet artist Yuri Yakulov. It was in two scenes and showed the workers in the fields and the factories. The complicated stage machinery hampered the action and the ballet was neither a scandal (as might have been expected with so many émigré Russians in the Paris audience) nor a flop. It soon disappeared.

Much more exciting was Massine's next work, *Ode*. This owed much of its success to the strange, inventive designs of Pavel Tchelitchev, who was working for Diaghilev for the first time but was to design for ballet for the rest of his life.

Ode was a parable about man's struggle with nature, but W. A. Propert gave a very fair idea of what a late Diaghilev creation was like when he said that the theme was less important than

> . . . the dancing stars that were upheld in their courses by invisible hands, and a dozen other passages of pure delight, inconsequent and irrelevant though they seemed to be.
>
> Light played a great part in it, and most strikingly perhaps in a scene called 'Flowers of Mankind', in which intricate and lovely figures of flowers and men were projected onto the deep blue background, while in front of it Nature and the 'Light Speck' played ball with an immense crystal sphere that glittered with all the colours of the prism; and again in the closing scene, when the final catastrophe was heralded by quivering tongues of flame on the pearl-grey sky. Then there was a scene in which masked women in wide silver dresses were multiplied endlessly by lines of receding puppets, while in front of them, with white cords patterning the whole height of the stage, took place a dance of white figures, also masked.

It was Massine's last ballet for Diaghilev. To Balanchine fell the responsibility, and the glory, of the last four productions. With *Apollon Musagète (Apollo)*, first produced on 12 June 1928 at the Théâtre Sarah Bernhardt, Paris, he first stated his creed of neo-classicism, using the traditional vocabulary in a new and austere, yet profoundly moving way to show how the young god was born and instructed the Muses in their arts before his ascent to Olympus. It was Stravinsky's music which inspired Balanchine to make this enduring masterpiece and Stravinsky himself conducted the first performance by the Diaghilev ballet (the work had already been staged in Washington by Adolph Bolm). It was a landmark in twentieth-century ballet, the beginning of the great Stravinsky–Balanchine friendship and collaboration, and a triumph for Serge Lifar as the young god.

The Gods go a'Begging, to Handel's music arranged by Sir Thomas Beecham (later used with success by Ninette de Valois), was first produced in London in 1928, conducted by Beecham. It was a charming pastoral, very different from *Le Bal* which followed – a strange, haunting work with music by Rieti and a superb setting and fantastic costumes by the Italian painter de Chirico. *Le Bal* was shown first in Monte Carlo on 9 May 1929, nearly twenty years after Diaghilev had first brought Russian ballet to the West. He refused any anniversary celebrations; he was a superstitious man and never liked to look back.

For the Paris season was saved the next – and last – big première, *Le Fils prodigue*. It was a re-telling of the parable in a majestic setting by Georges Rouault and to a powerfully theatrical score by Prokofiev. Balanchine proved

108. Pavlova and Novikov in *Flora's Awakening* at Covent Garden during the 1925 London season. Compared with *Giselle* this was artistic slumming, but such was the ballerina's genius that she could transform trumpery ballets through her impeccable style.

that he could make a 'story ballet' as well as any other choreographer, and Lifar, once again, had a fantastic triumph in the title role.

The Diaghilev ballet returned to Covent Garden that summer to show its new productions and some old favourites. The success was as great as ever – if Paris was the arbiter of taste, London was always more faithful. The last night of the season was a great one. The Diaghilev ballet ended as it had begun, with total triumph.

Diaghilev said goodbye to his company and, disobeying doctors' orders, went off to his beloved Venice. He was a dying man, prematurely aged by twenty years of endeavour and uncertainty; aged too, perhaps, by his eagerness in later years to keep young company and keep abreast of all that was new in the world of art. His dancers gave some performances in Vichy and then dispersed for the holidays. To them, in all parts of the world, came the news that Diaghilev had died on 19 August 1929. He was buried on the island of San Michele, in the Venice lagoon. So the prophecy came true and his last journey was by water.

The Diaghilev ballet, as such, could never be reassembled. There was no one of sufficient stature to take up his task. Moreover, although the company since the mid-1920s had had a permanent base for part of the year in Monte Carlo, it had no real roots. There was no school to feed it with dancers. The company had great stars in the 1920s, but both Balanchine and de Valois insist that the *corps de ballet* work became weak, and Grigoriev, Diaghilev's company manager throughout the existence of the troupe, sagely said that it is always easier to engage stars than to recruit a good *corps de ballet*.

However, if Diaghilev's company had to disperse, his work was to be continued by people who had learned from him what artistic achievements were possible within the ballet theatre. He had insisted for twenty years on productions as near to perfection as he could make them, and in retrospect his record is staggering. Arnold Haskell has said that the list of his collaborators reads like 'an index to the cultural history of the first three decades of the century', but their influence continues today. Most of Diaghilev's collaborators were young; he was starting them on their careers and many were to outlive him by nearly half a century. Even Virginia Zucchi outlived him, dying in Monte Carlo in 1930. They were able to pass on to younger generations his artistic ideals. In the year of the centenary of his birth, 1972, his reputation stood as high as ever and he is, significantly, revered as much by young people as by those who remember, with such nostalgia and pleasure, the most gorgeous of his productions.

ANNA PAVLOVA (1881–1931)

Anna Pavlova, who danced outside Russia before Diaghilev took his exotic troupe to Paris (she visited Stockholm, Copenhagen, Prague and Berlin in 1908), was the other great influence on ballet in the early part of the twentieth century. Her influence was quite different from that of Diaghilev, artistically perhaps not so deep but in some ways more far-reaching. She was a genius who could make anything she chose to dance seem magical. And she danced all over the world, inspiring young people in places as far apart as Australia and Peru to make a career in ballet. Her name has become synonymous in the minds of the non-balletgoing public with the word 'ballerina' and she was unquestionably the best-known dancer of her age.

Born in St Petersburg, the sickly daughter of poor parents, Pavlova was accepted in 1891 into the Imperial Ballet School, where her talent was soon recognized by Johansson and Gerdt and also by Cecchetti, who was to become her favourite teacher. She first appeared at a benefit for Johansson, entered the company as a *coryphée* in 1899 and by 1905 was a ballerina. Her repertory at the Mariinsky included the great classical ballets – *Giselle, The Sleeping Beauty, Raymonda, Paquita, Esmeralda, Le Corsaire* and *La Bayadère*.

109. The Ballets Suédois in *Relâche* (1924). The Swedish millionaire Rolf de Maré (1898–1964) decided to start a ballet company which he hoped might emulate Diaghilev's success and unite new choreography with the finest design and new scores. Despite its Swedish origins and its roster of Swedish dancers the company was strongly oriented towards the Parisian art world which de Maré knew well – hence its French title. Its leading dancer and choreographer was de Maré's friend Jean Borlin (1893–1930), who created the entire repertory of twenty-four ballets in the five years (1920–1925) of the company's existence. Apart from a handful of works concerned with Swedish folklore, the ballets called upon French talent for music and design, which was very fine. *Relâche* (French for 'theatre closed') was an experiment largely conceived by the artist Francis Picabia to tease the public. Picabia produced the design, Borlin the dances, Satie the score, and René Clair the filmed interlude (called, naturally enough, *Entr'acte*).

She celebrated her ten years of service as an artist of the Imperial Theatres with a performance of *La Bayadère*, and it is important to remember that she was a great ballerina in Russia before she embarked on the twenty years of touring that were to win her a special place in ballet history. Without those years of experience and, above all, careful training in St Petersburg, her subsequent successful career would have been quite impossible.

110. Anna Pavlova with her favourite teacher, Enrico Cecchetti, who devoted three years of his teaching life to working with her. Cecchetti (1850–1928) is a link through his teacher, Lepri, with Carlo Blasis whose pupil was Lepri. Tiny, bounding, with phenomenal *ballon* and pirouettes, Cecchetti had a remarkable career in the Italian theatres and in London before going to St Petersburg in 1887, as dancer, mime and then as teacher. His 'Method' was codified by Cyril Beaumont and Stanislas Idzikowski and published, with a preface by the Maestro, as *A Manual of The Theory and Practice of Classical Theatrical Dancing (Cecchetti Method)* in London in 1922. The 'Method' still helps in the formation of many dancers to this day.

It was customary for artists of the Imperial Theatres to appear outside Russia during their vacations or on leave of absence. Pavlova followed up her first tour with another European one the following year and by 1910 had been signed up by Otto Kahn to appear at the Metropolitan Opera House, New York. In April 1910 she was in London, where one of her many thousand converts to ballet was the English critic and historian, Cyril Beaumont. She danced in the early Diaghilev seasons in Paris and London but preferred to go her own way, forming a company and engaging, over the years, such celebrated partners as Bolm, Legat, Mordkin, Novikov, Volinin and Vladimirov. Although the touring became more frequent she maintained her contact with the Mariinsky Theatre until 1913.

By then she had bought a house in London (Ivy House, formerly the home of the painter J. M. W. Turner) and this was the base to which, all too infrequently, she returned for rest and rehearsals. She recruited many English dancers for her company and all seem to have worshipped her. Her tours were probably more widespread than those of any other ballerina before or since. She would dance anywhere she could find a stage, appearing throughout the United States (where her fame preceded that of the Diaghilev ballet) and widely in South America, the Orient and Australia. Everywhere she left indelible memories.

About Pavlova's repertory there are conflicting opinions. Much of it was undoubtedly trashy, but she did also present a number of classical ballets, or extracts from them, and even the most sentimental of her numbers, which would have been intolerable if performed by an inferior artist, were transformed by her genius. There exists a short film, made in Hollywood by Douglas Fairbanks in 1924, which captures her magic, especially in the little extract from *Christmas*.

Pavlova's taste in choreography, music and costumes may sometimes have been questionable; about her standard of dancing there can be no doubt. Cyril Beaumont (whose little monograph, published in 1932, is one of the most vivid evocations of her art) wrote: 'She was always exercising, always rehearsing. She never rested on her laurels; she must live up to, and not on, the golden legend of her name.' She herself had said, many years before, 'The true artist must sacrifice herself to her art', and this she did. She travelled from the Riviera to The Hague in January 1931 to begin yet another tour. A chill turned to pneumonia and she died on Friday 23 January, shortly before her fiftieth birthday. Her ashes were placed in Golders Green Crematorium, London, near Ivy House.

6 Bridging the Gap: The Baby Ballerinas

Diaghilev died in August 1929, Pavlova only eighteen months later. To the big, international ballet audience there seemed, as Arnold Haskell put it, 'a terrifying silence'. Haskell was already involved with endeavours which would result in the remarkable achievements to be described in the next chapter, but the people working to build a British ballet were very, very few and their ambitions were known to only a small circle of friends and well-wishers. The task and the triumph of holding and greatly enlarging the ballet public in the West fell to the émigré Russians.

The Ballets Russes companies of the 1930s and 1940s have by now slipped almost into oblivion except in the memories of those who saw and enjoyed their performances, but their place in ballet history is vital. We have seen, throughout this book, how the tradition of ballet has been handed on over the centuries from teacher to pupil: the pupil becomes a dancer and then in turn a teacher, for the dancer's performing life is short. A forgetful generation (Haskell's phrase again), and the art could be lost. The technique of the *danse d'école*, established by Blasis, requires careful and highly specialized training from an early age. It cannot be self-taught. Ballet has survived great wars and revolutions fundamentally because the schools and the teachers have survived. Brief absence from the theatre is less serious than cessation of work in the ballet studios. For a ballet company to endure it is vitally important that it should have behind it a school to feed it with dancers and to prepare the next generation.

Neither Diaghilev nor Pavlova had such a school. The renaissance that took place in the early 1930s was made possible by a generation of teachers who had had little contact with Diaghilev but who had brought to Paris the traditions of their Mariinsky school. Kshessinska, Preobrazhenska and Egorova, to name but three, had fled Russia and were teaching in Paris to earn a living. From their studios it was possible to recruit a new company.

The man who deserves the greatest credit for re-starting the Ballets Russes is René Blum (1878–1944: he was a victim of the German occupation of France and died in Auschwitz). After Diaghilev's death Blum was appointed director of ballet at the enchanting little Monte Carlo Opéra, a theatre rich in ballet tradition for it had offered Diaghilev the nearest thing he ever had to a permanent base. Blum was a man of wide culture and exquisite taste. The Ballets Russes companies with which he was associated (for there were a number of rifts and splits) maintained the highest artistic standards during the 1930s.

The first company, called the Ballets Russes de Monte Carlo, was run jointly by Blum and Vasily Grigorievich Voskresensky (1888–1951), who chose to be called Colonel W. de Basil. He had been associated with the arrangement of seasons of opera and ballet in Paris, and when he heard of Blum's appointment he hurried to Monte Carlo to take part in the enterprise. Blum was an artist, de Basil a shrewd showman, and to call the latter a mountebank at this time would not be too strong. His name has tended to overshadow that of the gentler Blum, for his character was undoubtedly the more colourful. Kathrine Sorley Walker's excellent history, *De Basil's Ballets Russes*, provides a fascinating portrait of the Colonel as well as the definitive study of his company and its many vicissitudes, and she says of him, 'De Basil's character is painted black, white and every shade of grey.'

Together Blum and de Basil engaged as choreographers George Balanchine, and then Léonide Massine, and – a scoop – Grigoriev, Diaghilev's *régisseur* from 1909 to 1929. Grigoriev, with his famous memory and with the aid of his wife Lyubov Tchernicheva, was able to reconstruct many of the ballets from the Diaghilev repertory. A giant of a man, a quietly spoken bear, Grigoriev stayed with de Basil until the end, then worked for other companies, including Britain's Royal Ballet, to help keep alive the great ballets of the early Diaghilev epoch. He died in London in 1968; Tchernicheva died eight years later.

Some of Diaghilev's best dancers were recruited for the revived Ballets Russes, and the Paris studios where the one-time Imperial ballerinas taught were combed for young talent. Alexandra Danilova was the principal ballerina. Trained in the Imperial Ballet School and graduating into the ballet company in Soviet Petrograd, she had left Russia in 1924 as a member of the quartet of dancers, led by George Balanchine, who were in due course recruited by Diaghilev. In Diaghilev's troupe she soon became a leading

111. Alexandra Danilova as the Firebird in Fokine's ballet of the same name. Danilova first danced this role with Diaghilev; her magnificent elevation and the authority of her style made her an ideal interpreter of the bird in the revivals presented by de Basil in the 1930s.

112. M. F. Kshessinska in her Paris studio in 1935, working with the young Tatiana Riabouchinska. Riabouchinska (b. 1917) was the oldest of de Basil's 'baby ballerinas'.

113. (Above) *Le Cotillon* (choreography by Balanchine, music by Chabrier, décor by Christian Bérard) was first performed by the Ballets Russes de Monte Carlo in Monte Carlo on 12 April 1932. Baronova is in the centre, holding the mandolin; David Lichine and Olga Morosova are on the left. The ballet had a libretto by Boris Kochno and was ostensibly a suite of dances touched by hints of mystery. It was a ballet of bittersweet charm, with incidents – such as the 'hand of Fate' sequence about fortune-telling – which could disturb as well as enchant. The choreography was intimately linked to the radiant youth and talents of its first cast. More than forty years after it was first performed, when the ballet had long fallen from the repertory, *Le Cotillon* was recreated from fragments of film and dancers' memories of the choreography and presented by the Joffrey Ballet in 1989.

114. (Right) *Jeux d'Enfants* (choreography by Massine, music by Bizet, décor and costumes by Joan Miró), was first produced in Monte Carlo on 14 April 1932. This ballet contained a ravishing role for Riabouchinska as the Child and, like *Cotillon*, it exploited the formidable technique of the young dancers. The role of the Top (centre, kneeling) was created by Baronova and gave a pretext for innumerable *fouettés*. Toumanova also danced the role, and she also had a remarkable series of *fouettés* at the end of *Cotillon*.

dancer, and throughout the 1930s she was a senior ballerina of the new Ballets Russes, an inspiration to younger dancers (on whom the brightest light of publicity fell) and a marvellous link with the grandest traditions of her great school. Her popularity in America, where she chiefly worked, during the 1940s and 1950s was phenomenal, and she taught in New York until 1988. Her artistry and her example – true wit and true elegance in performance – have remained a powerful influence on generations of dancers. One of the trump cards in the revived Ballets Russes company was the presence of the 'baby ballerinas'. These were Tatiana Riabouchinska, born in 1917, a pupil of Mathilde Kshessinska; and Irina Baronova and Tamara Toumanova, both born in 1919 and from the studio of Olga Preobrazhenska. Their youth and brilliant technique, and the fact that at the age of fourteen or fifteen they could create and carry major roles with extraordinary aplomb made them a startling injection of new blood into the ballet. The press adored them, and the wily Colonel obtained for them interviews and pictures in the newspapers which undoubtedly helped to make the public aware of the rebirth of the Russian ballet. On stage they were glamorous creatures, but off stage they were well-chaperoned if lively girls. Baronova tells an endearing story about a musician in the orchestra who from

115. David Lichine (1910–1972) and Irina Baronova in the second movement of *Les Présages*, Massine's first 'symphonic' ballet, to Tchaikovsky's Fifth Symphony. It was produced in Monte Carlo on 13 April 1933. The way in which Lichine is carrying Baronova has passed into the vocabulary of ballet and is known to dancers as 'the *Présages* lift'.

116. Nina Verchinina and the *corps de ballet* in the first movement of *Les Présages*. The scenery and costumes, brilliantly coloured and filled with explosive images of stars and comets, are by the French painter André Masson. Massine was continuing the Diaghilev tradition of employing easel painters for his ballets. In 1989, the former Ballets Russes dancer Tatiana Leskova revived *Les Présages* very successfully for the Paris Opéra Ballet.

117. The closing moment of *Choreartium*, choreographed by Léonide Massine to Brahms's Fourth Symphony. Décor and costumes were by Constantin Terechkovich and Eugène Lourié, and the ballet was first produced at the Alhambra Theatre, London, on 24 October 1933. This was the second of Massine's 'symphonic' ballets, staged towards the end of the de Basil company's fantastically successful first season in London. It was this work which sparked off great controversy among music critics about the use of symphonic scores for ballet. Leskova also revived this work, with success, for Birmingham Royal Ballet in 1991.

his desk in the pit fell in love with the pretty *midinette* she danced in *Le Beau Danube*. One day he summoned up courage to wait for her at the stage door; out came a fourteen-year-old in white socks, no make-up, and with a mother in firm attendance.

The young dancers, characteristically, delighted Balanchine, and for the first season in Monte Carlo in the spring of 1932 he made *La Concurrence* (Auric–Derain) and *Cotillon*. Boris Kochno and Christian Bérard collaborated on *Cotillon*, which was a ballet true to Diaghilev's ideals, a continuation of his work.

After these two ballets, Balanchine left the enterprise to work for Les Ballets 1933, a company which he founded with Kochno to produce new ballets, and which was aptly named since it did not last out the year of its

118. Irina Baronova and Léonide Massine in *La Symphonie fantastique*. The ballet, with choreography by Massine, was danced to the Berlioz symphony of the same name, but was accepted by the music purists because the symphony did have a very definite story-line: the romantic hallucinations of a poet in search of an unattainable beloved. It was first performed by the de Basil company at Covent Garden on 24 July 1936. Bérard's setting included a particularly striking red ballroom scene with the dancers all dressed in black and white; this scene stopped the show on the opening night. The theme was very similar to Ashton's *Apparitions* and Nijinska's *La Bien Aimée*, all of about the same date. Toumanova was the most celebrated in the ballerina role. In the early 1930s audiences were divided in their admiration of Toumanova and Baronova much as in earlier times they had fought over Taglioni and Elssler, Pavlova and Karsavina.

title. During 1933 he was invited to America, where he took up residence and set about creating the school and company which made classical ballet an American art. Massine succeeded Balanchine as choreographer of the Ballets Russes, and was also a star performer. He revived *Le Beau Danube*, made *Jeux d'Enfants*, gradually restored some of his Diaghilev creations to the repertory, and in this same year (1933) he sparked off a new adventure with *Les Présages*, which he choreographed to Tchaikovsky's Fifth Symphony.

119. *La Boutique fantasque* with Alexandra Danilova and Léonide Massine as the Can-Can Dancers and Jan Hoyer as the Shopkeeper. Baronova is the tarantella dancer (next to Massine), a role created by Lydia Sokolova in 1919. It was revivals of ballets such as these from the Diaghilev repertory which gave the Ballets Russes companies of the 1930s the hard core of their repertoire.

On 4 July 1933, the Ballets Russes de Monte Carlo came to London, to the old Alhambra Theatre in Leicester Square. The season opened with *Les Sylphides*, *Les Présages* and *Le Beau Danube*. The triumph was complete. Audiences, suspicious at first, took the young dancers to their hearts, as well as welcoming back such favourites as Danilova, Massine, and the great Polish character dancer Leon Woizikowski, who was to be a stalwart member of the company. The season was extended – it was eventually to run for four months – and ended with a bang with Massine's second 'symphonic' ballet, *Choreartium*. This caused an immense rumpus among music critics. How dare a choreographer tackle Brahms's Fourth Symphony? The audience was more interested in the dancers and the dancing, and the Colonel enjoyed the publicity. The success of this London season encouraged the impresario Sol Hurok to take the company to America later in the year, where a season opened at the St James Theatre, New York, and

120. *Beach* (choreography by Massine, music by Jean Françaix, costumes and décor by Raoul Dufy) was first produced on 19 April 1933. It was a charming balletic evocation of the Monte Carlo beach, complete with Oriental Carpet-seller. Baronova was the Rose Maid and Lichine the handsome Swimmer.

121. Léonide Massine revived his *Three-Cornered Hat* for de Basil, and he is seen here as the Miller, with Tamara Toumanova as the Miller's Wife.

122. *Union Pacific* (choreography by Massine, music by Nicholas Nabokov, décor and costumes by Albert Johnson and Irene Sharaff) was first performed by the de Basil company in Philadelphia on 6 April 1934, during the company's first American tour. This comedy ballet dealt with the laying of the transcontinental railroad and was one of the first Ballets Russes productions to have an American theme. In the centre: Baronova, the Lady Gay; Toumanova, a Mexican; Massine, the Barman. Kneeling, right: Sono Osato as the Barman's Assistant.

---

was followed by a successful tour. Although at first tours did not prove financially very rewarding, Hurok (a genuine devotee of ballet as well as a great impresario) persisted in travelling the Ballets Russes companies, and by this means built an audience for ballet throughout the United States. In the following years the Ballets Russes tours of Australia were also to prove enormously successful; they implanted a ballet tradition there which first flowered in the work of a one-time Ballets Russes dancer, Édouard Borovansky,

123. *Protée*, with choreography by David Lichine, music by Debussy ('Danse Sacrée et Profane'), and scenery and costumes by Giorgio de Chirico, was first performed by the de Basil company at Covent Garden on 5 July 1938. Anton Dolin was the Sea God who was able to change his personality at will. The role was created by Lichine, the one really gifted new choreographer to emerge from the de Basil company.

who founded a school and, in 1944, a company, which were vital elements in establishing a native Australian ballet.

In addition to its ballerinas, the Ballets Russes de Monte Carlo boasted a roster of handsome, virile male dancers such as David Lichine and Yurek Shabalevski. There was an intense glamour about the Russian ballet in the 1930s that won it a huge popular audience. London seasons at Covent Garden, usually in high summer, attracted a vast public. In those days the old gallery of the Royal Opera House (now entirely reseated as the Amphitheatre) was not bookable in advance, so every night there was a long queue of fans down Floral Street at the side of the theatre waiting to climb the stairs and cheer their favourites.

The artistic politics of the Ballets Russes were such that, as the years passed, disagreements between Colonel de Basil and René Blum and Léonide Massine led to extreme shifts of allegiance and ruptures between these leading figures. In 1936 Blum split from de Basil, taking with him the magic Monte Carlo connection. He started a second company, the Ballets de Monte Carlo, while de Basil re-named his troupe several times as finance and policy dictated; from 1939 his company was called the Original Ballet

124. Mikhail Fokine's ballet *Thamar* was first staged in Paris by the Diaghilev ballet in 1912. It told a dramatic tale of Thamar, Queen of Georgia, who lured men to her castle and, having sated her passion, stabbed them and had their bodies flung into the river flowing below the castle walls. Set to Balakirev's symphonic poem of the same title, with stunning designs by Léon Bakst (the sloping brick walls of Thamar's castle were a brilliant visual coup), the ballet was unashamed melodrama, sustained originally by the performances of Tamara Karsavina and Adolph Bolm. With de Basil, the revival of *Thamar* was somewhat tame, though the beauty and dramatic power of Lyubov Tchernicheva – seen here as the Georgian Queen stabbing the Young Man – were greatly admired.

Russe. By this time Léonide Massine had also left him and joined forces with Blum, becoming artistic director of his troupe, now retitled the Ballets Russes de Monte Carlo. Dancers moved variously between the rival companies: Danilova, Markova, Toumanova, Youskevitch and Eglevsky joined Massine, while Baronova, Riabouchinska, Lichine and Dolin were part of the de Basil company. In 1938 there was a hectic summer when both companies were in London at the same time, de Basil at Covent Garden, Blum–Massine at the Theatre Royal, Drury Lane. Balletomanes scurried round the corner from

125. (Above) *Rouge et Noir*, or *L'Étrange farandole*, with choreography by Massine, music by Shostakovich (First Symphony), and décor and costumes by Henri Matisse, was first performed by the René Blum (later Sergei Denham) company in Monte Carlo on 11 May 1939. From left to right: André Eglevsky, Igor Youskevitch, Alicia Markova and Frederic Franklin. With this star-studded cast, the ballet was very popular in America. It was never seen in London, as war broke out in September 1939 two days before the company was due to open at Covent Garden.

126. (Right) Alexandra Danilova and her partner, the English dancer Frederic Franklin, were to be enduring and greatly loved stars of the Ballets Russes de Monte Carlo, which took up permanent residence in the United States in 1939. They are seen here in George Balanchine's *Danses concertantes* to Stravinsky's score of the same name. The ballet was created for the Ballets Russes de Monte Carlo in New York in 1944, with designs by Eugene Berman.

127. *Colloque Sentimentale* was choreographed by George Balanchine, though it was listed in theatre programmes as having been created by André Eglevsky. Based on a poem by Paul Verlaine, it had a score by Paul Bowles, and setting and costumes by Salvador Dali. It was first performed in New York in 1944 by Ballet International. The dancers are Eglevsky and Rosella Hightower, who are here seen in a revival by the de Cuevas company. At the right is a turtle topped by a dressmaker's dummy which featured in the action, as did a gentleman riding a bicycle. During the 1940s the surrealist painter Salvador Dali became involved in ballet, providing what can best be described as unusual settings for several works by Léonide Massine – *Bacchanale* (1939), *Labyrinth* (1941) and *Mad Tristan* (1944). His sets were often brilliant but completely extinguished the ballets they accompanied.

one house to the other to catch one ballet and one group of dancers here, another there.

For London this was indeed the end of an exciting decade. The outbreak of war in 1939 found the two companies again on their travels. The de Basil troupe went first to Australia, then toured North and South America, while

128. *Graduation Ball* (choreography by David Lichine, music by Johann Strauss, décor and costumes by Alexandre Benois) was first produced by the Ballets Russes de Monte Carlo in Sydney, Australia, on 28 February 1940. Lichine is the First Cadet and his wife Tatiana Riabouchinska the Junior Pupil. The de Basil company had a tremendous success in Australia during this tour.

the Ballets Russes de Monte Carlo was taken over by Sergei Denham (1897–1970), a Russian-American banker, as manager. The company remained thereafter in the Americas, touring with great success until the late 1950s, by which time the repertory was emaciated and the expenses of touring the United States became crippling. The company disbanded in 1962.

Colonel de Basil travelled widely with his ballet company throughout the Americas during the Second World War, and made a disastrous visit to Cuba, when the troupe was stranded without money and the dancers went on strike. The Original Ballet Russe survived the war and returned to Europe and the Royal Opera House, Covent Garden, in 1947. Alas, the ballets that London had loved in the 1930s were in poor shape, the sets and costumes had faded, the company consisted mostly of newcomers who lacked the style and theatricality to give the ballets their rightful glamour. The old audience was sadly disillusioned. The new, young audience that had grown up during the war years with the Sadler's Wells Ballet wondered what the fuss had been about. Russian ballet, as Diaghilev and his heirs had shown it, was dead. The next Russian ballet London would love was the real ballet from Russia brought by the Bolshoy and Kirov companies.

 # 7 The Building of British Ballet

British ballet, today celebrated, popular and influential throughout the world, was a decidedly late starter. The *ballet de cour* was virtually unknown at the English court. No royal patron of the arts (of whom there were depressingly few) thought to establish and endow a ballet school or ballet company. Queen Victoria doted on the charming ballets of the Romantic period but took it for granted that the ballerinas and the ballet-masters would be from the Continent. At the beginning of this century ballet meant either an extravaganza in the great music-halls, notably the Empire and the Alhambra Theatres in London, or a visiting ballerina from Denmark or Russia.

The Diaghilev ballet did not reach London until 1911. By then Adeline Genée had been the supreme favourite at the Empire Theatre for over a decade. She was succeeded by an English dancer, Phyllis Bedells, who also appeared during the 1920s with Anton Dolin in seasons of variety at the London Coliseum. Their dancing was the staple fare. The visits of the Diaghilev company were something marvellous and strange. It was not until the early 1920s that a few enthusiasts began to wonder if they could not establish a national company in England. An Association of Teachers of Operatic Dancing (now the Royal Academy of Dancing) had been founded in 1920 by Philip Richardson (editor of the *Dancing Times*) and Édouard Espinosa (1871–1950), who was the foremost teacher of the day. Espinosa, who had been born in Moscow and was of a famous dancing dynasty, was concerned about the correct teaching of classical dancing. Richardson supported his campaign and the Association was formed with representatives of the French, Russian, Italian and Danish academies on the board and with Genée as the first president. Its concern was only with teaching. The initiative in production, and in the maintenance of schools from which dancers and choreographers might emerge, was taken by two remarkable women: Dame Ninette de Valois (born 1898) and Dame Marie Rambert (1888–1982). Significantly, both had worked with Diaghilev.

NINETTE DE VALOIS AND THE ROYAL BALLET

Chronologically, Rambert may have been the first to stage genuinely British ballets; she presented the earliest work of Ashton and Tudor, for which service alone she deserves her place in history. But both she and de Valois were working, in their very different ways, at the same time towards the same object. De Valois built the huge edifice which is today the Royal Ballet, Britain's National Gallery of the dance; Rambert once compared her company to the Tate Gallery. We will discuss the larger institution first.

De Valois, herself an excellent dancer (she had studied with Espinosa, Cecchetti and Legat), was assisted at the start of her enterprise by another great woman of the English theatre, Lilian Baylis, C H (1874–1937), founder

129. Adeline Genée (1878–1970). The porcelain charm of this Danish ballerina, her neat, light technique and the irreproachable respectability of her private life, helped greatly at the beginning of this century, during her reign at the Empire Theatre, Leicester Square, to win a new audience for ballet in London. She toured America twice with enormous success and in 1913 visited Australia and New Zealand where her name became legendary. After marriage and retirement she worked tirelessly for the Royal Academy of Dancing in London, becoming its first president and holding office until she handed over to Margot Fonteyn in 1954. She is seen here in the full splendour of her costume for *The Pretty Prentice* at the London Coliseum in 1916.

130. The Vic-Wells Ballet's first production of the full-length *Swan Lake*, on 20 November 1934, was designed by Hugh Stevenson. Robert Helpmann is seen as Prince Siegfried and Alicia Markova as Odette, protecting her swans, among whom was the very young Margot Fonteyn. On the back of the photograph, taken from the *Dancing Times* archives, an illuminating press handout is pasted. It reads in part: 'The most epoch-making event in the history of British ballet takes place tonight at Sadler's Wells Theatre, when Petipa's famous *Lac des Cygnes* will be presented in its entirety for the first time by an all-British company. (There will be a very distinguished audience of Society people and though the best seats were priced at three guineas each, the whole house has been sold out for a fortnight. We could have sold as many seats again.)' Over half a century later, the drawing power of *Swan Lake* remains undiminished.

of the Old Vic and Sadler's Wells companies and thus founder of Britain's National Theatre, English National Opera and Royal Ballet. She first met de Valois in 1926 and promised her that if she would help in staging dances for the plays and operas then being given at the Old Vic Theatre she would try and do more for her later. De Valois accepted the offer, ran her own ballet school, and learned her craft of choreography by working at the Abbey Theatre in Dublin (with W. B. Yeats) and at the avant-garde Festival Theatre, Cambridge. In 1931, when Lilian Baylis rebuilt and re-opened the derelict Sadler's Wells Theatre in Finsbury (now Islington), London, she included a

131. *Douanes* (choreography by Ninette de Valois, music by Geoffrey Toye, designed by Hedley Briggs) was first performed on 11 October 1932. Ninette de Valois is seen here with Robert Helpmann, Harold Turner (the company's first virtuoso male dancer) and Frederick Ashton.

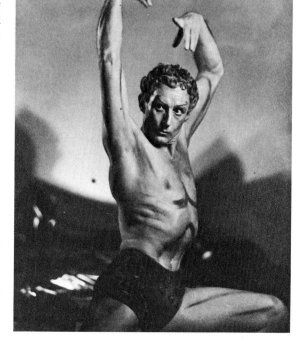

132. Anton Dolin as Satan, the role he created in Geoffrey Keynes's 'masque for dancing', *Job*, first produced by the Camargo Society on 5 July 1931, with choreography by Ninette de Valois to the music of Vaughan Williams. Dolin later danced the ballet at the Old Vic and Sadler's Wells, and is seen here in a post-war production at Covent Garden.

133. Robert Helpmann, Moira Shearer and Léonide Massine in the ballet sequence from *The Red Shoes*. This Michael Powell–Emeric Pressburger film was a huge success when it was shown in 1948, and has remained one of the key works in filmed ballet. Its influence was considerable: it led young people to watch ballet and, in some instances, to become dancers. It brought film stardom to Moira Shearer, who was a ballerina of exceptional gifts with the Sadler's Wells Ballet. Though its story is unredeemed kitsch, the film preserves some fascinating sequences of Massine dancing and a brief clip of Marie Rambert and the Mercury Theatre. Shearer's dazzling qualities as a ballerina – speed, lightness, clarity of style – are matched by her dramatic sincerity. Well worth watching, even today.

ballet studio. De Valois moved in with her school and, with six other girls, founded a little company to dance in the operas. From that tiny beginning, helped by guest artists and friends, she was soon able to produce whole evenings of short ballets and then to embark on re-staging the great classical ballets. The Russian classics and *Giselle* were mounted for the company by Nicholas Sergueyev, from notation, but the success of the first big productions, *Giselle* (at the Old Vic on 1 January 1934) and the complete *Swan Lake* (at Sadler's Wells on 20 November the same year), was almost entirely due to Alicia Markova.

Born in 1910 as Alicia Marks, Markova had trained with Astafieva in London and joined the Diaghilev ballet when only fourteen years old. Diaghilev prophesied a great future for her and she fulfilled his confidence. Forgoing more lucrative engagements, she danced for the young Vic-Wells Ballet (as it was then called) long enough to establish it and long enough to set an example of exquisite classicism and purity of style to her successor, Margot Fonteyn (1919–1991). Later, with Anton Dolin (1904–1983), another pioneer in British ballet, she toured widely in the British Isles with the Markova–Dolin company. In the war years she achieved perhaps the highest point of her career in America, but returned to England to help found Festival Ballet. Her contribution was of inestimable importance in the early days: she was the first great British ballerina, and has become a wise and popular teacher in America and England.

De Valois based the repertory of her company on the classics, rightly believing them to be essential for the education of the audience as well as the dancers. To them she added native works – at first mostly by herself for economic reasons; money was desperately short and there was no Arts Council in those days. By 1935 she could afford a resident choreographer and with unerring good sense chose Frederick Ashton. She already had Constant Lambert (1905–1951) as conductor and musical

134. *Dante Sonata* (choreography by Frederick Ashton, music by Liszt, décor and costumes by Sophie Fedorovitch after Flaxman) was first produced at Sadler's Wells Theatre on 23 January 1940. The photograph shows Margot Fonteyn and Michael Somes as two of the Children of Light.

135. (Above) *Hamlet* (choreography by Robert Helpmann, music by Tchaikovsky, décor and costumes by Leslie Hurry). Helpmann's first work for the theatre was originally performed at the New (now Albery) Theatre, London, on 19 May 1942. Robert Helpmann is seen on the left as Hamlet, with David Paltenghi at his feet as the dead Claudius; on the right, Celia Franca (later to become director of the National Ballet of Canada) is Gertrude. The designs remain among the finest ever made for a British ballet.

136. (Right) *The Rake's Progress*, a ballet by Gavin Gordon (with choreography by Ninette de Valois, music by Gavin Gordon, and superb scenery and costumes by Rex Whistler, after Hogarth) was first performed by the Vic-Wells Ballet on 20 May 1935. The first Rake was Walter Gore, but when he left the company Robert Helpmann soon made the part very much his own. He is seen here in the 'orgy' scene, in a wartime production. The ballet's scenery and costumes were lost on tour in Holland in 1940 when the Vic-Wells company had to flee the German invasion; they were recreated in 1942, and the ballet has remained in the repertory ever since.

adviser. The three of them were the architects of the Royal Ballet we know today.

The progress of the little Vic-Wells Ballet, dancing one or two nights a week in London, to the Sadler's Wells Ballet, which became nationally famous during wartime tours and internationally famous after it had moved to Covent Garden and conquered New York (the first triumphant visit was in 1949), is fully described in Mary Clarke's book *The Sadler's Wells Ballet*, which takes the story up to 1955. By that time a second company, the Sadler's Wells Theatre Ballet, under the direction of Peggy van Praagh, was staging the first ballets of John Cranko and Kenneth MacMillan.

The Sadler's Wells Ballet School had its own premises in two buildings, the junior school at White Lodge in Richmond Park (residential and day pupils, with a full education programme and a special wing for the boys) and a senior school in West London from which dancers would graduate into the companies; the two schools and the two Sadler's Wells companies were separate entities, however, under different managements, namely the directors of the Royal Opera House and the governors of Sadler's Wells Foundation, and the directors of Sadler's Wells Trust and the governors of Sadler's Wells School. Sadler's Wells Theatre could (and did) throw out the Sadler's Wells Theatre Ballet if it wished. There was no formal link between the two companies and the two schools. This was put right and the whole

137. *Pineapple Poll* (choreography by John Cranko, music by Sullivan arranged by Charles Mackerras, designed by Osbert Lancaster) was first performed by the Sadler's Wells Theatre Ballet at Sadler's Wells on 13 March 1951. Here we see David Poole as Jasper, Elaine Fifield as Poll and, to the right, David Blair as Captain Belaye, Sheila O'Reilly as Mrs Dimple and Stella Claire as her niece Blanche. This was Cranko's first smash-hit comedy character ballet.

enterprise safeguarded for the future in 1956 by the granting of a Royal Charter of Incorporation by 'Elizabeth the Second by the Grace of God of the United Kingdom of Great Britain and Northern Ireland and of Our other Realms and Territories, Queen, Head of the Commonwealth, Defender of the Faith'. It was made Patent 'at Westminster the thirty-first day of October in the fifth year of Our Reign'. The Charter is reprinted in full in *Ballet Annual* No. 12.

Britain at last had a Royal Ballet. Princess Margaret, president of the Royal Ballet, takes an active interest. Unlike the other royal ballet companies, however, it had been created by the director, dancers and choreographers. Having proved their worth, they won their royal accolade.

138. *The Sleeping Beauty* at Covent Garden in 1946. The photograph shows Act III of the ballet with Oliver Messel's setting and costumes. Fonteyn and Helpmann are in the centre of the picture and on their left are Violetta Prokhorova (later Violetta Elvin) and Alexis Rassine as the Blue Bird and his Princess. Violetta Prokhorova danced with the company for the first time on the second night of this production of *The Sleeping Beauty.* She provided Britain's first glimpse of a Bolshoy-trained dancer.

Dame Ninette de Valois retired as director of the Royal Ballet in 1964, but remained in charge of the school until 1970. She had seen her bigger company conquer Russia in 1961; the 'second company', under the direction of John Field (1921–1991), had mounted and toured the big classics as well as the native repertory. Margot Fonteyn was acknowledged as the leading ballerina of the Western world. Rudolf Nureyev (b.1938) made his first home in the West with the Royal Ballet after he defected from the Kirov Ballet, and formed a hugely popular partnership with Fonteyn. Frederick Ashton (1904–1988), who was to succeed Dame Ninette as director of the Royal Ballet, was acknowledged to be a choreographer of genius.

Ashton led the Royal Ballet company until 1970. During his time in office

139. *Cinderella* (choreography by Frederick Ashton, music by Serge Prokofiev, décor and costumes by Jean-Denis Maclès) was produced at Covent Garden on 23 December 1948; it was the first British three-act ballet. Moira Shearer is in the centre as Cinderella with Michael Somes as her Prince. The ballet was intended for Fonteyn, who later gave the definitive interpretation, but her indisposition gave the première to Shearer, a dancer of crystalline clarity and elegance.

he brought Bronislava Nijinska to Covent Garden – repaying an artistic debt he felt he owed: she had been markedly influential on the young Fred Ashton who had danced with the Ida Rubinstein Ballet in the late 1920s, when La Nijinska was company choreographer. So the Royal Ballet acquired *Les Biches* and *Les Noces*, two Nijinska masterpieces, from their creator. And Ashton, as well as making his enchanting ballet *The Dream*, also commissioned Kenneth MacMillan's tremendously successful version of *Romeo and Juliet*. Ashton's retirement was marked with a gala performance at Covent Garden on 24 July 1970, organized by his own colleagues, which was the happiest survey of his choreographic genius.

This 'danced anthology' of Ashton's career to that date contained tiny extracts from some ballets, larger sections from others. He could be witty in *Façade* and *A Wedding Bouquet*; romantic in *Apparitions* and *Marguerite and*

140. Dame Ninette de Valois retired as director of the Royal Ballet in July 1964 and was honoured with a *grand défilé* of the entire Royal Ballet organization – companies, staff and school. All came on stage in a massive procession to pay homage to this great woman. The date was 7 May 1964.

Armand; sublimely lyrical in *Symphonic Variations* – the epitome of the English classical style which he and Margot Fonteyn did so much to engender; pastoral in *La Fille mal gardée*, which was funny, and beautiful as well; while in *Enigma Variations* he created a ballet about friendship which had at its heart the loneliness of the creative artist. A few months earlier Ashton had been honoured differently, but no less rapturously, with a gala performance by the Royal Ballet at the Metropolitan Opera House, New York, to which the company have been frequent and greatly loved visitors. Ashton's contribution to the building of the Royal Ballet helped to show it to the world as a great classical ensemble.

The year 1970 also saw the retirement of Sir David Webster (1903–1971), who had been general administrator of the Royal Opera House, Covent Garden, since its re-opening after the war in 1946. Webster had played no

141. Margot Fonteyn and Rudolf Nureyev with the *corps de ballet* of the Royal Ballet in the 'Kingdom of Shades' scene from *La Bayadère*. Nureyev's staging of this ravishing Petipa choreography was first performed by the Royal Ballet on 27 November 1963. It was an important acquisition for the repertory and provided sensational roles for soloists and *corps de ballet*. In 1989, Natalya Makarova staged the full-length *Bayadère* for the Royal Ballet in her adaptation of the Petipa original.

small part in the growth and fame of the Royal Ballet, and in the development of its audience, and he was particularly aware of the vital importance of the school. He was succeeded by John Tooley; at the same time Kenneth Mac-Millan, after a three-year stint as director of the ballet at the Deutsche Oper in Berlin, assumed direction of the Royal Ballet in partnership with John Field. Field resigned a few months later, and the Royal Ballet was reorganized so that the touring section became a smaller and more flexible travelling group with a more contemporary repertory.

This policy was not successful. A second company had been formed to maintain performances at Sadler's Wells Theatre in 1946 when Dame Ninette de Valois took her original company to Covent Garden. The new Wells Theatre troupe was largely made up of young dancers and students from the company school, and the company had functioned admirably as a cradle and nursery of talent, both interpretative and creative. It was here

142. *Romeo and Juliet* (choreography by Kenneth MacMillan, music by Serge Prokofiev, décor and costumes by Nicholas Georgiadis) was first produced at Covent Garden on 9 February 1965. Left: Lynn Seymour and Christopher Gable, for whom the roles of the lovers were created, although in fact they did not dance in the first performance; on that occasion the parts were taken by Fonteyn and Nureyev.

that John Cranko and Kenneth MacMillan had composed their first ballets, and such eminent artists as Nadia Nerina, David Blair, Svetlana Beriosova, Lynn Seymour and David Wall had learned their craft as young dancers. The link with Sadler's Wells Theatre was lost in 1955, when the company came under the aegis of the Opera House, and the ensuing years found it touring extensively through Great Britain under the directorship of John Field, taking Royal Ballet standards and a traditional repertory to many cities. To a large and devoted public, this was the Royal Ballet; with the popularity of such artists as Doreen Wells and David Wall, and the well-reasoned repertory comprising traditional classics and new creations, it was greatly loved. The change in 1970 to a smaller, more experimental identity did not find favour with the public, and under the direction of Peter Wright the company soon restored the established mixture of classical ballets and popular revivals, as well as new creations. The success of this policy, together

143. Svetlana Beriosova (1932–) as Perséphone in Frederick Ashton's staging of Stravinsky's melodrama first produced by the Royal Ballet at Covent Garden in 1961. Beriosova not only danced the title role but also spoke the André Gide text. Lithuanian born, the daughter of the ballet master Nicholas Beriozoff, Beriosova's career began as a child. After dancing with various companies she joined the Sadler's Wells organization in 1950 and became one of the Royal Ballet's greatest classical ballerinas. Her Odette-Odile in *Swan Lake* was a performance of rare distinction. She created many roles; memorable were her Lady Elgar in Ashton's *Enigma Variations* and Tsarina in MacMillan's *Anastasia* in which she played mature roles with exceptional dignity, beauty and charm.

with the discovery of new choreographers such as David Bintley, made the Sadler's Wells Royal Ballet an increasingly significant and influential company.

Kenneth MacMillan remained as director of the Royal Ballet until 1977. During his years in office he not only served as administrator, but continued as principal choreographer. His output included two important full-length ballets, *Anastasia* and *Manon*, and several shorter pieces; he re-staged *The Sleeping Beauty*, produced new one-act works both for the Covent Garden

144. *Symphonic Variations* (choreography by Frederick Ashton, music by César Franck, setting and costumes by Sophie Fedorovitch) was first performed at Covent Garden on 24 April 1946. The original cast, from left to right: Moira Shearer, Michael Somes, Margot Fonteyn, Brian Shaw and Pamela May. The sixth member of the cast (who stood just to the left of Moira Shearer) was Henry Danton.

and touring companies, and ensured that other choreographers contributed to the repertory: a notable acquisition was Jerome Robbins's *Dances at a Gathering*. In 1977, MacMillan was succeeded by Norman Morrice as director and celebrated his release from time-consuming administrative work by creating the magnificent full-length *Mayerling* in 1978, and several important one-act works (*La Fin du Jour*; *My Brother, My Sisters*, for the Stuttgart Ballet; *Gloria*). He made a further full-length piece, *Isadora*, in 1981. MacMillan continues as principal choreographer of the Royal Ballet, and his creations have been crucial in shaping the dramatic abilities of the company as well as markedly influential in finding an emotionally expressive manner for the

145. Margot Fonteyn and Rudolf Nureyev in *Marguerite and Armand*, created by Ashton as a showpiece for their combined talents.

146. *La Fille mal gardée* (choreography by Frederick Ashton, music by Herold, décor and costumes by Osbert Lancaster) was first produced on 28 January 1960. In scene i, shown here, Nadia Nerina is Lise with Stanley Holden as Mother Simone and David Blair, perched in the hayloft, as Colas. The picture is from Margaret Dale's television production for BBC TV, one of the most successful early transfers of a large-scale ballet to the small screen. It remains a priceless record of the tremendous original cast.

147. *La Fille mal gardée*: the end of the ballet. Alexander Grant as Alain claims his red umbrella.

classical academic dance. From his early and psychologically acute *The Invitation*, and by way of such daring pieces as *Playground* (for the Sadler's Wells Royal Ballet) to the spiritual concern of *Requiem* and the piercing emotions of *Song of the Earth*, MacMillan has sought to extend the range and possibilities of ballet. He has always been aware of the classical foundation of his art, as he demonstrated in his version of *The Prince of the Pagodas*, with its implicit tribute to Petipa.

In the Royal Ballet generation following MacMillan, the work of David Bintley (b. 1957) has been of especial note. On graduating from the Royal Ballet School, the young Bintley seemed to plunge almost immediately into creativity. His début with *The Outsider* for the Sadler's Wells Royal Ballet was of exceptional promise. There followed ballets in each succeeding year which confirmed that the Royal Ballet had found a fruitful new creative talent. With the full-length *Swan of Tuonela* (1982) Bintley told a Nordic

148 (Left). The second scene of Ashton's *Ondine*, with Margot Fonteyn as the water sprite above one of the many fountain-shaped groups of the *corps de ballet* which Ashton created to suggest the watery nature of the scene. Alexander Grant as Tirrenio, King of the Mediterranean, watches, right.

149 (Above). Ashton's version of Turgenev's play *A Month in the Country* was illuminated by exceptional emotional insight into the characters, exquisite choreography, and by interpretations no less remarkable. Lynn Seymour is seen here as Natalya Petrovna with her son's tutor Belyayev (Anthony Dowell) in the scene in which they disclose their feelings for each other. These were the roles they created.

150. (Above) Monica Mason as the Chosen One in the second scene of Kenneth MacMillan's *The Rite of Spring* for the Royal Ballet. With designs by Sidney Nolan, this staging moved away from the Ancient Russian connotations of the score to something more universal in its portrayal of tribal ritual. Monica Mason was twenty-one when she created the central role of this fine production: her performance was astonishing in its hieratic power.

151. (Right) Antoinette Sibley as Manon, David Wall as her brother, Lescaut, and Derek Rencher as Monsieur G. M. in MacMillan's *Manon*, a hugely successful and popular three-act version of the Abbé Prévost tale, for the Royal Ballet.

saga in bold theatrical terms. In *The Snow Queen* (1986) he produced a popular fairy-tale work, and in his third long piece for the Sadler's Wells Royal Ballet, *Hobson's Choice* (1989), he contrived a jovial narrative based on Harold Brighouse's play, which again delighted the public. A dance-actor of rare gifts (his Petrushka is very fine), Bintley shows a comparable feeling for the dramatic in his creations, but he has also made plotless works for the Royal Ballet and the Sadler's Wells Royal Ballet, with fluent classical writing in such pieces as *Flowers of the Forest*, *Young Apollo* and *Allegri Diversi*.

152. Kenneth MacMillan originally staged a one-act *Anastasia* in Berlin when he was director of the ballet at the Deutsche Oper in 1967. On his return to London as director of the Royal Ballet this became the final act of a full-length study of the life of the Grand Duchess Anastasia and the woman, Anna Anderson (the heroine of the Berlin staging), who believed herself to be the Grand Duchess. Lynn Seymour is seen here in the last act of the *Anastasia* staged for the Royal Ballet in 1971; David Adams partners her as her husband.

153. Darcey Bussell and Tetsuya Kumakawa as Princess Rose and the Fool in Kenneth MacMillan's *The Prince of the Pagodas*, first produced at the Royal Opera House, Covent Garden, in December 1989.

154. David Bintley made *Choros* for the Sadler's Wells Royal Ballet in 1983. It combined ideas from classic Greek dance with a sense of athleticism, as this picture shows, with Iain Webb partnering Susan Lucas, and Marion Tait supported by Nicholas Millington.

155. David Wall as Rudolf and Merle Park as Countess Larisch in Kenneth MacMillan's *Mayerling* for the Royal Ballet. Created in 1978, this full-length ballet concerned the tragic history of the Austrian Archduke Rudolf who killed himself and his mistress, Mary Vetsera, at a royal hunting-lodge at Mayerling. As Rudolf, David Wall had one of the most taxing roles ever created for a male dancer, which he performed with magisterial power and astonishing emotional force. As Rudolf's mistress, Merle Park was given one of the most rewarding modern roles of her career.

156. David Bintley's *The Flowers of the Forest*, for Sadler's Wells Royal Ballet.

157. In 1967 Antony Tudor was invited to create a work for the Royal Ballet at Covent Garden. The result was *Shadowplay*, with music by Charles Koechlin, whose Buddhist theme was a journey of self-discovery by the Boy with Matted Hair (Anthony Dowell). Dowell is seen here with Derek Rencher as the commanding figure of the Terrestrial, one of the figures on the Boy's pilgrimage.

158. Antoinette Sibley as Titania with Alexander Grant (as Bottom with the ass's head) in *The Dream*. The choreography was by Frederick Ashton, music by Mendelssohn, and décor and costumes by Henry Bardon and David Walker; the ballet was produced at Covent Garden on 2 April 1964. This was Sibley's first important creation in an Ashton ballet and it marked the beginning of her great partnership with Anthony Dowell, who created the role of Oberon.

159. Dancers of the Royal Ballet in Ashley Page's *Pursuit*, which was first performed at the Royal Opera House, Covent Garden, in 1987. The hard-edged classicism of Page's choreography was matched by the vivid shapes in the designs by the abstract painter Jack Smith.

160. The closing moments of *Swan Lake,* staged by Peter Wright and Galina Samsova for Sadler's Wells Royal Ballet. Design is by Philip Prowse.

Norman Morrice remained director of the Royal Ballet until 1986, when he was succeeded by Anthony Dowell (b. 1943), who had, since his earliest appearances with the company, typified the finest qualities of the company's classical style. The elegance and aristocracy of Dowell's dancing, his partnership with Antoinette Sibley in the classical and modern repertory, had made him an exemplar of the Royal Ballet manner, and he was the natural successor to Morrice as director of the company.

One of the most important developments in the Royal Ballet's history took place in 1990. For several years the Sadler's Wells branch of the company had found an eager audience and an admirable stage in the Hippodrome Theatre, Birmingham. Thanks to the enterprise of Birmingham's municipal authorities an invitation was made to Sadler's Wells Royal Ballet to establish a more permanent relationship between theatre and ballet company. Funding, a constant and constantly aggravating bugbear for all dance activity in Britain, was generous; the stage and working facilities

161. *Jardin aux lilas*, with choreography by Antony Tudor, music by Chausson ('Poème' for violin and orchestra), and scenery and costumes by Hugh Stevenson. The ballet was first produced by the Ballet Rambert at the Mercury Theatre on 26 January 1936, with Maude Lloyd as Caroline, Hugh Laing as her Lover, Antony Tudor as the Man She Must Marry, and Peggy van Praagh as an Episode in His Past. The ballet retains its place in the repertory today, notably with American Ballet Theatre. It was a forerunner of those 'psychological' ballets in which Tudor so acutely explored the emotional world of his characters; with telling gesture, quick meetings and partings, Tudor conveyed deep feelings. This picture shows a 1944 revival by the Ballet Rambert with Sally Gilmour (right) as Caroline, Frank Staff (centre) as her Lover, and Sara Luzita (left) as the Episode in His Past. Frank Staff, a dancer of romantic good looks and fine technique, later contributed several successful ballets to the Rambert repertory before returning to his native South Africa, where he died in 1971 at the age of fifty-three.

were infinitely more extensive than at the ancestral Sadler's Wells Theatre; a regional identity would be generated that was more permanent in its implications than that of a mere touring company. So in October 1990 the Birmingham Royal Ballet came into existence, with increased numbers and increased opportunities for performance and for creativity. After sixty years, Britain's National Ballet had a regional base as sound and significant as that of the Royal Ballet at Covent Garden.

162. *Dark Elegies*, with choreography by Antony Tudor, music by Mahler (the 'Kindertotenlieder'), and décor and costumes by Nadia Benois. These 'Songs on the Death of Children' were first staged by the Ballet Rambert in 1937, and they reflect in part the influence on Tudor of the American dancer and choreographer Agnes de Mille, who was with Rambert at that time and who discussed American modern dance techniques with Tudor. *Dark Elegies* survived in the repertory of the re-named Rambert Dance Company of the 1980s, and it has been staged by several other companies, notably in Tudor's own production for American Ballet Theatre. Originally produced on the small stage of the Duchess Theatre in London, with American Ballet Theatre it could command the expanse of the Metropolitan Opera House, New York.

THE BALLET RAMBERT

The Ballet Rambert not only played an exciting and influential part in impressing upon the public, around 1930, that British dancers, choreographers and designers could produce chic and beautiful works, but has continued over the years to act as a very necessary goad to the 'Establishment' forces of the Royal Ballet. If the big company showed the way, Rambert

163. *Lady into Fox* (choreography by Andrée Howard, music by Honegger, décor and costumes by Nadia Benois) was first produced at the Mercury Theatre in London on 15 May 1939. Here Sally Gilmour is in the title role, which she created. The part of the Husband is danced by Walter Gore. It was a remarkably effective translation of David Garnett's novel to the ballet stage.

164. *Antonia* (choreography by Walter Gore, music by Sibelius, designed by Harry Cordwell) was first produced at the now demolished King's Theatre, Hammersmith, on 17 October 1949 with Paula Hinton and Walter Gore in the principal roles, as in this picture. It was a ballet of jealousy, with a powerful dramatic role for Paula Hinton, a superb dance-actress. She became the muse (and the wife) of Walter Gore, dancing in many of his ballets with his own company and also when he worked in Portugal and Germany.

165. The Ballet Rambert in the closing moments of Glen Tetley's *Pierrot Lunaire*, the first ballet they acquired from an American choreographer after their reorganization as a company specializing as much in contemporary dance techniques as in classical ballet. The dancers are Jonathan Taylor (Brighella), Gayrie MacSween (Columbine) and Christopher Bruce (Pierrot), who first danced *Pierrot Lunaire* for the Ballet Rambert in 1967. The score is the Schoenberg song cycle; the elegant designs are by the American artist, Reuben Ter-Arutunian.

166. Siobhan Davies's *Embarque* was created for Rambert Dance Company in 1988, after the choreographer had returned from a year's visit to America. It conveyed a sense of the vast distances covered by the choreographer on her travels. Sara Matthews and Paul Old are seen here, in costumes by David Buckland.

167. Guy Detot and Nelson Fernandez in Richard Alston's *Rainbow Ripples*, for Ballet Rambert.

demonstrated an alternative. A personality of incredible energy, erudition and perception, Marie Rambert discovered talents in dancers and choreo-graphers – Ashton, Tudor, Howard and Gore – who were themselves unaware of their potential. Her happiest years were probably the early ones of the Ballet Club in the Mercury Theatre at Notting Hill, where she watched her young company of immensely gifted artists creating the first British ballets and where she could sustain personal contact with nearly everyone in the audience in that tiny theatre. Her early career and the work of her company up to 1961 is described and illustrated in Mary Clarke's *Dancers of Mercury*. Significantly, when the company tried to move into the domain of the Royal Ballet with such large and expensive productions as *Don Quixote* (1962), after a first happy acquisition of *La Sylphide*, it began to lose its own identity. In 1965, under the joint direction of Rambert herself and her new choreographer Norman Morrice, the company was re-formed as a smaller

168. (Above) Richard Alston made *Dangerous Liaisons* for Rambert Dance Company in 1985. Catherine Becque and Ian Stewart are seen here in Richard Smith's costumes.

169. (Right) Mona Inglesby as Giselle, with Wanda Evina (1891–1966) as Berthe, in the first act of *Giselle*. Mona Inglesby's own ballet company, International Ballet, which she directed from its inception in 1941 until its dissolution in 1953, toured extensively throughout Britain, concentrating on the full-length Russian classics. These were staged by Nicholas Sergueyev from his notebooks which contained a record of the St Petersburg stagings in the Stepanov script. During its twelve years International Ballet did much to encourage the interest of audiences outside London in the full-length classics. The company also danced in vast arenas to thousands of spectators on the Continent. Madame Evina started her career with Diaghilev and was later greatly valued as a pianist for ballet classes, especially those of Stanislas Idzikowski. Her understanding of classic mime brought new life to a part that had become stereotyped.

troupe, effectively bridging the gap between classical and modern dance and concentrating almost entirely on the production of new works by their own and visiting choreographers.

It was to take some five years for the company to find a new identity. Morrice's choreographies indicated the path the company would now follow, and his artistic decisions were much strengthened by the example of the works by Glen Tetley, which enhanced the repertory. The American-born Tetley (b. 1926) had evolved a creative style which made use of both classical and modern elements, and his work for Nederlands Dans Theater had been influential in guiding Morrice's feelings about the future for the Ballet Rambert. Such creations as Morrice's *That is the Show,* and Tetley's *Pierrot Lunaire, Ziggurat* and *Embrace Tiger and Return to Mountain* confirmed the new possibilities of the Rambert company's artistic policy. These were further extended when Christopher Bruce (b. 1945), a leading male dancer, showed a marked choreographic talent in his first works. His *George Frideric, Ancient Voices of Children* and *Ghost Dances,* among other pieces, helped to win a new audience for the Rambert ensemble. After Morrice's move to the Royal Ballet in 1977 the company was to have several changes of artistic director – with inevitable changes in artistic policy; John Chesworth held the position until

170. Alicia Markova and Anton Dolin dancing the second act of *Giselle* in Festival Ballet's first season at the old Stoll Theatre in the autumn of 1950. The Stoll Theatre, which stood at the southern end of Kingsway, was the company's London home in its early years. Built as an opera house, it had a splendid stage and auditorium for ballet.

1981, when Robert North succeeded him; he in turn was succeeded in 1986 by Richard Alston.

Alston (b. 1948) had been trained at the London School of Contemporary Dance. He was the first of the young creative artists produced by that organization to seek a stylistic break with the school and company ethos. Influenced by Merce Cunningham's linear and structural qualities, Alston established his own experimental group before working in New York with Cunningham himself. On his return to Britain his choreography was increasingly used by London Contemporary Dance Theatre and then by Ballet

171. Anton Dolin was a firm believer in the star system, and by inviting great artists to dance with Festival Ballet as guests he did much to set standards and to give inspiration to the young company. As late as 1955, Alexandra Danilova was able to conquer a new generation with her irresistible performance as the Street Dancer in *Le Beau Danube.* The Hussar here is John Gilpin, Festival Ballet's own brightest star.

Rambert for which he made such works as *Bell High*, *Rainbow Ripples* and *Chicago Brass*. In Alston's years with Ballet Rambert, his wish to show dance as dance, devoid of literary or dramatic connotations, has created a considerably leaner company, typified by his own productions (*Strong Language*, *Dangerous Liaisons*, *Zansa*), by works acquired from Cunningham and Trisha Brown, and by a change in the company's name to Rambert Dance Company.

OTHER COMPANIES

The Sadler's Wells Ballet and the Ballet Rambert were the dominant and formative companies in Britain during the 1930s and 1940s. During the war, when ballet boomed as never before and a new audience was discovered in the many cities visited by touring companies, the increased opportunities led to the appearance of various new ensembles. The Anglo-Polish Ballet

172. John Gilpin (1930–1983) in Harald Lander's *Études*. Gilpin was a most elegant classical virtuoso and a star of London Festival Ballet, of which he was also briefly artistic director.

173. Toni Lander (1931–1985) in dances from Bournonville's *Napoli*, as staged by her husband, Harald Lander, for Festival Ballet. A Danish ballerina of superlative gifts, she starred with London Festival Ballet and American Ballet Theatre, where her technical authority and the integrity of her interpretations gained her much acclaim.

174. In 1977 Rudolf Nureyev staged his version of Prokofiev's *Romeo and Juliet* for London Festival Ballet, with designs by Ezio Frigerio.

(1940–1947) showed, in its early years, lively Polish dancing from its two star performers, Czeslaw Konarski and Alicja Halama; the International Ballet (1940–1953) was formed by Mona Inglesby and toured with a repertoire largely consisting of classical revivals, mounted by Nicholas Sergueyev from his Stepanov notations of the Mariinsky Theatre ballets. Sergueyev, in charge of productions at the Mariinsky, had fled St Petersburg at the time of the 1917 Revolution, taking with him that theatre's priceless records of the repertoire. With these he was to work in Europe, and perhaps his most significant contribution was to mount the classical ballets for Ninette de Valois's young Vic-Wells Ballet. It is not an exaggeration to say that the West's understanding and appreciation of the classics, and our knowledge of the basic texts, is owed to Sergueyev's notations which preserved in Stepanov script much of the essential choreography of the old ballets.

The most important company to emerge was Festival Ballet, now English National Ballet. Founded by Alicia Markova and Anton Dolin with the impresario Julian Braunsweg in 1950, the year before the Festival of Britain, it was of course a showcase for its two stars, but from the first it offered serious stagings of the traditional repertory together with

175. Galina Samsova in a characteristically exultant leap. Samsova, born in Stalingrad and trained in Kiev, came to the West in 1961, and became a leading ballerina with London Festival Ballet and subsequently with Sadler's Wells Royal Ballet, as well as touring with the New London Ballet, which she led with André Prokovsky. She is seen here in Prokovsky's *divertissement, Vespri*.

important works of the Ballets Russes years by Fokine and Massine, which deserved to be seen in reputable productions. Markova and Dolin invited many illustrious guests to appear – Massine, Danilova, Chauviré, Toumanova, Riabouchinska, Lichine, Mia Slavenska – and the company nursed some talented new dancers, notably Belinda Wright and John Gilpin, and the Danish ballerina Toni Lander, all of whom were to become tremendously popular. Despite financial problems – Festival Ballet had no immediate subvention – Dr Braunsweg managed admirably to develop a

176. In 1979, Peter Schaufuss produced Bournonville's *La Sylphide* for London Festival Ballet, with designs by David Walker. Schaufuss inserted sequences that had been omitted from the traditional Copenhagen version, and created passages of his own in Bournonville-inspired choreography. The result was an expansive staging, admirably danced at its première by Schaufuss as James and by Eva Evdokimova (who had been trained in Copenhagen) as an ethereal sylph. They are seen here in the closing moments of the second act as the Sylphide dies. Happily, the staging and these interpretations have been preserved on film.

company, a repertory and an audience, and the ballet was soon a considerable force, nationally and internationally. Financial crises were frequent; in 1966, after an ambitious and ill-judged staging of *Swan Lake*, the company had to be rescued from near-bankruptcy. With the help of Donald Albery, an experienced man of the theatre, Festival Ballet was put on a more secure commercial footing. In 1968 Beryl Grey became artistic director and for the next decade was markedly successful in building a repertory and in developing the company's activities. For several years her star dancers were

177. Natalya Makarova as Tatyana, with Alexander Sombart, in Cranko's *Onegin*, staged by London Festival Ballet. Makarova demonstrated a profound sympathy with the role of Tatyana, and on her return to her native Leningrad and the Kirov Ballet in 1989, after an absence of eighteen years, she danced the two great *pas de deux* from the ballet with Sombart as a magnificent partner.

178. Elaine MacDonald in Bournonville's *La Ventana* with Scottish Ballet. Elaine MacDonald was for many years the leading ballerina of the companies directed by Peter Darrell (Western Theatre Ballet, Scottish Ballet) and was his muse, creating memorable leading roles in his works. But her range also encompassed a more traditional repertory, and she was admirably seen in *La Sylphide* and *Les Sylphides* in which her lightness and musicality were especially fine.

179. Paula Hinton with Peter Cazalet in *The Prisoners* by Peter Darrell (1929–1987), with Western Theatre Ballet. This dramatic ballet, first staged in 1957, told of two prisoners sheltered by the wife of one of them, and it typified Peter Darrell's quest for serious modern themes for choreography. Paula Hinton, one of the most subtle and powerful dramatic ballerinas, was especially associated with the roles created for her by her husband, Walter Gore. As a guest in Darrell's tautly conceived work, she gave a distinguished performance.

180. Dancers of Western Theatre Ballet in Walter Gore's *Street Games*. Gore initially made this ballet for his own New London Ballet in 1952; its gentle humour and resourceful, imaginative choreography were typical of Gore's work.

181. (Above) In 1990 Scottish Ballet acquired Balanchine's *Scotch Symphony*, which the choreographer had created after his company, New York City Ballet, visited the Edinburgh Festival in 1952. It is a charming comment on balletic Scottishness, danced to the last three movements of Mendelssohn's Scottish Symphony.

182. (Right) Patrick Harding Irmer and Anca Frankenhauser in Robert Cohan's *Forest*, created for London Contemporary Dance Theatre in 1977.

Galina Samsova and André Prokovsky, and the identity of the company continued happily to be that which Markova and Dolin had created. Beryl Grey was succeeded in 1979 by John Field, and in 1984 Peter Schaufuss, the Danish dancer who had already appeared with the company and had mounted a successful version of *La Sylphide* during Beryl Grey's directorate, was invited to take over the reins of the company. Schaufuss sought to galvanize the troupe, bringing in new dancers and new stagings, not all of them successful, and made the unwise decision to change the name of the company to the improbable 'English National Ballet'. In 1990 disagreements with the company's board precipitated his resignation, and he was succeeded by Ivan Nagy.

A vital move towards the idea of regional ballet had been made in 1957 when Elizabeth West (1927–1962) had founded the Western Theatre Ballet.

Based in Bristol, the company was dedicated to the idea that 'theatre' was to be as important as 'ballet' in the repertory. Despite great financial hardship in the early years, the company developed into a notable force in British ballet, with Peter Darrell (1929–1987) as its choreographer from the earliest days. Darrell's ability to produce highly dramatic or entertainingly lively work was essential to the Western Theatre Ballet's eventual success, a success which led in 1969 to its relocation by the Arts Council to Glasgow, where it became Scottish Theatre Ballet (now the Scottish Ballet). Under the guidance of Peter Darrell, who had assumed artistic responsibility for the company after Elizabeth West's death, Scottish Ballet developed a strong identity. Drama remained important, but the company now had a responsibility to put on classical ballets, which were imaginatively presented, and to invite other choreographers to create and re-stage other works for the company. Darrell continued to provide a large and vital part of the repertory, producing the full-length *Tales of Hoffmann* and *Mary, Queen of Scots*, as well as many shorter pieces. In these his muse was the company's ballerina, Elaine MacDonald, an artist of rare clarity of style and dramatic sensitivity.

183. Christopher Gable and members of Northern Ballet Theatre in *A Simple Man*, a ballet about the painter, L. S. Lowry, choreographed by Gillian Lynne and originally conceived for television in 1987.

184. Siobhan Davies as the Lady with the Deck Chair in Robert Cohan's *Waterless Method of Swimming Instruction*, for London Contemporary Dance Theatre in 1974. A *capriccio* set in the dry pool aboard an ocean liner, the piece was witty, and nowhere wittier than in Siobhan Davies's attempts to put up her deck chair, which activity soon resembled a fight with a sea-monster. It was very stylish clowning.

185. Julian Moss and Charlotte Kirkpatrick in Richard Alston's *Doublework*, staged for the London Contemporary Dance Theatre in 1984.

After Peter Darrell's death, Scottish Ballet appeared to have lost artistic momentum. It experimented with guest directors, but no coherent policy for the company emerged, until the appointment of Galina Samsova as artistic director in 1991.

At the same time that Western Theatre Ballet transferred its activities to Scotland, a former dancer of the company, Laverne Meyer, set about forming another regional company in Manchester. This was Northern Dance Theatre, whose aim was similar to that of Western Theatre Ballet: to show strong theatrical works to an audience outside London. The company laboured long and hard, and created interesting new work without winning a large enough public following. In 1976 Robert de Warren was appointed director; he changed the company's title to Northern Ballet Theatre, which suggested an altered artistic alignment. Generally undistinguished classical stagings became the company diet; and in 1988

186. Tracey Fitzgerald as Eurydice in Kim Brandstrup's *Orfeo*, a poetic recension which combined modern and baroque dance forms, created for London Contemporary Dance Theatre in 1989. Brandstrup, a Danish choreographer trained at the London School of Contemporary Dance, has also made a series of noteworthy productions for his own Arc Dance Company during the 1980s. The beautiful costume is by Craig Givens.

Christopher Gable, a former principal of the Royal Ballet who was also a film and stage actor, took charge of the company, which moved its base of operations to Halifax in 1990. Gable has initiated productions – *Giselle, Romeo and Juliet, Don Quixote* – which stress the dramatic aspect of ballet.

One other highly significant development of the post-war years was sparked off by the first visit of the Martha Graham Company to London in 1954. That season had been disastrous in financial terms, but though audiences were small, they numbered many theatre figures who were to be greatly appreciative of Graham's work, among them Robin Howard (1924–1989). Howard was a member of a distinguished family; he was a man of great energy, in spite of having lost both legs during war service. He was profoundly impressed by the emotional and physical weight of Graham's dance-pieces. As a result he underwrote further seasons by Graham and other American modern dancers, and eventually succeeded in establishing the London School of Contemporary Dance to teach the Graham technique. Howard asked Robert Cohan, one of Graham's leading dancers, to come to London to teach in the school, and from his endeavours, and with Howard's tireless energy, idealism and private fortune, London Contemporary Dance Theatre emerged as a showcase for the artists produced by the school. Between 1964 and 1969, the foundations were laid; in 1969 Robert Cohan arrived in London to work, and the Contemporary Dance Trust found itself a home at The Place, near Euston Station. This former drill-hall of the Artists' Rifles was to be the cradle from which emerged a splendid company and a magnificent school, masterminded by Howard and Cohan. From the activities of these two enterprises came choreography – from Cohan, of course, as the guiding spirit, and then from Siobhan Davies, Richard Alston, Robert North, Jonathan Lunn and several other company members – and a dance ensemble which won international praise. But more significantly even than this, the Contemporary Dance Trust had by its teaching, its performances and its educational work altered the way a whole nation thought about dancing, and had extended that influence into Europe. Since 1969, dance has become a major factor in the artistic experience of a generation of young people in schools and colleges in Britain, and it has gained an audience very different (though no less dedicated) from that devoted to classical ballet. That dance is now an integral part of national experience, and a vital part in many areas where the other arts do not penetrate, is due to the selfless work of Robin Howard, Robert Cohan and their colleagues. Superlative performance has been matched by creative energy, and the proliferation of modern, post-modern and 'new' radical dance in Britain can be attributed to the groundwork of the Contemporary Dance Trust.

8 America:
Two Kinds of Dancing

It is a curious fact that America is a country possessing two vital but diametrically opposed systems of dancing: the classic *danse d'école* imported from Europe, and a native tradition of free or modern dance that owes nothing to European attitudes. It is also worth noting here that the two styles, which had seemed in complete opposition for many years, have inter-reacted; there is a welcome cross-fertilization between the two schools in America and, very interestingly, in Europe too.

Of course ballet was known in America during the nineteenth century. Certain of the Romantic stars appeared there, notably Fanny Elssler; American ballerinas like Mary Ann Lee and Augusta Maywood (who made a fine career in Europe) knew real success. But it was the reaction, late in the century, against the artificialities of 'toe-dancing' that brought about the phenomenon that we must – for the sake of convenience, though no other – call modern dance. Two interesting precursors of the modern dance movement were American, although they both made their careers in Europe: Isadora Duncan and Loie Fuller. Duncan (1878–1927) achieved her fame in Europe, where her highly personal interpretations of serious music (in itself a rarity at a time when the prosaic output of Minkus and Pugni was still a musical norm for ballet), her Greek-inspired draperies and tunics, her bare feet and her tremendous personality enraptured audiences. Her dances were emotional interpretations of moods suggested to her by nature or by music; of technique she possessed little, but her phenomenal presence and her quality of movement, plus her daring, her absolute scorn for conventional morality, and the personal tragedies that dogged her life, lent an added excitement to her appearances.

Loie Fuller (1862–1928), the darling of the art nouveau age, had even less technique, but her inspired use of lighting to play over the filmy draperies that she manipulated by means of long canes suggested a new vision of light and of abstract shapes as part of dancing. The native American tradition had its beginnings in the work of Ruth St Denis (1877–1969) and her husband Ted Shawn (1891–1972). St Denis started out as an exotic dancer performing oriental solos, but gradually her interest in Eastern philosophy led her into more ambitious dances and to international fame in the years before the First World War. In 1914 she entered into partnership with the dancer Ted Shawn, and from this developed a company and a school, under the name Denishawn, which was to become the most important and most inspiring in the United States during the 1920s. Tours, which helped to keep the flame of public interest alight, were followed by years in which they separated, St Denis turning towards the study of dance in relation to religious experience and Shawn continuing to tour with a group of male dancers, teaching, writing, inspiring audiences wherever he found them and

187. Isadora Duncan (1878–1927). The intensity of her personality and a natural power and grace of movement overcame many of her physical and technical limitations. Although no film exists of her dancing, the magic of her image still persists. Reconstructions of her dances have become increasingly popular in recent years; a most touching (and convincing) evocation of her presence is owed to the *Five Brahms Waltzes in the manner of Isadora Duncan* which Frederick Ashton composed for Lynn Seymour and which that illustrious dancer marvellously interpreted.

188. Ruth St Denis and Ted Shawn in *Egyptian Suite* (1919), one of the many works inspired by ethnic dance with which they delighted audiences during the 1920s.

later initiating the influential Jacob's Pillow summer school and Dance Festival which still teaches and presents all forms of dance – modern, ethnic and ballet.

It was from the Denishawn company of the 1920s that the real pioneers of American modern dance were to come: Martha Graham and Doris Humphrey. Both graduated from the company with a desire to explore their own individual ideas of what dance could be, and the vital development of technique which each was to contribute to modern dance was the result of their need to impress their own ideals and style on their supporting groups. In teaching the dancers who were to work with them, a set technique had to be developed which could be used as a daily discipline in class, and the expansion of modern dance owes much to this fact. It also owes much to the interest in dancing as an educative and artistic experience in American colleges, where dance performance and creation has made an important link between students and choreographers.

Martha Graham (1894–1991) is accepted as the most influential figure in modern dance; for more than fifty years the Graham school and the various incarnations of her company have been the nursery for an extraordinary collection of talented dancers who have moved on from the Graham style and

189. *Appalachian Spring*, one of Martha Graham's most celebrated pieces, was created in 1944, with a score by Aaron Copland and design by Isamu Noguchi. In it a newly married pioneer couple set up house in a new land: the original cast, seen here, had May O'Donnell as the Pioneer Woman, Martha Graham as the Bride and Erick Hawkins (the first male dancer to join the Graham company) as the Husbandman.

190. Martha Graham as Jocasta, Robert Cohan as Tiresias and Bertram Ross as Oedipus in Graham's *Night Journey*. Created in 1947, this work was one of Graham's boldest exercises in re-telling Greek myth – in this case the story of Queen Jocasta, her marriage with her own son, Oedipus, and the intervention of the blind seer Tiresias. Robert Cohan was eventually to become the founding artistic force behind the London Contemporary Dance Theatre and its school.

191. Doris Humphrey and members of her group in her dance inspired by Bach's Air on the G String, created in 1928.

technique to contribute to the present lively dance tradition in the USA. Merce Cunningham, Pearl Lang, Erick Hawkins, Paul Taylor and Robert Cohan are all graduates of the Graham academy. Besides establishing a system of training, Graham's considerable output has covered a remarkable range, from specifically American pieces like *Appalachian Spring* to dances based on myths which became the subjects of later works – versions of the Greek tragedies (*Clytemnestra* and *Phaedra*, for example) that enabled her to show their universal connotations and reveal the inner conflicts of personality, a favourite theme with her.

Doris Humphrey (1895–1956) was a notable theorist of modern dance, much concerned with the choreographic possibilities implied in the idea of balance and fall. For some years she joined forces with Charles Weidman (1901–1975), an accomplished mime and a master of comic effects, and they exerted a remarkable influence on their students. Humphrey's most famous disciple was José Limón (1908–1972), an outstanding dancer, and for his company she created many of the works in the repertory, as well as acting as

192. The original cast of José Limón's *The Moor's Pavane*. Telling the story of *Othello* in succinct form, to a Purcell Chaconne, this is one of the key works by Limón (1908–1972). He is seen as Othello, with Lucas Hoving as Iago and Betty Jones as Desdemona. Missing from the group is Pauline Koner, who created the role of Emilia.

193. *Revelations*, choreographed by Alvin Ailey (1931–1989) to Negro spirituals. This was the most famous – and justifiably so – of Ailey's creations for his own company: still wonderfully vivid and sincere in revealing the faith that inspired the spirituals.

artistic director. Doris Humphrey was an influential figure at the Connecticut College Summer School of the Dance, the most important institution of its kind, at the New York Young Men's and Young Women's Hebrew Association (the famous New York 'Y') and in the dance section of the Juilliard School in New York.

The expansion of modern dance was in part the result of dancers moving away from their parent company in which they had made reputations as soloists and forming small and often temporary groups for which they in turn became choreographers. If not particularly stable – financial difficulties have always taken a toll – the tradition is lively, and the post-Graham/Humphrey generation included some notable artists. Beside José Limón we must place his most famous soloist and an outstanding dancer in her own creations, Pauline Koner. Sybil Shearer was a former student of Humphrey and is recognized as one of the great modern dance figures; since leaving New York she has been artist in residence at the National College of Education in Evanston, Illinois. Another Graham artist is Anna Sokolow. Hanya Holm came initially from Germany to direct the Mary Wigman School in America; the influence of this great German free dancer was considerable during her visits to the United States during the 1930s.

The tradition of Negro dance has had a wide application: for Katherine Dunham it meant a brilliant theatricalization of American Negro and Caribbean themes; for Pearl Primus it implied a dance based on African styles,

194. Merce Cunningham's choreographies have been acquired by several ballet companies, who find in the clean, pure lines of his work a style which accords happily with classically trained bodies. His own company, though, provides the ideal means of enjoying Cunningham's dance vocabulary: Alan Good, Rob Remley and Victoria Finlayson of the Cunningham company are seen here in Cunningham's *Pictures*.

195. Merce Cunningham in his *Antic Meet*, with music by his long-time collaborator, John Cage. First performed in 1958, this comedy satirized the plight of the 'little man'.

196. Members of the Merce Cunningham Dance Company in Cunningham's *Travelogue*.

197. Members of the Alwin Nikolais Dance Company in his *Imago*. This picture shows the closing Arcade sequence in which a city's population is seen as a collection of fantasy creatures.

while Alvin Ailey's American Dance company has been concerned not only with Negro dance (as in his beautiful *Revelations*, which explores the emotional world of spirituals) but with building a repertory that offers a wide view of much American dance of all kinds.

The proliferation of American dance during the 1960s, and after, was remarkable. A survey by the New York critic Don McDonagh, *The Rise and Fall and Rise of Modern Dance* (1976), conveyed much of the vitality as well as the waywardness of the most advanced practitioners of that decade, who were moving away from the formal vocabulary established by Graham and Humphrey into the field of 'happenings', where elements of chance were all-important – and pretentiousness was not avoided. In the group of creators who were associated with the experiments undertaken in New York at Judson Church, there were many figures who were later to be markedly influential

198. The joyous Paul Taylor in his own *Book of Beasts*, a wonderfully happy work created in 1971.

in the emergence of 'new dance', a style radically different from that of accepted modern dance. The new generation of free dancers – eager to rethink the rules of movement and how it could be used – were nevertheless influenced by the work of one senior figure of modern dance. This was Merce Cunningham.

Merce Cunningham represented a conscious break with many of the accepted trappings of modern dance; he uses chance techniques with musical accompaniment (he has long been associated with John Cage, the avant-garde

199. For thirty years Paul Taylor has continued to astonish his audiences by the imaginative vitality of his creations. In 1988 he produced *Counterswarm*, to music by Gyorgy Ligeti, which dealt with humanity in terms of insect life.

composer who specializes in random musical effects) in the choreographic make-up of his theatre works, where the position of a dance in the ensemble is varied from night to night; he aims to use everyday activity as well as dance movement; he shows a basic concern to make his audience look at dancing with fresh eyes, freed from any literary or emotional associations. The result, in his latest work, is serene and beautiful dances that are both cool in manner and radiant in effect.

Among the magicians of the dance theatre is Alwin Nikolais (b. 1912), who is responsible for the entire composition of his works – electronic score, design, lighting and movement. His 'sound and vision pieces', as he calls them, are virtuoso exercises in illusion, in which, with skilled use of projections and lighting, he creates a kaleidoscope of shapes, colours and movement that beguiles audiences world-wide.

Paul Taylor (b. 1930), a graduate of the Cunningham and Graham companies, is a masterly choreographer with a predilection for good music for his

200. Twyla Tharp (centre) with members of her company in *Eight Jelly Rolls*.

work, a rarity in an art where, from the very beginning, scores have been the weakest element. Taylor dared to use late Beethoven quartets for his two-act *Orbs*, and his choreography did not minimize the score. His creations range from the fresh, heart-lifting *Aureole* (which has entered the repertory of ballet companies) and *Arden Court*, to the humours of *Three Epitaphs* or *Minikin Fair*, the darker pieces like *Churchyard* or the bleak *Last Look*. All are shaped by an exceptional musical sensitivity and theatrical integrity, the dance always resourceful and fresh.

From the Taylor company came Twyla Tharp (b. 1942), who started her choreographic career after leaving Taylor in 1965 with work that examined the elements of dancing with a beady and inquiring eye. By the early 1970s she was creating those blazingly energetic and fast dances – *Eight Jelly Rolls*,

201. The American Mark Morris has been hailed as one of the most significant and innovative choreographers to spring from the modern dance discipline. In 1986 he presented this *Pièces en Concert* in New York as part of the Next Wave Festival at the Brooklyn Academy of Music. He is seen here in the centre with Susan Hadley and Rob Besserer.

The Bix Pieces – which won her fame. There followed works for ballet companies – *Deuce Coupe* for the Joffrey Ballet (1973); *Push Comes to Shove* (1976) for American Ballet Theatre – that demonstrated to a larger audience the meticulous craft and physical bravura of her style. Since then Tharp, herself an inimitably alert and combative performer, has choreographed for her own company and, as a result of a developing interest in the classic academic dance, for the New York City Ballet and the Paris Opéra Ballet. Her dances show the performers as bright and daring in a uniquely American way, and her work has rightly been recognized as a vital reflection of the dance of her time.

From the experimental work which continued at Judson Church came many of the leading figures of the new dance of the 1970s and 1980s. Trisha Brown (b. 1936) has moved from an early simple, gestural style to a manner more accessible in its fluidity and vitality (as in *Set and Reset*, and *Opal Loop*

202. In November 1989 Mikhail Baryshnikov joined Mark Morris's Dance Group in Brussels for the creation of *Wonderland*, a piece inspired by the Hollywood gangster films of the 1940s. Baryshnikov is seen here with Olivia Maridjan-Koop, and the shadow of Rob Besserer.

which is performed by Rambert Dance Company). Lucinda Childs (b. 1940), also a graduate of Judson Church, has produced work austere in line and coolly minimalist; in 1984 she created *Premier Orage* for the Paris Opéra (which has been adventurous in acquiring choreographies from several American 'moderns': among the most important creations have been Merce Cunningham's *Un Jour ou Deux*, Andrew deGroat's *Nouvelle Lune* and Mark Morris's *Ein Herz*).

Mark Morris (b. 1956) excited much interest among audiences in America and Europe in the 1980s. The influences on Morris's style range from folk-dance, ballet and modern dance to the imagery of popular music, and his musical taste is similarly catholic. He has shown a particular sympathy with baroque music, and his dance-pieces have explored the world of Tamil love-songs, spuriously religious folk-music, and a wide variety of classical texts. In 1988 he was invited to bring his company to the Théâtre Royal de la Monnaie

203. Mikhail Baryshnikov and Kathleen Moore with members of American Ballet Theatre in Mark Morris's *Drink To Me Only With Thine Eyes*, created for American Ballet Theatre in 1988. Set to Virgil Thompson piano preludes – which are performed on stage – Morris's dances are intense in their musicality and taxing in their demands on the white-clad cast. The result is exhilarating and beautiful.

in Brussels, to replace the Béjart troupe, and there he produced a masterly visualization of Handel's *L'Allegro, il Penseroso ed il Moderato*, and a cinema-inspired *Wonderland* which starred Mikhail Baryshnikov. For American Ballet Theatre he has also staged a classically deft and ebullient *Drink To Me Only With Thine Eyes*.

Parallel with this activity has been the remarkable expansion of the classic dance in America since the 1930s. The key event which sparked off this development was the arrival in the United States of George Balanchine; he had been invited there by two wealthy dance-lovers, Lincoln Kirstein and Edward M. M. Warburg, to start a school of ballet and if possible extend it into a company. The School of American Ballet opened its doors on 1 January 1934; from it a small company was formed, the American Ballet, whose chequered career ended in 1938 following a disastrous liaison with

204. The architects of the New York City Ballet: Lincoln Kirstein and George Balanchine.

the Metropolitan Opera, New York. For the next eight years Balanchine's career lay largely on Broadway and in Hollywood, composing dances – and very good ones – for musical comedies and films. There were some opportunities for creating ballets, but it was not until the foundation in 1946 of Ballet Society (an enterprise launched by Kirstein and Balanchine to give subscription performances of new works) that Balanchine really returned to ballet. By the end of 1948 an invitation to perform at the New York City Center transformed Ballet Society into the New York City Ballet.

Thereafter the company, under the guidance of Balanchine and Kirstein, rapidly developed into the great ensemble that we know today. For his dancers Balanchine composed a massive body of work which must be accounted one of the supreme artistic achievements of this century.

205. Members of the New York City Ballet in Balanchine's *Serenade*. The dancer's fall to the ground was an incident kept in the choreography from the time of the original rehearsals of this ballet, when a student fell in the studio.

Balanchine was a classicist. For him the choreography was the thing: on the foundation of the score he erected dance structures of amazing beauty and complexity, which were for him extensions of the *danse d'école* he had learned as a pupil and performer in the Mariinsky Theatre company. Innovation, experiment and a continual concern for the classic dance itself were the characteristics of Balanchine's choreography, from *Apollo* onwards. Generally plotless, although there was often an inner dramatic tension to his work, Balanchine's creations made the classic ballet American. On his return to his native Russia with his company in 1962, Balanchine was greeted by an interviewer who said to him, 'Welcome to Moscow, home of the classic dance.' 'I beg your pardon,' replied Balanchine, 'Russia is the home of the Romantic ballet. The home of classical ballet is now America.'

Just as the different elements of the old, noble French school – the Italian virtuosity of such ballerinas as Legnani, the Bournonville teaching of Christian Johansson – were transformed by the bodies and temperaments of Russian dancers at the end of the nineteenth century to make the Russian classical

206. Nicholas Magellanes and Tanaquil LeClercq in Balanchine's *Orpheus*, first produced by Ballet Society in New York in 1948. The score by Stravinsky was one of several he composed especially for Balanchine; the sets and costumes are by Isamu Noguchi.

207. Judith Fugate, Mikhail Baryshnikov and Coleen Neary in Balanchine's *The Four Temperaments* with the New York City Ballet. Between 1978 and 1980 Baryshnikov was a member of Balanchine's company which he had joined in order to work with the master choreographer.

208. (Above) *Agon* (choreography by Balanchine, music by Stravinsky) was first performed by the New York City Ballet in 1957. The score was dedicated by Stravinsky to Balanchine and Kirstein, and the ballet epitomizes their conception of classical dancing in America in the mid twentieth century.

209. (Right) *Liebeslieder Walzer* (choreography by Balanchine, music by Brahms, setting by David Hayes, costumes by Karinska) was first performed at the New York City Center on 22 November 1960. Diana Adams and Bill Carter are seen in the first part of this enchanting picture of nineteenth-century manners; the setting is a naturalistic drawing-room with the dancers wearing conventional evening dress of the period. In the second part the mood changes, the dancers' costumes (and the dances) become balletic, but the ballet ends with a return to the real world of the drawing-room.

school, that schooling was itself transformed by the athletic prowess of the American body to produce, under Balanchine's guidance, dancers who were leaner, faster, longer-legged, more brilliant in physical cut-and-thrust and, curiously, more democratic. Intensely musical, and inspired chiefly by the female dancer, Balanchine made ballets that had a clarity and an uncluttered air so that they seemed an effortlessly right realization of the score. They were music made flesh, visible and beautiful.

Balanchine's output was so massive – in the splendid catalogue of his creations published in New York in 1983, the year he died, 425 works are listed, from the slightest solo to the grandest masterpiece – that any proper study would take a book rather than part of one chapter. But in considering his American achievement it is significant that the first work he made after his arrival – *Serenade*, staged for his pupils at the School of American Ballet in 1934 – was dedicated to demonstrating the ennobling discipline of the classic academic dance. This was a theme that constantly ran through his later work.

With the music of Stravinsky, a composer he greatly admired and who returned his admiration, Balanchine produced more than twenty ballets, from *Apollo*, the first, in which he saw clearly his way forward as a classicist, to such marvels as *Orpheus* and *Agon*, and the monumental creations (*Violin Concerto*; *Symphony in Three Movements*) staged for the 1972 Stravinsky Festival in which the New York City Ballet saluted the composer so gloriously.

With such romantic composers as Tchaikovsky in *Ballet Imperial* (now known as *Piano Concerto No. 2*), or Bizet (*Symphony in C*), or Mendelssohn (*Scotch Symphony*), Balanchine devised exhilarating displays to lift heart and mind. With more advanced compositions – Webern, late Stravinsky, electronic music – he made ballets of bracing intellectual vigour, although his dance language here naturally acquired distortions and extensions of the academic vocabulary. Dramatic ballets were rare – *La Sonnambula* (also known as *Night Shadow*); the full-length *Don Quixote*; the early *Prodigal Son* – but each was as sure in effect as the plotless works. Balanchine's achievement was that of a man who furthered the classic dance more than any choreographer since Petipa. He gave it fresh impetus, a new image, by taking it to America, and his influence, no less than his attainment, was immense.

210. One of the greatest creations to come from the 1972 Stravinsky Festival staged by the New York City Ballet was Balanchine's *Violin Concerto*. Bart Cook and Karin von Aroldingen are seen in the first aria. The title was subsequently amended to *Stravinsky Violin Concerto*.

After Balanchine's death in 1983, the direction of the New York City Ballet passed jointly to Jerome Robbins and Peter Martins, who had been nominated for the post during Balanchine's lifetime. Martins (b. 1946) is a Danish *premier danseur* who joined the New York City Ballet in 1969 and was soon recognized as an outstanding Balanchine dancer. (The Bournonville link is a fascinating one here: Bournonville schooling, by way of Christian Johansson, shaped the dancers of the St Petersburg ballet which produced Balanchine, and the outstanding Bournonville teacher, Stanley Williams, has been a leading pedagogue with the New York City Ballet and its School of American Ballet. And another eminent Danish dancer, Ib Andersen, joined the company in 1979. Such bloodlines are essential in making a company style.)

211. *Dances at a Gathering* (choreography by Jerome Robbins, music by Chopin, costumes by Joe Eula) was first produced by the New York City Ballet on 8 May 1969. The dancers in this picture are (left to right): Violette Verdy and John Clifford, Kay Mazzo and Anthony Blum, Sara Leland and John Prinz, Patricia McBride and Robert Maiorano, and Allegra Kent with Edward Villella. When staged by the Royal Ballet in 1970 the work acquired a slightly stronger emotional flavour and also more humour.

Robbins (b. 1918) was initially discovered by another company which has reflected the expansion of ballet throughout the United States: American Ballet Theatre.★ The company was founded in 1940 by Lucia Chase (1907–1986) as a determinedly American troupe, although it called upon foreign stars (Markova, Dolin, Alicia Alonso) and choreographers (Fokine, Tudor, Massine) as well as native talent. In its half-century, the company has fostered many American dancers, notably the dramatic ballerina Nora Kaye (1920–1987), and called upon many native choreographers (Agnes de Mille, Eugene

★ Originally known as Ballet Theater, the company name was changed after its successful London season in 1946 to Ballet Theatre. Subsequently the title was expanded to American Ballet Theatre in 1957.

212. *Bugaku* (choreography by Balanchine, music by Mayuzumi, décor and lighting by David Hayes, costumes by Karinska) was first performed by the New York City Ballet on 20 March 1963. Allegra Kent and Edward Villella are seen in the marvellously erotic *pas de deux* which is at the centre of this ballet. It was inspired by the attitudes, though not the technique, of the Japanese Gagaku court dances.

213. Suzanne Farrell and Peter Martins in Balanchine's *Agon* with the New York City Ballet.

Loring, Michael Kidd, Herbert Ross, William Dollar, Eliot Feld, together with such modern dance creators as Merce Cunningham, Twyla Tharp and Mark Morris). The pattern of invitations to foreign stars and choreographers, initiated in the first seasons, has continued: among the company's distinguished visitors have been Natalya Makarova, Carla Fracci, Toni Lander, Erik Bruhn, Fernando Bujones, Anthony Dowell, Julio Bocca and Mikhail Baryshnikov (who directed the company throughout the 1980s).

A developing concern of American Ballet Theatre over the years has been the presentation of the traditional classical repertory, and in 1967 came the production of a full-length *Swan Lake* (a necessity, it seems, for every ballet company, large or small, if the box-office is to be kept happy). Thereafter the company continued to add full-length productions, most notably Natalya Makarova's handsome version of *La Bayadère*, Kenneth MacMillan's *Romeo and Juliet*, and his staging of *The Sleeping Beauty*, all of which have proved huge attractions for its audiences. Despite its eclectic repertory and roster of dancers, American Ballet Theatre has retained an American identity that

214. Merrill Ashley of the New York City Ballet in Balanchine's *Allegro Brillante*. Merrill Ashley's dancing has a speed and absolute clarity that dazzle the eye, and Balanchine paid tribute to these qualities in *Ballo della Regina*.

215. In 1941 Mikhail Fokine was in Mexico City to create a new work for Ballet Theater. This was *Bluebeard*, with music by Offenbach and designs by Marcel Vertès. Its action was comic, though too complicated, but it gave fine roles to Anton Dolin as Bluebeard and Irina Baronova as Boulotte, a peasant girl whom he marries. They are seen, centre, with Miriam Golden and Margaret Banks as two of Bluebeard's other wives. The piece was not a great success, but the performances of Baronova and Dolin were wonderfully merry.

216. *Pillar of Fire* (choreography by Antony Tudor, music by Arnold Schoenberg (Transfigured Night), décor and costumes by Jo Mielziner) was first produced by American Ballet Theatre in 1942. The ballet was inspired by the poem by Richard Dehmel, which had also inspired Schoenberg's score. The heroine, Hagar, is an unhappy woman whose desperate search for love brings disillusion and then final happiness. Nora Kaye is seen here as Hagar, with Antony Tudor as the man to whom she owes her eventual happiness. *Pillar of Fire* was the work which first revealed Nora Kaye as a great dramatic dancer.

can be seen in such old favourites as Agnes de Mille's *Rodeo* and Jerome Robbins's *Fancy Free*. The latter was Robbins's first piece for the company, staged in 1944, and it was an instantaneous smash-hit. A virtuoso comic study of three sailors on shore leave in wartime New York, it became a classic of our time. With its combination of academic dance and contemporary movement, it offered a new approach to ballet as something specifically American in feeling and expression – a quality which was also to be found in Eugene Loring's *Billy the Kid* (1938), Lew Christensen's *Filling Station* (1938) and Agnes de Mille's *Rodeo* (1942). The style of *Fancy Free* was extended by Robbins in a series of works for ballet and for the Broadway stage, notably *West Side Story. Interplay* (1945) and *New York Export: Opus Jazz* (1958) revealed how well Robbins could unite jazz and popular dance forms with ballet.

Other Robbins choreographies made social comment – as in *The Guests*, which dealt with intolerance, and *The Cage*, which, showing female predators,

217. Mikhail Baryshnikov and Natalya Makarova in the *pas de deux* from *Don Quixote*. With American Ballet Theatre, these two stars brought the splendid elegance of their Kirov training to this flashy *pas de deux*, and made art out of its most meretricious moments.

was like the second act of *Giselle* performed by an insect colony – while his *Afternoon of a Faun* updated the idea of Nijinsky's original to provide a portrait of two young dancers in a rehearsal studio, delicately aware of their bodies and of each other. American Ballet Theatre's tragedy was that Robbins left in 1950, and thereafter the company failed to find a permanent choreographer who could help to form a distinctive identity for the troupe. A widely based repertory served as a showcase for its home-grown and imported talent, and during the decade in which he directed the company Mikhail Baryshnikov sought to ensure a stronger classical style for his dancers; but despite efforts to encourage creative talent within its ranks, the company has not developed a clear 'house-style' in choreography.

218. Erik Bruhn (1928–1986) and Lupe Serrano (b. 1930) in the final pose of the *pas de deux* from *Don Quixote*. Bruhn, the Apollo among male dancers of his generation, trained in the school of the Royal Danish Ballet and became an impeccable exponent of Bournonville style. He also developed on the international stage a large repertory of classical and modern roles which he danced with superlative grace and integrity. Lupe Serrano was a ballerina of rare virtuosity who spent much of her career with American Ballet Theatre.

219. Fernando Bujones and Gelsey Kirkland in the *pas de deux* from *Don Quixote*, with American Ballet Theatre.

220. *Fancy Free*, with choreography by Jerome Robbins, music by Leonard Bernstein, and décor and costumes by Oliver Smith. The first performance of this ballet, on 18 April 1944 at the old Metropolitan Opera House, New York, heralded the arrival of Jerome Robbins, then aged only twenty-three, as a major choreographer. Robbins was one of the sailors in the original cast, dancing the third variation. In this picture, taken in 1950, the three are Paul Godkin, John Kriza (who created the sentimental role and danced it for twenty years) and Eric Braun. The girls are Norma Vance and Allyn McLerie.

Robbins's association with the New York City Ballet began in 1950, and except for periods when he worked with immense success on Broadway or when he devoted himself to experiment, the company remained an essential base for his creativity for forty years. In 1990 Robbins announced his retirement from active participation as one of the New York City Ballet's joint ballet-masters, and a fortnight's retrospective season during that summer enabled the company to pay tribute to a man who has enhanced the repertory with many ballets, from *Dances at a Gathering* (1969) and *Goldberg Variations* (1971) to *The Four Seasons* (1981) and the hilarious *The Concert* (1956).

Robbins's co-director, Peter Martins, consolidated much of the company repertory in the years after Balanchine's death. He had the unenviable task of succeeding a genius as artistic director of the company. However, Martins has annually produced new works since his *Calcium Light Night* of 1977, which first indicated his creative manner. In his later ballets, *Barber Violin Concerto*,

Les Gentilshommes and *Ecstatic Orange*, Martins can be seen to be continuing and adapting the creative policies established during the Balanchine years. In 1988, Martins organized another festival devoted to a single musical theme (earlier ones had been dedicated to Stravinsky, Ravel, and Tchaikovsky), which enabled many choreographers to work for the company. This American Music Festival attracted a great deal of new work: no fewer than seventeen choreographers (they included such 'moderns' as Paul Taylor and Laura Dean, as well as the more classical Eliot Feld, William Forsythe and Martins himself) were invited to provide twenty-one ballets.

The New York City Ballet stands, of course, as a pinnacle of classic ballet, significant not least in showing America (and the world) the power of academic dance.

Other American companies have sought to encourage and satisfy the public taste for dancing. The Joffrey Ballet had a modest beginning in 1956, when Robert Joffrey (1930–1988) formed a small performing ensemble to show his choreographies, and subsequently those of Gerald Arpino (b. 1928), a dancer in the company. Despite one major disaster when private funding was withdrawn, the company has expanded to become a major force in American

221. Gerald Arpino's full-length *Clowns* was staged by the Joffrey Ballet in 1968. Robert Blankshine is seen here amid the plastic shapes which represent both a Big Top and the World in this allegorical ballet.

222. Members of the Dance Theatre of Harlem in Balanchine's *Agon*.

ballet. In addition to the choreographies by Joffrey and Arpino, the company undertook revivals of historically significant works by Ashton, Fokine, Massine, Tudor and Jooss, and staged a fascinating reconstruction (the work of the dance-scholar Millicent Hodson) of Nijinsky's *Le Sacre du printemps* in 1987.

Throughout America, both classical and modern dance abound. Universities have been centres of activity since the 1930s, when Bennington College, Vermont, offered a summer school in modern dance and invited Graham, Humphrey, Weidman and Hanya Holm to work there. Major ballet troupes exist in San Francisco (which boasts the oldest professional company in America), Houston, Washington and Boston, and in other cities smaller companies perform invaluable work. Of exceptional interest has been the Dance Theatre of Harlem, founded by Arthur Mitchell – a leading dancer with the New York City Ballet – which made its début in 1971 as America's first black classical dance ensemble, and has since gained an enthusiastic following nationally and internationally.

9 Soviet Ballet:
Vaganova and her Pupils

The last years of the Imperial Russian Ballet saw a few reforms, notably in the ballets staged by Fokine, but the pattern had changed very little from the Petipa era. The old generals were in the front seats to applaud the ballerinas, of whom there was still a galaxy. Pavlova maintained her connection with the Mariinsky until 1913; Karsavina did not leave Russia until 1918 (her second husband was H. J. Bruce, an English diplomat, and it was in England that she made her home, helping the young English ballet in innumerable ways). The Russians claim that because Fokine continued to work there until 1918 his reforms were reflected in their repertory as much as in the West, but in pre-revolutionary Russia he was as handicapped as Diaghilev had been by bureaucracy. During the war and the Revolution there was little opportunity for artistic experiment. All energy was spent on survival. Somehow the dancers, and above all the school, emerged safely from those terrible times.

It was estimated, however, that the Revolution robbed the ballet of about forty per cent of its personnel; many left the country either during or immediately after the Revolution. The ballet-masters and the teachers who were left fought valiantly for the survival of their art and their champion was Anatoly Lunacharsky, formerly a professional theatre and music critic, who became the first Soviet Commissar of Enlightenment. Speaking in March 1921, he said of the Russian school of ballet: 'To lose this thread, to allow it to break before being used as the foundation of new artistic culture – belonging to the people – this would be a great calamity ... Can ballet be

223. (Above) Marina Semyonova (b. 1908) the first great Soviet ballerina, is seen here as the heroine in the second act of Petipa's *Raymonda* in its revival at the Bolshoy Theatre, Moscow, in 1945.

224. (Right) Galina Ulanova was born in 1910 and graduated into the Leningrad ballet in 1928, after studying with Agrippina Vaganova. For the next thirty-five years her name was associated with many of the greatest triumphs of Soviet ballet. A dancer of glorious gifts, she gave every role total conviction and grace of spirit. She is seen here in the adagio from the second act of *Swan Lake*, partnered by Konstantin Sergeyev. Sergeyev (1910–1992) was an illustrious male dancer, the husband of Natalya Dudinskaya, who became director and choreographer of the Leningrad Kirov Ballet and artistic director of the Vaganova School.

abolished in Russia? No, this will never happen.' The doors of the Mariinsky were thrown open to the people. The ballet-master Leontiev did his best to sustain a repertory, calling on the help of those of his colleagues who remained in Russia. The ballerina Elizaveta Gerdt (1891–1975) carried the main burden of the repertory.

Attempts were made to produce heavily symbolic ballets, indoctrinated with Soviet political beliefs, but in 1922 a revival of Petipa's *The Sleeping Beauty* was a tremendous success (Spessivtseva was one of the Auroras) and henceforward the company continued to revive its old masterpieces as well as to create new works which inevitably reflected the changed spirit of the times.

The direction of the former Mariinsky ballet was offered to Fokine, but he could not agree with the authorities either about money or the roles given to his wife and finally left Russia. He was invited back, but never returned. Under a succession of 'caretaker' directors emerged the most powerful influence on Soviet ballet, the great teacher Agrippina Vaganova, who was to mould the ballerinas who became the glory of Soviet ballet.

A former soloist of the Imperial company and appointed a ballerina in 1915, Vaganova had retired early from the stage but returned to teach when she found that a new type of school was being founded and that skilled teachers were in desperately short supply. She began teaching at the Petrograd State Choreographic School in 1921 and the first of her famous pupils was Marina Semyonova. Her method evolved from her own experience and from knowledge gained from working with her pupils. She kept an open mind and absorbed the methods of all schools, herself constantly learning and passing on her knowledge to grateful pupils. Natalia Roslavleva, critic and historian, in her book *Era of the Russian Ballet*, 1966, prepared for English

225. Tatyana Vecheslova (1910–91) was an eminent member of that generation of Leningrad ballerinas who graduated from Vaganova's classes in the late 1920s (she was a contemporary of Ulanova and Dudinskaya). Her repertoire included all the great classical roles as well as the heroines of the new Soviet ballets, her every interpretation marked by vivid dramatic feeling. On retiring from the stage in 1953 she became a teacher, and among her pupils was Natalya Makarova. She is seen here in one of her favourite roles, that of Esmeralda.

publication by Novosti Press Agency, which describes the Soviet ballet in great detail and is required reading for this period, says:

> Vaganova pupils acquired the space-conquering amplitude of movement that became a sign manual of the Soviet school. Their *tours* were more impetuous, the elevation more soaring, the back and head posed, the arms more fluid and expressive. The classical line remained as pure as ever, but it allowed greater variety. Soviet choreographers started taking advantage of Vaganova-trained pupils (they expressed not only the Vaganova system, but the *age* they lived in, with its soaring spirit). Vaganova, in turn, was also influenced by the style of Soviet choreography and this did not fail to be reflected in her work.

226. Natalya Dudinskaya (b. 1912) in the first act of *La Bayadère* at the Kirov Theatre, Leningrad. A pupil of Vaganova, Dudinskaya astounded audiences by her transcendental technique and the strength of her characterizations. She danced the classic repertory in Leningrad and created many roles in the new Soviet ballets before retiring in 1962. She then became teacher of the 'perfection class' for the Kirov Ballet and later chief instructress at the Vaganova School, passing on the precepts of Vaganova as well as her own deep understanding of ballet.

As a teacher she was not only eloquent in the classroom but was also able to put down her precepts in writing. Her book *Fundamentals of the Classic Ballet*, first published in 1934, has been translated into many languages and is still the basis of Soviet teaching. After her premature death on 5 November 1951, the school over which she had presided – in later years she taught only the senior students and the 'class of perfection' – was re-named after her, and in 1958 a book of essays about her work was published by the Russian Theatrical Society. In it, Semyonova wrote: 'She demanded that the image, emotions and content of the dance be conveyed by the *entire body*. The body was our instrument. Therefore, her main concern was that this instrument of ours be developed to perfection.'

227. Many experiments were made during the 1920s as choreographers searched for new dance forms to express the ideals and emotions of the emergent Soviet society. The work of Kasyan Goleizovsky (1892–1970) was among the boldest at this time, and his *Joseph the Beautiful*, staged at the Bolshoy Filial Theatre in Moscow in 1925 with music by Seregey Vasilenko and design by Boris Erdman, was an attempt to express in sculptural terms a theme concerning freedom of feeling in the light of the biblical story. Our picture shows only half the stage; the ramps and the curving lines of dancers were repeated again on the right, in a mirror image.

It was brought to perfection by Semyonova, and then by that extra-ordinary first generation of magnificent ballerinas – Galina Ulanova, Natalya Dudinskaya, Tatyana Vecheslova, Olga Lepeshinskaya – and by their pupils and successors, who are the present stars of the Kirov and Bolshoy Ballets.

Although the most celebrated, and certainly the most influential, Vaganova was not the only great teacher to emerge after the Revolution. In Moscow, where the Bolshoy Theatre remained open throughout the darkest days, Tikhomirov was still teaching; the young Asaf Messerer (1903–1992), a

228. *The Red Poppy* was first staged in Moscow in 1927, with choreography by Lev Lashchilin and Vasily Tikhomirov to a score by Glière. It was the first successful Soviet ballet, its three acts telling the story of a Soviet warship in a Chinese port, and how the sailors came to the aid of oppressed Chinese workers. Subsequently staged by other Russian companies, the ballet was revived at the Bolshoy Theatre in Moscow in 1950, with choreography by Leonid Lavrovsky. This picture shows the famous *yablochko* – the sailors' dance from Act I of this production.

dazzling virtuoso dancer, started to give classes in the 1920s, and his teaching continued to be honoured in our own times. The Bolshoy was to benefit very considerably in the post-revolutionary years. Under the Tsars, Moscow's ballet had suffered because St Petersburg was the seat of court and government, and the St Petersburg ballet received the lion's share of patronage and interest. A stylistic difference developed between the cool, classic St Petersburg style and the more vital dramatic manner of the Moscow dancers. This meant that when Marius Petipa created his *Don Quixote* in Moscow in 1869, he produced a strongly dramatic staging which, when he

229. *The Flames of Paris* (choreography by Vasily Vainonen, music by Boris Asafiev, décor by Vladimir Dmitriev) was first produced at the Kirov Theatre, Leningrad, in 1932. Its four acts relate the people's triumphs and dramas during the French Revolution.

230. Olga Lepeshinskaya and Yury Zhdanov in the Diana and Actaon *pas de deux* choreographed by Vaganova for her revival of *Esmeralda* at the Kirov Theatre in 1935. Zhdanov was one of the leading dancers of his day, and partnered Ulanova in many roles. Their performance in *Romeo and Juliet* has been filmed.

231. *The Fountain of Bakhchisaray* (choreography by Rostislav Zakharov, music by Boris Asafiev, décor by Vladimir Khodasevich) was first produced at the Kirov Theatre, Leningrad, in 1934. Based on Pushkin's poem, this four-act ballet told of a Khan who fell in love with a captive Polish princess. Here we see the Khan's soldiery wrecking the Polish manor house at the end of Act I: the house went up in flames in a spectacular manner as the curtain fell. The ballet remains in the Soviet repertoire.

mounted it in St Petersburg two years later, was made more academic in style to suit court taste. The Bolshoy company experienced continuing neglect until, in 1900, Alexander Gorsky arrived from St Petersburg to undertake new productions of some of Petipa's ballets. Gorsky had been a pupil and assistant to Petipa, but he developed these revisions to suit his own ideas about dramatic expression and Moscow found them very much to its taste.

Invited to take responsibility for ballet at the Bolshoy, Gorsky made a basic repertory for the theatre through revivals and new works until his death in 1924. He was the vital bridging figure between Imperial and Soviet times, providing both continuity and innovation. After the October Revolution of 1917, Moscow became the seat of government and the artistic centre of the

232. Vakhtang Chabukiany (1910–1992) as the hero, Frondoso, in his own three-act *Laurencia*, first produced at the Kirov Theatre, Leningrad, in 1939. Born in 1910, Chabukiany was one of the greatest of Soviet male dancers, and also created ballets for the Tiflis Ballet in his native Georgia which he directed for many years.

USSR. Artistic experiment marked the emergence of a new era for the arts in Russia. Eager experimentation began when what had seemed the dead hand of Tsarist officialdom was removed. (That it was to be replaced by the even more oppressive hand of Stalinist doctrine is one of the tragedies of art in Russia in this century.)

Balletic novelty in Moscow was particularly associated with the work of Kasyan Goleizovsky (1892–1970), who sought to give the academic language a richer and more physically luxuriant outline, together with a more modern dynamic which reflected the turbulent times in which he lived. The erotic elements in his *Joseph the Beautiful* (1925) – a re-telling of the Bible story – and the poster-like political manner of *The Whirlwind* (1927) were a vivid response to the new challenges he felt were offered to Soviet artists. Alas, his choreography found little official favour; he laboured in the regional and remoter opera houses of the Soviet Union before, late in life, he returned to Moscow to work once again in his native city.

In Leningrad, fascinating experimentation was carried out by Fedor

233. A dramatic moment from Chabukiany's *Laurencia*, with Maya Plisetskaya, left, being accused while Chabukiany, right, is restrained by soldiery. The plot dealt with a peasant rising in Castile. The original production was performed in Leningrad in 1939, and this illustration shows the later Moscow staging, in which Plisetskaya was memorably brilliant. A film clip exists of her dancing a variation with astonishing bravura.

Lopukhov (1886–1973), a member of a distinguished dancing family which also included his sister, Lydia Lopokova. His work was concerned with the preservation and renovation of the classical heritage left to the St Petersburg/Leningrad ballet by Petipa – Lopukhov was notable in seeking to conserve and illuminate what Petipa had created – and also to devise a classic manner suited to the new Soviet society. One of his most daring creations was *The Magnificence of the Universe*, set to Beethoven's Fourth Symphony. Shown only once, in 1923, this extraordinary work on a cosmic theme sought to interpret the music in plotless movement. It was a bold experiment, but one which was instantly dismissed by critics and political authorities, who prevented any favourable comment appearing in newspapers. More relevant to the political conditions of the time was Lopukhov's *Red Whirlwind*, first shown in 1924, and like Goleizovsky's ballet of similar title concerned with the sweeping away of the old by the irresistible wind of revolutionary change. Finally, in 1927, Lopukhov staged *The Ice Maiden*, a far more traditional piece which showed his mastery of academic forms and

234. A scene from the second act of Leonid Lavrovsky's celebrated production of *Romeo and Juliet*. First given at the Kirov Theatre in Leningrad in 1940, with music by Prokofiev and designs by Pyotr Williams, the ballet was mounted in Moscow in 1946. This picture of the production at the Bolshoy Theatre, Moscow, shows the discovery of Tybalt's body, and conveys the grandiloquent scale of the presentation.

acknowledged his debt to the old ballet of Petipa. But by this time a ballet had been staged in Moscow which was to show rather more practically the way forward for Soviet ballet. This was *The Red Poppy*, by Vasily Tikhomirov and Lev Lashchilin. First produced in 1927, it revealed how political ideology might be given sound theatrical form. It must be recognized as the first truly successful Soviet ballet, and it held its place in the repertory of Russian theatres for many years. Here was the correct socialist message – Russian sailors coming to the aid of oppressed Chinese workers – and the correct directness of means and accessibility of musical style. At a time when ballet was still being attacked by certain left-wing intellectuals as an unwelcome survival from Imperial days (as it had been ever since the Revolution), the directness and suitability of the message of *The Red Poppy* served to drown protest. The combined labours of Lunacharsky and Vaganova to preserve the ballet as a great manifestation of Russian art, and the début of Marina Semyonova, gradually won official approval. When Stalin came to power, his promulgation of the dreadfully stultifying doctrine of 'socialist realism' limited all the arts in Russia to the most slavish literalism and hidebound socialist ideology; ballet in Russia now had to concern itself with large-scale dramas

235. Ulanova as Juliet – a role she created in Lavrovsky's version – with Alexander Lapauri as Paris.

whose politically correct message was more significant than their artistic means.

The Flames of Paris by Vasily Vainonen (1901–1964), produced in 1932 at the Kirov Theatre, Leningrad, glorified the French revolutionaries. An inadequate film exists of part of the ballet (with the splendid Muza Gottlieb and Vakhtang Chabukiany) which suggests something of its style, and the final jubilant *pas de deux* can still be seen in concert programmes given by Soviet dancers.

The dramatic ballets of the 1930s often looked to Russian and world literature for subject-matter. *The Fountain of Bakhchisaray*, based on Pushkin's poem, was the subject of Rostislav Zakharov's first ballet. Theme and music were by Boris Asafiev, a prolific and distinguished composer of ballet music at this time. The ballet was first seen at the Kirov Theatre in 1934, and remains in the Leningrad repertory to this day. The role of Maria, the heroine, was created by Galina Ulanova, and confirmed her as a supreme dance-actress. Zakharov (1907–1984) produced three other Pushkin ballets: *The Prisoner of the Caucasus* in Moscow in 1938; *Mistress into Maid*, also in Moscow, 1946; and *The Bronze Horseman* in Leningrad in 1949. Other choreographers turned

236. Irina Kolpakova, principal ballerina of the Kirov Ballet, as Aurora in *The Sleeping Beauty*, a performance of perfect classic style. For nearly forty years, Kolpakova was an exemplar of the purest academic dancing: she was the last of Vaganova's own pupils to achieve ballerina status.

237. Alexander Pushkin (1907–1970) was the chief male dancer in Leningrad and a teacher of genius. Among his pupils were Rudolf Nureyev (who called him 'gentle, trusting') and Mikhail Baryshnikov. He is seen here giving a class with, behind him, Yury Solovyov, one of the most gifted of Leningrad *premiers danseurs*, who committed suicide in 1977 at the age of thirty-six.

238. Galina Ulanova coaching Ekaterina Maximova and Vladimir Vasiliev of the Bolshoy Ballet in Yury Grigorovich's staging of *The Nutcracker*.

to Lermontov, Shakespeare (admired and understood in Russia), Lope de Vega (for Chabukiany's *Laurencia*) and Victor Hugo.

It was in another Shakespeare ballet, *Romeo and Juliet*, to Prokofiev's score and with choreography by Leonid Lavrovsky (1905–1967), that Ulanova created another famous role at the Kirov Theatre. Born in 1910, the daughter of Mariinsky dancers, Ulanova studied first with her mother and then spent the last four years of her training with Vaganova. She epitomized many of the achievements of Soviet ballet during her theatrical career. Vaganova called this era 'the new spring of our ballet', and Soviet historians consider Ulanova to be as significant in the history of ballet as Chaliapin had been in that of opera. As the Russian critic Natalia Roslavleva wrote, 'in her sphere, Ulanova had proved that the most complicated, deep and psychologically subtle emotions may be conveyed through the medium of classical dance'. Ulanova retired from the stage in 1962 – happily her Giselle and Juliet have been worthily preserved on film, and she continues to coach the young artists of the Bolshoy, a theatre to which she transferred in 1944 after wartime evacuation. She was first seen in the West in 1951 in Florence, but her genius was fully revealed when the Bolshoy Ballet made their first major visit to the West in 1956 at the Royal Opera House, Covent Garden. The impact was as great as that of the Diaghilev ballet, and Ulanova, no longer young, had the greatest triumph of all.

In 1961 London also received a first visit from the Leningrad State Kirov Ballet. Here was a company at the height of its powers, with a galaxy of stars – although it was without one of its youngest and most gifted members, Rudolf Nureyev, who had chosen to defect while the company was in Paris just before its London season. But with Irina Kolpakova, Alla Ossipenko, Inna Zubkovskaya, Alla Sizova, Natalya Makarova, with Vladilen Semenyov, Oleg

239. (Above) Yury Solovyov as the Blue Bird and Alla Sizova as Princess Florine in the Kirov Ballet's *Sleeping Beauty* in London in 1961. Solovyov was a dancer of genius, wonderfully matched by the enchanting and gifted Sizova. The first performance by the Kirov Ballet in London featured the pair as a memorable leading couple in Grigorovich's *The Stone Flower*.

240. (Right) Ekaterina Maximova and Vladimir Vasiliev in the final *pas de deux* from *Don Quixote*; the joyous bravura and sparkling high spirits which these two glorious dancers generated in this duet were marvellous to behold, as delighted audiences round the world could testify.

Sokolov and the angelic Yury Solovyov, it was a troupe whose classical productions and classical dancing excited intense admiration for the dancers' serene grace and theatrical elegance. The production with which the company opened the season, Yury Grigorovich's *The Stone Flower*, which starred Sizova, Ossipenko and Solovyov, was much praised.

The Leningrad tradition of choreography, maintained in Soviet times by Lopukhov and then by Lavrovsky, was developed by Yury Grigorovich (b. 1927). His earliest success was *The Stone Flower* (1957), and two years later he followed it with *Legend of Love*. Then in 1964 he was invited to become director of the Bolshoy Ballet, and in 1968 he produced for the company his vastly popular version of *Spartacus*. The Khatchaturian score had previously been used by other choreographers, with little success: in his staging for the Bolshoy, Grigorovich created a work as significant to Soviet ballet as the Lavrovsky *Romeo and Juliet*. The massive scale of Grigorovich's dances, the broad sweep of the action filled with racing lines of male dancers,

241. The Bolshoy *corps de ballet* in the second act of Lavrovsky's staging of *Giselle*, with Rimma Karelskaya (second from the left) as Myrtha: one of the wonders of ballet in our time.

242. Maya Plisetskaya in the third act of *Swan Lake*. For once, the often misused term *prima ballerina assoluta* can properly be applied to Plisetskaya. Born in 1925, her career has blazed with the splendour of her technique and her fiery temperament. In the traditional repertory she has given interpretations of memorable power; in more modern work – as Laurencia; and in roles made for her in Russia and by European choreographers – she has been no less effective. She has continued to dance with undiminished grandeur in the autumn of her career.

243. Raissa Struchkova (b. 1925) and Alexander Lapauri (1926–1975) in their most celebrated concert number, the *Moskowski Waltz*. Superb dancers in the Soviet repertoire, both artists brought tremendous style and excitement to this showpiece. Their fine qualities, though, were properly to be seen in full-length ballets, Lapauri as a powerful character dancer, and Struchkova as a wonderfully warm-spirited Juliet and Cinderella.

244. (Above) Nina Ananiashvili as Raymonda in Yury Grigorovich's excellent staging for the Bolshoy Ballet of the old Petipa classic. The Georgian-born Ananiashvili is one of the brightest young ballerinas of the Bolshoy troupe.

245. (Right) Natalya Bessmertnova and Mikhail Lavrovsky in the opening scene of *Giselle*, which they danced together for the first time at the Bolshoy Theatre, Moscow, on 15 September 1963. 'All Moscow' was there to witness their début. They had been coached by Leonid Lavrovsky – Mikhail's father – in this, his famous staging of the old ballet.

of Roman armies and nobility and rebellious slaves, and the superlative interpretations he inspired in his dancers, gripped audiences wherever the ballet was performed, and it became a certain success for the Bolshoy on every tour. The original cast was led by the Bolshoy's two young stars, Vladimir Vasiliev (b. 1940) and Ekaterina Maximova (b. 1939), and their interpretations in this, as in many other ballets, made them the darlings of a world audience.

The size of the Bolshoy company – 250 dancers – meant that there were also lustrous figures of an earlier generation whom the West learned to love just as the Moscow public had done. Maya Plisetskaya (b. 1925) and Raissa Struchkova (b. 1925) were outstanding. The fiery Plisetskaya came to early fame as a prodigious virtuoso, and as a proudly beautiful interpreter of a great range of roles, from Juliet to Aurora, from Kitri in *Don Quixote* to Laurencia. She has continued to dance indomitably at an age when many other ballerinas

246. (Above) A moment of confrontation in Yury Grigorovich's *The Golden Age* (for the Bolshoy Ballet). The heroine, Rita (Natalya Bessmertnova), stands between the hero, Boris (Irek Mukhamedov, right), and the degenerate forces of the cabaret with its villain Yashka (Gediminas Taranda) and the dancers who foxtrot so elegantly through the song 'Tea for Two'. Grigorovich, director and chief choreographer of the Bolshoy, made his new version of this Shostakovich ballet in 1983 as a portrait of Soviet society in the 1920s. He produced a brilliant commentary on Soviet art and manners of the time with a dazzling central role for Mukhamedov, then the Bolshoy's new hero.

247. (Right) Lyudmila Semenyaka as Aurora and Alexey Fadeyechev as Désiré in the 'Vision' scene of *The Sleeping Beauty* as staged for the Bolshoy Ballet by Grigorovich. Semenyaka, Leningrad-trained, is a consummate classical ballerina; Fadeyechev is a noble Prince, and son of another *danseur noble* of an earlier generation, Nikolay Fadeyechev.

---

have retired. Struchkova won her public by a sparkling technique and an irresistible charm of personality. She was a beguiling Juliet, a touching Giselle, and a delightful film exists of her Cinderella.

Under Grigorovich's direction over more than twenty-five years, the Bolshoy Ballet has become a leaner and younger company than that which the West first saw. Grigorovich has frequently been the subject of controversy as director and choreographer, reproached by certain factions who resent the predominance of his stagings in the repertory, but – like Balanchine or Béjart – he had set a style for his company which was reflected in his creations, and such productions as *Ivan the Terrible* (1975) and *The Golden Age* (1982) have been notably successful. His muse in many later works has been his wife, Natalya Bessmertnova (b. 1941), a ballerina of exquisite line and dramatic presence. Another outstanding Moscow star has been Lyudmila Semenyaka (b. 1952), trained in Leningrad, and the pre-eminent classical ballerina in Russia. Of male stars, Irek Mukhamedov (b. 1960) has been seen to marvellous effect in the entire Bolshoy repertory. Creator of the hero, Boris, in *The Golden Age*, Mukhamedov provided both superb physical skill and intense dramatic artistry in his interpretations. In 1990, he decided to work in the West and joined the Royal Ballet.

The history of the Kirov Ballet, after its initial triumphs on visits to the West in the 1960s, was punctuated by dramas associated with the repressive atmosphere in Russia at that time. In 1970, during a Kirov season in London, Natalya Makarova (b. 1941), already acknowledged as a great ballerina, decided to stay in the West in order to confront greater challenges and take part in a less stultifying repertory. Four years later the prodigious Mikhail Baryshnikov (b. 1943), who had been recognized as a marvellous talent at an

248. (Above) The Kirov *corps de ballet* in *Chopiniana* (*Les Sylphides*), a ballet which they dance with an ideal sensitivity.

249. (Right) Faroukh Ruzimatov as Ali in the Kirov Ballet's revival of *Le Corsaire* in 1988. Ruzimatov's exotic style, brooding and highly romantic, was excellently served in this wild and wonderful recension of the old ballet with its cast of pirates and beautiful slaves.

early age, also opted for the West during a concert tour of Canada. The loss of these two superlative dancers, and the suicide in 1977 of Yury Solovyov, whose soaring grace and beautifully pure personality had illuminated many leading roles at the Kirov, did much to lower the morale of the Leningrad ballet. Oleg Vinogradov (b. 1937), a dancer and choreographer who had also worked with Leningrad's second ballet company at the Maly Theatre, was appointed director of the Kirov. His task during the next decade was to pension off many older dancers and revitalize the company. By the 1980s he had succeeded, showing the world a new generation of Kirov luminaries, headed by such fine artists as Altynai Assylmuratova, Olga Chenchikova, Zhanna Ayupova, Yelena Yevteyeva and Tatyana Terekhova, with the exotic Faroukh Ruzimatov exciting much public interest. Vinogradov produced new ballets for the company – *Knight of the Tigerskin, The Government Inspector, Potemkin* – and invited both Roland Petit and Maurice Béjart to create ballets for the troupe.

In the age of *glasnost* and *perestroika*, Leningrad's ballet opened itself to the West, with increased opportunities for its dancers to venture forth and dance in London, Paris and New York, and for Russian teachers to work extensively in the West. A vital and significant historical link was established when the Kirov Ballet acquired two ballets by George Balanchine in 1989, *Scotch Symphony* and *Theme and Variations*; in a sense, Balanchine came back to his native city and to the theatre that first shaped him. And a final acknowledgement that the Cold War was dead for ballet came with the return of

250. Death (Gennady Babanin) stalks the crew of the battleship in Oleg Vinogradov's ballet *Potemkin*, which he staged for the Kirov Ballet in 1987.

Natalya Makarova to Leningrad to dance once more on the stage of the Kirov Theatre in February 1989.

There are many other ballet companies in the Soviet Union. Each republic boasts its own company; from major cities such as Perm and Novosibirsk, Riga and Minsk, ballet troupes have ventured into the West to show something of their art. The Maly Ballet from Leningrad and the Stanislavsky–Nemirovich-Danchenko Theatre Ballet in Moscow are significant ensembles. There is a richness in Soviet dance that Western audiences have still to discover.

10 Ballet Today ⟿⟨◉⟩⟾

Contemporary ballet and dance are so well documented in specialist magazines world-wide that it is unwise to dwell in too much detail here on the elements that make up today's dance scene. Companies rise and fall. Today's masterpieces are forgotten all too quickly. Reputations made in one country are unmade in another. One nation's balletic meat is another's poison – the contrasting critical reception of Maurice Béjart in mainland Europe and America is a case in point. As with monarchs of earlier times, audiences have favourites who can fall from grace. Throughout the world ballet and modern dance are increasingly popular, and there are national ensembles from Canada to China, Australia to Argentina, whose work is valuable and fascinating. This chapter can only suggest the broad outlines of events during the past decades; for detailed information, the reader should consult some of the many books, magazines and souvenir brochures that are now available.

For the twenty-year span of his Ballets Russes, Diaghilev was the supreme mentor of taste in Western ballet. His company was a vital and truly creative force, and after his death his associates were scattered over the Western world. Like seeds, they took root, and we have seen how they flourished in Britain and in the United States. In France, ancestral home of ballet, the significant figure was Serge Lifar.

Born in Kiev in 1905, Lifar studied briefly with Bronislava Nijinska, then fled Russia to join her in the Diaghilev company in 1923. He was to become the last great male star of the Ballets Russes. He made his first attempt at choreography with a new version of Stravinsky's *Renard* for Diaghilev in

251. Serge Lifar in his *Icare*, first produced at the Paris Opéra in 1935, with décor by Larthe, danced to rhythms suggested by Lifar and orchestrated by Szyfer. Lifar was a tireless theorist on the classic ballet, even going so far as to invent sixth and seventh positions of the feet. His magnetic presence and creative energy brought a serious dance audience back to the Opéra.

1929, but the death of Diaghilev in that year must have seemed to cast a blight on Lifar's career. But Lifar was soon engaged by Jacques Rouché, who had been endeavouring to restore the prestige of the Paris Opéra Ballet since he became director of the theatre in 1914. Lifar was invited to dance in a new production of *The Creatures of Prometheus*, whose choreography had been commissioned from Balanchine. Balanchine's illness meant that the work was entrusted to Lifar. The first performance was on 12 December 1929, and from then on, with brief intervals, Lifar was to dominate the Opéra Ballet until 1958. Lifar made many reforms, attracted great artists to work with him, and during the 1930s brought back to the Opéra some of its former glory

252. *Noir et Blanc*, whose choreography by Lifar made use of the wonderful score that Édouard Lalo had composed for Lucien Petipa's ballet *Namouna*, produced in Paris in 1882. First given under the title *Suite en Blanc* by the Paris Opéra Ballet in 1943, Lifar's plotless sequence of dances makes great technical demands on its interpreters. Lifar later staged this hymn to his own brand of neo-classicism for the de Cuevas company and for London Festival Ballet under the title *Noir et Blanc*. This illustration shows the de Cuevas production. From 1947 until 1962 the Grand Ballet du Marquis de Cuevas was a remarkable outpost of individuality and slightly old-fashioned glamour on the post-war international ballet scene. The Marquis de Cuevas, Chilean-born, married a Rockefeller and was a true patron of the arts, lavishing vast sums on 'his' ballet but in a slightly unpredictable way, depending on his tax situation. His company was star-studded and among its brightest luminaries were Rosella Hightower, Nina Vyrubova, Marjorie Tallchief, George Skibine, Serge Golovine, André Eglevsky, Tatiana Riabouchinska and Léonide Massine.

253. Yvette Chauviré in Serge Lifar's *Nautéos*. First produced in 1947 and revised for the Paris Opéra in 1954, the ballet gave 'La Chauviré Nationale' (as she was proudly named) a brilliant role as a sea nymph.

254. Elisabeth Platel and Charles Jude in the second act of Rudolf Nureyev's staging of *Swan Lake* for the Paris Opéra Ballet in 1984.

and a new audience. He was a superb dancer and took the principal roles in many ballets. He was also a prolific choreographer (the *liste non-exhaustive* of his works published in the French magazine *Les Saisons de la Danse* in 1970 is staggering). His first muse was Olga Spessivtseva, with whom he danced *Giselle*. He invited Marina Semyonova to appear with him, and his subsequent work with Yvette Chauviré, and the number of roles he created for her, contributed to her distinguished career. He danced with the Ballets Russes de Monte Carlo in 1938/1939, but he did not sever his connection with the Opéra; he remained at his post, serving the ballet faithfully during the years of the German occupation. Unjustly accused of collaboration, he was exiled for two years from his theatre, and went to Monte Carlo where he founded the Nouveau Ballet de Monte Carlo. That company was subsequently to form part of the Grand Ballet du Marquis de Cuevas, and Lifar returned to the Opéra to make a series of important works for Chauviré, for Nina Vyrubova (whom he recruited as an *étoile*) and for Toumanova. His most important ballets are described in C. W. Beaumont's *Complete Book of Ballets*

255. Jean-Yves Lormeau as Oberon, Noella Pontois as Titania and Patrick Dupond as Puck in John Neumeier's *A Midsummer Night's Dream*, staged by the Paris Opéra Ballet in 1983.

and its supplements. Lifar's autobiography should be read with caution, but a delightful portrait of the man was given by Maurice Tassart in *Ballet Annual No. 14*. Yet, as Tassart has said, the full Serge Lifar story has still to be written. After his death in 1986, a fine exhibition – *Une Vie pour la Danse* – was mounted in Lausanne (where Lifar had lived for some years) to display his collection of theatre material and celebrate his life; the Paris Opéra Ballet subsequently paid tribute to the man who revived its fortunes with programmes comprising such important works as *Suite en Blanc, Icare* and *Les Mirages*.

After Lifar's departure in 1958, the Opéra Ballet had a number of directors who were unable to master the labyrinthine politics of the theatre or to make full use of the company's enormous reserves of talent. It was not until Rudolf Nureyev was appointed director in 1983 that the company was again revitalized. Commanded by a star temperament as dominant as Lifar's, and by a man no less dedicated to the classic dance, the company blossomed. Nureyev brought in his own productions – *Raymonda, Swan Lake, Don Quixote,*

256. In 1985 Maurice Béjart choreographed a duet – *Rythme, Mouvement, Étude* – to celebrate the gifts of two exceptional young dancers at the Paris Opéra, Sylvie Guillem and Eric Vu An. This illustration gives a vivid impression of the gymnastic quality that Sylvie Guillem brought to this work.

Cinderella – but also made imaginative choices in repertory and casting; he educated a new generation of superbly talented young dancers, including Elisabeth Platel, Monique Loudières, Sylvie Guillem, Charles Jude, Manuel Legris and Laurent Hilaire, among many others.

But Nureyev's own career as a dancer sometimes conflicted with the Opéra's schedules, notably when a new opera house at the Bastille was opened in Paris in 1989 as a home for opera performance. As a result, the Palais Garnier (as the old Opéra is called) became exclusively a dance theatre and Nureyev departed in 1990, to be succeeded by Patrick Dupond, a very popular *étoile*.

France was also the home of the last manifestation of the old cosmopolitan touring company, the Grand Ballet du Marquis de Cuevas, whose stars and

257. Rosella Hightower in *Piège de Lumière*. John Taras created this ballet – the plot concerned convicts in the Brazilian jungle who set light-traps to catch the giant moths of the forest – for the de Cuevas ballet in 1952. As the Queen of the Morphides, Hightower had a role which displayed her technical and dramatic gifts. The Taras–Hightower collaboration produced several successful ballets for de Cuevas. John Taras was later to become a greatly valued ballet-master of the New York City Ballet and also of American Ballet Theatre.

whose wild and wonderful repertory thrilled audiences throughout the 1950s.

A renaissance of French ballet was heralded in 1945 when the end of the war released an effusion of talent. Roland Petit (b. 1924) emerged from the Opéra school and company to give recitals in Paris in 1944, which led swiftly to the creation of Les Ballets des Champs-Élysées. With the blessing and help of such eminent figures as Boris Kochno, Christian Bérard (an artist and gifted stage designer) and Jean Cocteau, Petit grouped around him some of the best young dancers and brightest talents in Paris. Superlatively decorated, his productions and his company had a wit and elegance uniquely French, and featured magnificent performers – Nina Vyrubova, Jean Babilée, Petit himself. In 1948 Petit separated from the troupe and formed the Ballets de Paris, with Renée (Zizi) Jeanmaire as his star in such ballets as *Carmen*. Visually, Petit's work has had no rival in ballet for the past half-century. An imaginative choice of the finest designers has meant that in the theatre, as in the cinema and music-hall in which he has also worked with great success, Petit's work has enchanted the eye. A commemorative volume by Gérard Mannoni,

258. (Left) *Les Forains* (choreography by Roland Petit, music by Henri Sauguet, décor and costumes by Christian Bérard) was first performed by Les Ballets des Champs-Élysées on 2 March 1945. If any ballet sums up the wonderful rebirth of French ballet after the German occupation, it is *Les Forains*. A group of young dancers in Paris were guided and helped by such distinguished figures as Boris Kochno, Christian Bérard and Jean Cocteau and, for a few exciting years, the Ballets des Champs-Élysées under Roland Petit seemed the most adventurous and decoratively brilliant in Europe. *Les Forains* had a typical Kochno libretto of utter simplicity, which matched the economy of Bérard's setting. A troupe of strolling players appear in a small town, perform, but get little reward for their pains. The dancers, from left to right, are Roland Petit, Solange Schwarz (of the great French dynasty of dancers), Micheline Morriss, Simone Mostovoy and Teddy Rhodolphe.

259. (Above) *Le Jeune Homme et la mort*, a ballet devised by Jean Cocteau with choreography by Roland Petit, décor by Wakhevitch and danced to a Bach Passacaglia, although it had deliberately been rehearsed to other music. Jean Babilée, a dancer of phenomenal technique and magnetic personality, was a revelation to post-war audiences in both classical and modern character roles. The role of the Young Man, to whom Death comes in the guise of his girlfriend, was an extraordinary display of acrobatic frenzy, which Babilée brought off in incandescent style. He is seen above with his wife Nathalie Philippart as the Young Girl in the original staging by Les Ballets des Champs-Élysées. In 1983 Jean Babilée returned to this role in performances with Roland Petit's Ballet National de Marseille. It was an astonishing recreation of the part of the Young Man, in which nearly forty years rolled away and the conviction of Babilée's interpretation won a new audience.

Roland Petit – un chorégraphe et ses peintres (1990), provides a most handsome survey of the design of Petit's works. Since 1972, Petit has been director of the Ballet National de Marseille, and has contrived a characteristically lively and imaginative repertory, with many large-scale works: a beguiling version of *Coppélia*; *Le Chat Botté*; *Ma Pavlova*; and the Proustian *Les Intermittences du Cœur*, as well as revivals of earlier successes – *Cyrano de Bergerac* and *Notre Dame de Paris*.

The other leading French choreographer of the post-war years is Maurice Béjart. Born in Marseille in 1927, Béjart danced and worked with his own group in Europe before staging *The Rite of Spring* in Brussels in 1959. The sexual energy of this version was exactly in tune with its time. As a result,

260. (Left) In 1946 Roland Petit took the remarkable step of reviving *La Sylphide*, using the Schneitzhöffer score that had been Filippo Taglioni's and with new choreography by Victor Gsovsky. The setting, based on old engravings, was by Serebriakov and the costumes by Bérard. The whole purpose of the production was to exploit the phenomenal Romantic style of Nina Vyrubova and her performance remains one of the outstanding achievements of ballet since the war. Although now lost, the Gsovsky version was remarkably faithful to the style of the period. This illustration gives a clear idea of the exquisite grace of Vyrubova's impersonation.

261. (Above) *Carmen* (choreography by Roland Petit, décor by Antoni Clavé, with music savaged from Bizet's opera of the same name) was first produced at the Princes Theatre, London, on 21 February 1949 by the Ballets de Paris de Roland Petit. Brilliantly theatrical, this Petit ballet created a sensation because of the décor, and the performances of Renée Jeanmaire (later Petit's wife) as Carmen, Petit himself as Don José and Serge Perrault as the Toreador. Jeanmaire cropped her hair for this production and seemed to discover for the first time the personality that was to be exploited later in ballets and revues staged for her by her husband. Jeanmaire and Petit are seen above with an Australian dancer, the late Gordon Hamilton, who was ballet-master to the company and later did important work in Vienna. *Carmen* was successfully revived by Petit for the Royal Danish Ballet, and effectively filmed as part of *Black Tights*.

262. In 1974 Roland Petit created a ballet on Proustian themes, *Les Intermittences du Cœur,* for his Ballet National de Marseille. In subsequent performances Maya Plisetskaya (for whom Petit had already created a ballet, *La Rose Malade,* in 1973) was unforgettable as the Duchesse de Guermantes.

263. Maurice Béjart created *The Kabuki* for the Tokyo Ballet in 1986, with the French *étoile* Eric Vu An as guest star. He is seen here with Yuko Tomoda of the Tokyo Ballet.

264. Maurice Béjart and Jorge Donn in Béjart's *Notre Faust* for the Ballet du Vingtième Siècle. Produced in 1975, the ballet was – characteristically, alas, for Béjart – danced to sections of Bach's B Minor Mass interspersed with tangos.

Béjart's company was soon transformed into the Ballet du Vingtième Siècle, and he started to create the massive spectaculars, combining dance, high drama, higher ideals and every sort of cross-cultural reference, which his company performed around the world in theatres, in sports stadia, in the open air, to vast popular acclaim (65,000 people saw three Béjart performances in Mexico City), notably from a young audience. No subject, no score, was sacred. A Bach Mass could be mixed with tangos in his treatment of the Faust legend (*Notre Faust*). Nijinsky, Baudelaire, Petrarch, Wagner's *Ring*, Kabuki drama, the Revolution of 1789, have all served as inspiration for spectacle and Béjart's very special kind of philosophizing. His work is adored in Europe, and finds hugely enthusiastic audiences around the world; it is viewed with rather more critical coolness in America and Britain. But there is no denying the impact of the Béjart style, and his choreographies have been well received at performances in Leningrad. It must be said, though, that Béjart's choreography favours the male dancer – who is displayed in physically striking

265. Dancers of Béjart's Ballet Lausanne in *Ring um den Ring*, Béjart's fantasy on Wagner's tetralogy.

movement – and that the message of Béjartian dance is always more important than the means.

In 1987, Béjart transferred his company to Lausanne, following a disagreement with the directorate of the Monnaie Opera House in Brussels. He was succeeded in that theatre by Mark Morris, whose entire creative manner is the antithesis of that of Béjart. In 1991 Morris returned to America, and Anne-Teresa De Keersmaeker with her company, Rosas, was installed at the Monnaie. In 1992 Béjart reduced the size of his company and announced the formation of a new theatre dance school, Rudra, in Lausanne.

In Germany, there was an exceptional upsurge of interest in classical ballet after the Second World War. Most German opera houses acquired a ballet troupe, its importance depending on the size of the theatre and the taste of the *Intendant*. Many British choreographers and dancers found work in Germany, but the pattern was a shifting one because personnel tended to move from city to city as contracts expired. However, three figures have been of special significance in the revival of Germany's ballet. John Cranko (1927–1973), the South African choreographer whose career had first blossomed with the Royal Ballet, was invited to Stuttgart in 1960 to stage his *Prince of the Pagodas*, and remained there. Under his guidance the Stuttgart company flourished, and with the Brazilian Marcia Haydée as his ballerina and with such exceptional male dancers as Egon Madsen and Richard Cragun, Cranko developed a repertory that made the company the leading

266. Marcia Haydée as Tatiana and Heinz Claus as
Onegin, the roles they created in John Cranko's
Onegin in 1965. Marcia Haydée joined John Cranko
in Stuttgart in 1961, and was his muse for a series
of important full-length ballets – *Romeo and Juliet*,
Onegin, *The Taming of the Shrew* – as well as for many
shorter ballets. She also created the leading roles in
other works staged for the Stuttgart Ballet: Mac-
Millan's *Las Hermanas*, *The Song of the Earth* and
Requiem, and John Neumeier's *Lady of the Camellias*.
Since 1976 she has been artistic director of the
Stuttgart Ballet.

267. John Neumeier as Christ, surrounded by
members of his company in his staging of Bach's St
Matthew Passion.

268. Dancers of the Stuttgart Ballet in Kenneth MacMillan's setting of the Fauré Requiem, staged for the company in 1977, with design by Yolanda Sonnabend.

ballet ensemble in Germany. Cranko recognized the vital importance of a school – a tenet he had learned from Dame Ninette de Valois – and his Stuttgart academy was formed to provide dancers for the company. For Marcia Haydée he created outstandingly popular full-length works – *Onegin*, *The Taming of the Shrew* (in which her Kate was matched by Richard Cragun's charm and physical bravura as Petruchio) and *Romeo and Juliet* – and a series of shorter ballets which benefited from the intense feeling of community that united his ensemble. Cranko also invited his friend and colleague, Kenneth MacMillan, to produce major works there, notably *The Song of the Earth*. Cranko's death on a flight bringing back his company from a triumphant visit to New York was a shattering blow, but in 1976 Marcia Haydée assumed direction of the company and has maintained and developed Cranko's traditions.

One of Cranko's dancers, the American John Neumeier (b. 1942), began his choreographic career in Stuttgart in the late 1960s. He became director of the Frankfurt Ballet in 1969 and then moved to Hamburg in 1973. Since

269. The Frankfurt Ballet in William Forsythe's *Impressing the Tsar*. In recent years the American choreographer William Forsythe has made his Frankfurt Ballet one of the most talked-about companies in Europe. His brand of classicism is marked by ferocious energy.

270. Ivan Liska as Peer Gynt. In his choreographies, John Neumeier has offered radical new versions of the classics and has also produced highly dramatic ballets (*The Lady of the Camellias*, *Medea* and *A Streetcar Named Desire*). For his *Peer Gynt* (1989) he commissioned a score from the Soviet composer Alfred Schnittke. Ivan Liska is a most sensitive and powerful dancer.

271. Alicia Alonso has been one of the most admired ballerinas of her time. She made her début in the late 1930s and has subsequently enjoyed a phenomenal and lengthy international career, first with American Ballet Theatre and then with the company she founded in her native Cuba, which was to become the National Ballet of Cuba. For more than forty years Alonso has been its director and ballerina, and has at the same time triumphed over near-blindness with immense bravery and dedication to her art. She is seen here in *La Diva*, choreographed by Alberto Mendez as a tribute to Maria Callas.

that time he has been director of the Hamburg Opera Ballet, and has gained a devoted following in that city and throughout Germany and much of Europe. Neumeier's creations are often intellectually fascinating – he favours themes of considerable complexity, combining the story of Manon Lescaut with that of Marguerite Gautier in his *Lady of the Camellias*, and turning his version of *The Nutcracker* into a commentary upon Petipa's ballets. Musically, Neumeier has opted for major scores and for the lengthy realizations this entails: he has choreographed no fewer than five Mahler symphonies, and he has set the whole of the Bach St Matthew Passion. For his *Peer Gynt* he commissioned a score from Alfred Schnittke, and his bardic *Amleth* for the

272. The charms of the Royal Danish Ballet, the Royal Theatre and of Copenhagen itself contribute to the nostalgic pleasure of watching ballets from the Bournonville era still being danced in faithful reproductions. *Napoli* (1842) is the most beloved of all the old ballets, and traditionally in the last act children from the Royal Danish Ballet school appear as onlookers on the bridge. In their time, nearly all great Danish dancers have stood there. The lovers in this picture are Henning Kronstam and Kirsten Simone; they are in the bridal cart with Lilian Jensen, who plays Teresina's mother. The tarantella dancers are (left to right) Niels Kehlet, Annette Weinrich, Flemming Ryberg, Mette Honningen, Anna Laerkesen, Jorn Madsen, Inge Olafsen and Flemming Halby.

273. Niels Kehlet, a star of the Royal Danish Ballet, in a typical Bournonville leap. He is seen in a studio of the Royal Theatre in Copenhagen, watched – surely approvingly – by portraits of the Bournonvilles, father and son. After a dazzling career as a virtuoso dancer Kehlet has moved on – in the Danish tradition – to a brilliant career as a mime artist with an outstanding gift for comedy.

274. *La Sylphide* with Margrethe Schanne as the Sylphide and Henning Kronstam as James in the Sylphide's death scene at the end of Act II. Schanne was the greatest Danish ballerina of her generation and enjoyed an international career in which her exquisite style was greatly admired. Kronstam, whose range has encompassed Bournonville heroes (beautifully danced) and comic cameos, was also the original Romeo in Ashton's *Romeo and Juliet*, staged by the Royal Danish Ballet in 1955, and was director of the company for several years. A film record exists of Schanne's farewell performance as the Sylphide – a heartbreaking interpretation.

275. Erik Bruhn as Don José in Petit's *Carmen* in Copenhagen, a role in which the impeccable stylist revealed himself as an impeccable actor.

276. Alexandra Radius and Han Ebbelaar in Hans van Manen's *pas de deux Twilight*.

Royal Danish Ballet used two Michael Tippett symphonies and the same composer's double concerto.

Another American choreographer, William Forsythe (b. 1949), is in charge of the Frankfurt Ballet. His early works were made for the Stuttgart Ballet, which he joined in 1971, and his most notable creation there was a full-length *Orpheus* with a score by Hans Werner Henze and libretto by the playwright Edward Bond. Its abrasive narrative told of the artist breaking entirely with the past in order to create a new order. The theme seems apt for the work that Forsythe has produced since then, in which the traditions of classic dance are ruptured and forms reshaped to make a harsh and uncompromising language – as in his *Impressing the Czar* and *In the middle, somewhat elevated*. Under Forsythe, the Frankfurt Ballet has now acquired international status, with regular seasons in Paris – a tribute to the anarchic and up-to-the-minute feel of its repertory.

The Royal Danish Ballet was 'discovered' in 1950 when Harald Lander (1905–1971) organized the first Ballet Festival there. Lander had been responsible for revitalizing the company in the twenty years during which he directed it (and its school) after the period of inanition which had overtaken the troupe in the years following Bournonville's death. He re-staged many Bournonville works, and revived Hans Beck's production of *Coppélia*. Before he left Denmark in 1951, he engaged the outstanding teacher Vera Volkova (1904–1975) to add the Russian Vaganova training to the Bournonville method still being taught at the Danish Ballet school. In the succeeding years, Niels Bjørn Larsen, Frank Schaufuss, Flemming Flindt, Henning Kronstam and Frank Andersen have in turn directed the company, adding to its repertory and nurturing the Bournonville canon and traditions. But the Danes have yet to discover a major native choreographer to help develop their ballet's identity, though they have a genius for giving definitive interpretations of works by visiting masters. The company continues to produce magnificent and buoyant male dancers and enchanting female stars.

Elsewhere in Scandinavia, traditional ballet has a home in the Royal Swedish Ballet, which can boast more than two centuries of performance and a repertory both classical and contemporary. Sweden has a more modern

277. (Left) The Dutch National Ballet in Rudi van Dantzig's *About a Dark House* (1978), which featured Rudolf Nureyev (right) in the leading role. The ballet told of an outsider (Nureyev) at a party, who imagines the stuffy guests as he would have preferred them to be.

278. (Above) Members of Nederlands Dans Theater in Jiri Kylian's *Falling Angels*, which is set to a Steve Reich score and was first produced in 1989 in Amsterdam.

company in the Cullberg Ballet. Founded by Birgit Cullberg (b. 1908) as a vehicle for her own strongly dramatic choreographies (*Miss Julie* remains her most celebrated piece), the company now features equally committed experimental pieces by her son, Mats Ek. His radical new productions of *Giselle* (its second act set in a madhouse) and *Swan Lake* have brought the company considerable public attention.

The balletic traditions in Holland have been concentrated in recent decades in the work of the Dutch National Ballet and Nederlands Dans Theater. The former was created in 1961 by the amalgamation of two existing companies in Holland. Its repertory was – and remains – broad in its perspectives, with traditional fare shown side-by-side with creations from three Dutch choreographers: Rudi van Dantzig (b. 1933), the company's director until 1990, who has produced pieces which express his strong social conscience; Hans van Manen (b. 1932), whose works frequently concern the tensions of human relationships; and Toer van Schayk, who has been dancer, stage decorator and choreographer.

279. Men of Nederlands Dans Theater in Jiri Kylian's *Soldiers' Mass*, a potent exposition of the feelings of men in battle, danced to Martinu's Field Mass.

280. Carla Fracci (b. 1936) as Bournonville's Sylphide. Carla Fracci's exquisite sense of Romantic style and her command of the traditional repertory have won her a world-wide public; in Italy, many roles have been created for her.

281. Among the choreographers who have worked regularly with the National Ballet of Canada is Glen Tetley. His *Alice*, based on Lewis Carroll's stories and his life, was staged in 1987 and featured the young Kimberley Glasco as Alice, seen here with Rex Harrington as Carroll and Owen Montague as the White Rabbit.

Nederlands Dans Theater was formed in 1959 as a splinter group from the main Dutch ballet scene. Devoted to a policy of intense creativity and to a dance language which sought a middle ground between classical and modern forms, the company was given an artistic identity by the choreographies of Glen Tetley and Hans van Manen. In the late 1970s, Jiri Kylian (b. 1947) became its choreographer and artistic director. Kylian, who is Czech-born, has provided a large body of work for his company which has won considerable international acclaim with this repertory. A style bold in both energy and emotion gives Kylian ballets their special attraction for audiences. His *Sinfonietta*, *Soldiers' Mass* and *Symphony of Psalms* have been widely seen and admired.

In the rest of Europe, as in the rest of the world, ballet and various forms of modern dance reflect national expectations and national needs. In France, determined financial support from governmental sources stimulated a buoyant creativity in modern dance during the 1970s and 1980s (this has been extensively charted in the pages of the magazine *Les Saisons de la Danse*). In Germany, an earlier tradition of free dance (*Ausdruckstanz*), led by Mary Wigman and her heirs, has surfaced again in the work of such creators as Pina Bausch in Wuppertal, where her angry, anguished dance theatre concentrates on the psychological tensions and isolations of modern life, and Johann Kresnik in Bremen, whose theatre is brutally forceful and intense. (His *Macbeth* is bloodstained even to the point of blood and viscera seeming to be poured from the stage into the orchestra pit.)

In Italy, the very cradle of European theatrical dance, ballet remains the eternal subsidiary and adjunct of opera. Despite occasional highlights – such grand spectaculars as Manzotti's *Sport* (Milan, 1891) and *Excelsior* (Milan, 1881), or the creativity of Aurel Milloss (1906–1990) – singing rather than dancing is the lyric entertainment for Italians. Schools produce excellent dancers who find their best opportunities abroad; Italian summer festivals, however, allow audiences to see a wide and fascinating selection of visiting companies and artists.

The influence of the Royal Ballet can be discerned in the national ensembles in Australia, Canada and South Africa. It was as the result of a

282. (Left) Kimberley Glasco and John Alleyne of the National Ballet of Canada in Glen Tetley's *La Ronde*, composed in 1987.

283. (Right) The first work choreographed by Robert Helpmann for the Australian Ballet was *The Display*, with designs by Sidney Nolan and music by Malcolm Williamson. Staged in 1964, it commented on the social and sexual manners of a group of young people by drawing a parallel with the behaviour of the Australian lyre-bird. Here, Kathleen Gorham is the leading girl.

direct appeal to Dame Ninette de Valois by dance-lovers in Toronto that Celia Franca (b. 1921), a former member of the Rambert and Sadler's Wells companies, was invited to Canada to form a company which it was hoped would become a national ballet. By dint of great determination, Franca succeeded. Her company was based, like Dame Ninette's own, on the classics; a school, headed by Betty Oliphant, flourished, and is today internationally admired. The National Ballet of Canada has toured extensively, showing a well-rounded repertory and a distinctive, honest, classical performance style.

284. David Ashmole and Ulrike Lytton in Glen Tetley's version of Stravinsky's *Orpheus*, made for the Australian Ballet in 1987.

But the company has yet to find a Canadian choreographic talent to confirm its creative identity.

The Australian Ballet was formed in 1962 when Peggy van Praagh (1910–1990), distinguished as a dancer and director with Rambert and the Sadler's Wells organization, took over the existing Borovansky Ballet and transformed it into a national troupe. Later, Robert Helpmann joined her in running the company, and its subsequent success was associated with the company's tours, both domestic and foreign. In 1983, Maina Gielgud assumed the direction of the company, and her broad experience (with Béjart and London Festival Ballet, among other European ensembles) is reflected in the increased breadth of the repertory, which encompasses the nineteenth-century classics and works by Tetley and Béjart, as well as Cranko, MacMillan and Ashton.

Thus theatre dance continues, adapts and expands around the globe. Ballet, as has so often been said, speaks an international language, but it speaks with very different accents in different countries. To enjoy ballet to the full we must remember this and accept the dancing of other nations on their own terms, avoiding that prejudice which can lead us to reject work that does not conform to preconceived notions of what 'ballet' should be. We have come a long way from the court of Lorenzo the Magnificent, but one factor remains unchanged: man's delight in dancing. So long as that delight continues, ballet will continue, too.

285. Maina Gielgud's fine staging of *Giselle* for the Australian Ballet, in designs by Peter Farmer. This illustration shows Miranda Coney (centre) as Giselle in the mad scene at the end of the first act with Adam Marchant (left) as Albrecht, Susan Elston as Berthe and Stephen Morgante as Hilarion.

Bibliography

We give here a list of books for readers who wish to study the different periods in ballet history in more depth. We have given some indication of their content. If they contain detailed bibliographies of their own we have not attempted to duplicate here. Many of the books are, alas, out of print but they should be available through good libraries and in good dance collections.

General

ANDERSON, JACK, *Ballet and Modern Dance: A Concise History* (Princeton, New Jersey, 1986). At the end of each chapter is a selection of brief related readings which give a taste of the works listed in the excellent bibliography.

AU, SUSAN, *Ballet and Modern Dance* (London, 1958). With many fine illustrations, the author, who is a dancer as well as an historian, traces the story of theatrical dance in the Western world.

BEAUMONT, CYRIL W., *The Complete Book of Ballets* (London, 1937). *Supplement to the Complete Book of Ballets* (London, 1942). *Ballets of Today* (London, 1954). *Ballets Past and Present* (London, 1955). *The Complete Book* and its three supplements are invaluable for Beaumont's detailed descriptions of the action of the ballets included. *The Complete Book* has in places been superseded by later scholars but it remains a fascinating work of reference. *Ballet Design Past and Present* (London, 1947) is exactly what the title says.

CHUJOY, ANATOLE, AND MANCHESTER P. W., *The Dance Encyclopaedia* (New York, 1967). A greatly enlarged and updated edition of Chujoy's *The Dance Encyclopaedia* of 1949. Contains authoritative long articles as well as shorter entries.

CLARKE, MARY, AND CLEMENT CRISP, *Making a Ballet* (London, 1974). Based on the testimony of choreographers, dancers, musicians and designers who describe their creative processes. Not How to Make a Ballet, but How Ballets are Made. *Design for Ballet* (London, 1978). Superbly illustrated with almost 300 designs, 35 in colour, ranging from the Renaissance to Rauschenberg. *The Balletgoer's Guide* (London, 1981). An introduction for the newcomer with stories of the ballets, sections on the choreographer and the stars, and an illustrated glossary of dance steps. *The History of Dance* (London, 1981). An outline guide to a vast subject, which places ballet in the context of other dance forms, from primitive to television and video.

CLARKE, MARY, AND DAVID VAUGHAN (EDS.), *The Encyclopedia of Dance and Ballet* (London, 1977). Contains entries on some 350 ballets and modern dance works, together with longer articles contributed by specialist writers worldwide. Well illustrated.

COHEN, SELMA JEANNE (ED.), *Dance as a Theatre Art: Source Readings in Dance History from 1581 to the Present.*

GUEST, IVOR, *The Dancer's Heritage: A Short History of Ballet* (London, 1960). Sixth edition fully updated 1988. *Le Ballet de l'Opéra de Paris: Trois siècles d'histoire et de tradition* (Paris, 1976). Traces the 'official' history of one of the most important and influential companies.

HASTINGS, BAIRD, *Choreographer and Composer: Theatrical Dance and Music in Western Europe* (Boston, 1983).

KIRSTEIN, LINCOLN, *The Book of the Dance* (New York, 1935). Published as a paperback under the title *Dance* (New York, 1969). Ranges from myth and ritual and the Greek theatre to the emergence of the American classical ballet school. *Movement and Metaphor* (New York, 1970; London, 1971). A superbly illustrated survey of ballet through four centuries and fifty seminal works.

KOEGLER, HORST, *The Concise Oxford Dictionary of Ballet* (Oxford, 1977; latest edition, 1987). Indispensable.

MASON, FRANCIS (ED.), *Balanchine's Complete Stories of the Great Ballets* (New York, 1954; latest edition, 1978). Contains some interesting comments by George Balanchine on his own works. With a detailed chronology.

MOORE, LILLIAN, *Artists of the Dance* (New York, 1938; paperback, 1969). A series of essays on great dancers from La Camargo to Martha Graham.

ROBERT, GRACE, *The Borzoi Book of Ballets* (New York, 1946). A lively account of selected ballets by a discerning member of the audience.

ROBERTSON, ALLEN, AND DONALD HUTERA, *Dance Handbook* (London, 1988). With an introduction by Merce Cunningham, this is not only a reference book but a guidebook to performance and follow-up study. Ideal for newcomers as well as aficionados.

WILSON, G. B. L., *A Dictionary of Ballet* (London, 1957; last edition, 1974). A pioneer work and of lasting value as Wilson never deleted an entry. Particularly good on the nineteenth century.

Periodicals and Annuals

The Ballet Annual: A Record and Year Book of the Ballet, 18 vols. (London, 1947–63). Edited by Arnold L. Haskell, assisted by G. B. L. Wilson, Ivor Guest and Mary Clarke. The editor contributed most of the reviewing of each year's events but the *Annual* contained a number of important articles by specialist writers.

Two important periodicals are now defunct but are worth seeking out in dance libraries. *American Dance Index*, guided by Lincoln Kirstein under various editors, appeared in fifty-six issues between 1942 and 1948. In 1971 the entire series was published in New York by the Arno Press with an introduction by Bernard Karpel and a cumulative index. The historical and reference material is rich. In England, Richard Buckle's magazine *Ballet* contained historical articles as well as providing a lively (and very influential) view of the contemporary scene. Two issues appeared just before the Second World War, and publication resumed in 1946. The last issue came out in October 1952, and there were seventy-seven issues in all. Also defunct, but probably more accessible in dance libraries, is *Dance Perspectives* (New York, 1958–75, 64 issues), founded by Selma Jeanne Cohen to continue the ideals of *Dance Index*.

Existing periodicals

Great Britain: *Dancing Times*, established as a national magazine in 1910 (it was formerly a house journal of a dancing school). Until 1956 the magazine covered all forms; then the ballroom coverage was split off into a separate magazine, the *Ballroom Dancing Times*. The magazine played an important role in the early years of British ballet and has always given space to historical material and dance teaching as well as international news and reviews. The issues from 1910 to 1951 are now available on microfilm. Monthly, illustrated. *Dance and Dancers*, established

in 1950. Monthly, illustrated, with extensive reviewing of the current scene and also historical articles. *Dance Research*, established 1983. The journal of the Society for Dance Research.

United States: *Dance Magazine*, established 1942. Monthly, illustrated. Claims to be the world's largest dance publication. With an international roster of contributors. *Dance Chronicle*, established 1977. Three issues a year. Subtitled *Studies in Dance and the Related Arts, Dance Chronicle* has published important articles by specialist writers and has done great service by making available studies too long for the monthly magazines, but too short for book form.

Elsewhere: Many countries which now have a lively dance scene have periodicals to chart its activities. For example, *Danser* in France, *Dance Australia*, *Ballett-International* (bilingual, German and English), *Vandance* in Canada, *Ballet 2000* for Italy and France, *Hungarian Dance News* and *Sovietskii Balet*.

Chapter 1

ARBEAU, THOINOT, *Orchesography*, translated by Cyril W. Beaumont from the French edition of 1588 (London, 1925; New York, 1965). 'A dialogue whereby all manner of persons may easily acquire and practise the honourable exercise of dancing.' Dealing with the society dances of the sixteenth century, it is the most valuable source material for those years. Funny little drawings and an entertaining text.

CHRISTOUT, MARIE-FRANÇOISE, *Le Ballet de Cour de Louis XIV, 1643–1672* (Paris, 1967). The definitive book on the period, meticulously documented.

LAMBRANZI, GREGORIO, *New and Curious School of Theatrical Dancing*, translated by Derra de Moroda from the German edition of 1716 (London, 1928; New York, 1966). Many illustrations by Johann Georg Puschner. More theatrical than its predecessors, it includes valuable material on the Commedia dell'Arte.

McGOWAN, MARGARET M., *L'Art du ballet de cour en France 1581–1643* (Paris, 1963). Deals in exemplary fashion with the period leading up to the Marie-Françoise Christout book.

RAMEAU, PIERRE, *The Dancing Master*, translated by Cyril W. Beaumont from the French edition of 1725 (London, 1931; New York, 1970). The standard work on the technique of eighteenth-century dancing by the dancing master to the Pages of Her

Catholic Majesty the Queen of Spain.

STRONG, ROY, *Splendour at Court: Renaissance Spectacle and Illusion* (London, 1972). Marvellous illustrations, many in colour, depicting the beauty of the entertainments.

Chapter 2

BLASIS, CARLO, *Traité élémentaire, théorique et pratique de l'art de la danse*, translated with a biographical sketch and foreword by Mary Stewart Evans from the Milan edition of 1820 (New York, 1968). The first practical treatise.

LYNHAM, DERYCK, *Ballet Then and Now* (London, 1947). An interesting study, particularly good on the eighteenth century.

The Chevalier Noverre (London, 1950). The only biography of Noverre in English and a useful guide to his life and work.

MAGRI, GENNARO, *Theoretical and Practical Treatise on Dancing*, translated by Mary Skeaping with Irmgard Berry from the Italian edition of 1779 (London, 1988). The most valuable eighteenth-century treatise on ballet technique.

NOVERRE, JEAN GEORGES, *Letters on Dancing* (London, 1930; New York, 1966).

RALPH, RICHARD, *The Life and Works of John Weaver* (London, 1985). The definitive work on the great English reformer.

SWIFT, MARY GRACE, *A Loftier Flight: The Life and Accomplishments of Charles-Louis Didelot, Balletmaster* (London, 1974). The book not only tells us much about Didelot but also describes this transitional period in ballet's development.

WINTER, MARIAN HANNAH, *The Pre-Romantic Ballet* (London, 1974). A meticulously researched and magnificently illustrated survey of the period.

Chapter 3

For writings on the Romantic Movement in ballet we refer you to the books of Ivor Guest. The titles speak for themselves; all are definitive works. They are listed here in chronological order of publication. *The Ballet of the Second Empire 1858–1870* (London, 1953). *The Ballet of the Second Empire 1847–1858* (London, 1955). The two volumes were subsequently published together under the title *The Ballet of the Second Empire 1847–1870*. *The Romantic Ballet in England* (London, 1954). *Fanny Cerrito: A Biography* (London, 1956). *The Romantic Ballet in Paris* (London, 1966). *Fanny Elssler: A Biography* (London, 1970). *Letters from a Ballet Master: The Correspondence of Arthur Saint-Leon* (London, 1981). A treasure trove of letters from the choreographer of *Coppélia*. Illustrated, annotated and with a list of Saint-Leon's ballets. *Jules Perrot: Master of the Romantic Ballet* (London, 1984). This monumental work about 'the most brilliant and the most influential choreographer of his age' includes Russian sources in its bibliography and published scenarios of ballets produced by Perrot. *Gautier on Dance* (London, 1986). A complete translation, annotated, of Théophile Gautier's writings on ballet and related dance taken from the newspaper articles he wrote at the time. From Taglioni in 1836 to *Coppélia* in 1871.

Other important sources are:

BEAUMONT, CYRIL W., *The Ballet Called Giselle* (London, 1944; New York, 1970).
BOURNONVILLE, AUGUST, *My Theatre Life* (Middleton, Conn., 1979; London, 1979). The great Danish balletmaster's account of his life and work. With a foreword by Erik Bruhn and an introduction by Svend Kragh-Jacobsen.
BRUHN, ERIK, AND LILLIAN MOORE, *Bournonville and Ballet Technique* (London, 1961; New York, no date). A collaboration appraising the Bournonville legacy to ballet-training by a dance historian and one of the greatest exponents of the Bournonville style.

HALLAR, MARIANNE, AND ALETTE SCAVENIUS (EDS.), *Bournonvilleana*. Thirty authors pay tribute to the life and work of Bournonville. Published in 1992 by the Royal Theatre, Copenhagen, in collaboration with Rhodos International Science and Arts Publishers, to coincide with the second Bournonville Festival.
JURGENSEN, KNUD ARNE, *The Bournonville Ballets: A Photographic Record 1844–1933* (London, 1987). A gorgeous collection of rare photographs, 478 of them, showing 24 ballets, 5 *divertissements* and 4 opera *divertissements* as danced through nearly a century. Compiled and carefully annotated by the author.

Chapter 4

BEAUMONT, CYRIL W., *The Ballet Called Swan Lake* (London, 1952). An excellent account of the history of the most popular of all ballets.
GUEST, IVOR, *The Divine Virginia: A Biography of Virginia Zucchi* (New York, 1977). A biography of the ballerina who made such a profound impact upon the artists who were later to help shape the Diaghilev Ballet.
KARSAVINA, TAMARA, *Theatre Street* (London, 1981). The best book of ballet memoirs ever written, telling the story of Karsavina's schooling in St Petersburg as well as the triumphs of her Diaghilev days.
LEGAT, NICHOLAS, *The Story of the Russian School* (London, 1932). A fascinating account of the greatest days of the Imperial Ballet by one of its greatest artists.
MOORE, LILLIAN (ED.), *Russian Ballet Master: The Memoirs of Marius Petipa* (London, 1958; latest edition, 1971). A querulous, sad, but revealing account of his career, written when Petipa had retired and saw the ballet he had built up going through dark days. Infuriating in some ways, but still fascinating reading about personalities rather than events.

ROSLAVLEVA, NATALIA, *Era of the Russian Ballet* (London, 1966; New York, 1966). An invaluable history and commentary on the whole history of ballet in Russia, but presented from the 'official' Soviet viewpoint.
WILEY, ROLAND JOHN, *Tchaikovsky's Ballets: Swan Lake, The Sleeping Beauty, The Nutcracker* (Oxford, 1985). A detailed description of the ballets and their scores by a distinguished musicologist. Invaluable. *A Century of Russian Ballet: Documents and Eyewitness Accounts 1810–1910.* (Oxford, 1990). A wonderful evocation of the period as recorded by dancers, choreographers, critics and balletomanes with many translations of printed libretti. Not only informative but highly entertaining.

Note: Many of the books listed under Chapter 5 contain relevant information about the last decades of the Imperial Russian Ballet, as from that source came the great émigrés.

Chapter 5

BEAUMONT, CYRIL W., *The Diaghilev Ballet in London* (London, 1940). Written many years after he had been so profoundly moved by the productions of the Diaghilev Ballet, this is one of Beaumont's most personal books. He describes not only the ballets but also his friendships with the dancers and the opportunities he had of watching them in rehearsal as well as in performance.

BENOIS, ALEXANDRE, *Reminiscences of the Russian Ballet* (London, 1941). Probably the most reliable of the memoirs about the early years of the Diaghilev enterprise. Especially good on the background to, and the preparations for, the first Paris season.

BUCKLE, RICHARD, *Nijinsky* (London, 1971; New York, 1975). The definitive biography, annotated with an exhaustive bibliography. *Diaghilev* (London, 1979). Here, a lifetime's pursuit of the great man and his achievements comes to fruition. Buckle is the supreme chronicler of Diaghilev and his Ballets Russes. Like his *Nijinsky*, the book has been scrupulously researched with help from innumerable people who knew and/or worked with Diaghilev.

GARAFOLA, LYNN, *Diaghilev's Ballets Russes* (New York and Oxford, 1989). The author claims to challenge the premises of 'the British school of Ballets Russes history' by relating her story to 'newer methods of social history, dance criticism and feminism that have vitalized American dance scholarship'. A sometimes infuriating book, but one which can not be ignored.

MASSINE, LÉONIDE, *My Life in Ballet* (London, 1968; New York, 1969). Gives an excellent account of how Diaghilev 'educated' his young choreographers. The early chapters on life in Russia are charming, but the later part of the book becomes somewhat dry.

MONEY, KEITH, *Anna Pavlova: Her Life and Art* (New York, 1982). A mammoth undertaking, superbly and lavishly illustrated, and, appropriately, dedicated to Frederick Ashton, who saw Pavlova as a youth in Peru and became infected with her magic.

NIJINSKA, BRONISLAVA, *Early Memoirs* (Boston, 1981; London, 1982). This book tells the story of the Nijinsky family and the involvement of Bronislava and her brother Vaslav with the Diaghilev Ballets Russes up to the break with Diaghilev and Nijinsky's breakdown. An intensely warm and human book.

HASKELL, ARNOLD L., *Diaghileff: His Artistic and Private Life* (New York, 1935; London, 1936). Written in collaboration with Walter Nouvel, Diaghilev's close associate, this was the first important biography to appear after Diaghilev's death. It remains essential reading; Haskell, unlike some later writers, actually knew the man.

KOCHNO, BORIS, *Diaghilev and the Ballets Russes* (New York, 1970; London, 1971). Lavishly produced, but with an inadequate text, the book is recommended chiefly for its illustrations. Kochno was later to give Buckle invaluable help on his life of Diaghilev.

LIFAR, SERGE, *Diaghilev* (London, 1940). A long and sometimes emotional biography by the last of Diaghilev's great male dancers. It contains quite a lot about Lifar too.

MACDONALD, NESTA, *Diaghilev Observed by Critics in England and the United States 1911–1929* (New York, 1975; London, 1975).

PROPERT, W. A., *The Russian Ballet in Western Europe 1909–1920* (New York, 1920; London, 1921). *The Russian Ballet 1921–1929* (London, 1931). Two rare and beautiful books, written at the time it was all happening. The first volume contains many gorgeous colour reproductions of designs and drawings. The second is illustrated with photographs.

SOKOLOVA, LYDIA, *Dancing for Diaghilev* (London, 1960; New York, 1961). In this book Lydia Sokolova, one of his most faithful dancers, gives a very warm picture of Diaghilev and his work.

Chapter 6

ANDERSON, JACK, *The One and Only: The Ballet Russe de Monte Carlo* (London, 1981). The history of the company which did more than any other troupe to spread and awaken a love of ballet throughout the United States.

ANTHONY, GORDON, *Russian Ballet* (London, 1939). Gorgeous camera studies of the glamorous dancers of the Ballet Russe companies of the 1930s, with an admirable text by Arnold L. Haskell.

BRAHMS, CARYL (ED.), *Footnotes to the Ballet* (London, 1936; New York, 1936). A collection of essays by a notable cast of writers. Particularly valuable is the one by Constant Lambert on 'Music and Action'.

DE MILLE, AGNES, *Dance to the Piper* (Boston, 1952). *And Promenade Home* (Boston, 1958). Two autobiographies by a popular choreographer that capture the spirit of the touring Ballet Russe companies.

GARCIA-MARQUEX, VINCENTE, *The Ballets Russes: Colonel de Basil's Ballets Russes de Monte Carlo 1932–1952* (New York, 1990). A detailed and fully illustrated chronology of the repertory, drawing on contemporary sources, photo archives and extensive interviews with the artists involved. To be read as a complementary volume to Kathrine Sorley Walker's book listed below.

HASKELL, ARNOLD L., *Balletomania: The Story of an Obsession* (London, 1934; New York, 1934). *Ballet* (London, 1938). These two best-selling books – the paperback *Ballet* sold more than a million copies – captured the excitement generated by the baby ballerinas and the legacy of Diaghilev.

WALKER, KATHRINE SORLEY, *De Basil's Ballets Russes* (New York, 1983). This authoritative book not only charts the story of the de Basil ballet but unravels all the tangles of name-changes and the ups and downs of a company that played such an important role in 'bridging the gap'. Excellent source notes and lists of the productions and the dancers.

Chapter 7

BLAND, ALEXANDER, *The Royal Ballet: The First Fifty Years* (London, 1981). A lavishly illustrated account with excellent statistical information. To be read in conjunction with the books by Kathrine Sorley Walker and Sarah C. Woodcock listed below.

CLARKE, MARY, *The Sadler's Wells Ballet: A History and an Appreciation* (London, 1955; New York, 1955). A detailed account of the company that is now the Royal Ballet from its beginnings until 1955. Written with help from many of the people who watched the whole development of the enterprise. *Dancers of Mercury: The Story of Ballet Rambert* (London, 1962). The story of the 'old' Rambert company and of Dame Marie herself, written with the collaboration of Dame Marie.

CLARKE, MARY, AND CLEMENT CRISP, *London Contemporary Dance Theatre: The First Twenty-one Years* (London, 1987). A year by year factual account of the company's history. Superbly illustrated – mostly by photographs by Anthony Crickmay.

CRISP, CLEMENT, ANYA SAINSBURY AND PETER WILLIAMS, *Fifty years of Ballet Rambert: 1926–1976* (London, 1976; revised and enlarged edition, 1981). Published originally to celebrate the first fifty years of Rambert's company, with an interview with Dame Marie and contributions from many colleagues.

DE VALOIS, NINETTE, *Invitation to the Ballet* (London, 1937; latest edition, 1953). Dame Ninette's first book, in which she described the principles on which her company was founded. *Come Dance With Me* (London, 1957). An enchanting autobiography.

FINDLATER, RICHARD, *Lilian Baylis: The Lady of the Old Vic* (London, 1975). A fascinating account of the life and work of the woman who made de Valois's dream of a national ballet come true.

GUEST, IVOR, *Adeline Genée: A Lifetime of Ballet Under Six Reigns* (London, 1958; New York, 1959). Based on Dame Adeline's personal reminiscences and covering the period from her early triumphs as a dancer at the beginning of the century to her work as President of the Royal Academy of Dancing. *Ballet in Leicester Square* (London, 1992). Two monographs on the Alhambra and Empire theatres in Leicester Square which presented ballet as part of their music hall entertainments at the turn of the century. Bridges the period between the Romantic Ballet and the arrival of Diaghilev and then the emergent British ballet.

HASKELL, ARNOLD L., *The National Ballet: A History and a Manifesto* (London, 1943, latest edition, 1947; New York, 1947). Written during the Second World War, when the Sadler's Wells Ballet had proved its artistic importance throughout the British Isles. It foreshadowed the company's move to Covent Garden as a national company.

HASKELL, ARNOLD L., MARK BONHAM CARTER AND MICHAEL WOOD (EDS.), *Gala Performance* (London, 1955). A largely pictorial celebration of the twenty-fifth birthday of the Sadler's Wells Ballet with an entertaining section by William Chappell on the early years.

MANCHESTER, P. W., *Vic-Wells: A Ballet Progress* (London, 1942; latest edition, 1949). This best-selling little book appeared at the height of ballet's wartime boom in Britain. It records the company's progress as watched by a critical member of the audience, based on her own diaries. Its judgements on the then repertory are still valid today.

RAMBERT, MARIE, *Quicksilver* (London, 1972). Dame Marie's autobiography and description of the work of her company to that date.

SHEAD, RICHARD, *Constant Lambert* (London, 1973). A biography of the man who shaped the musical policy of the (now) Royal Ballet. With a memoir by Anthony Powell.

VAUGHAN, DAVID, *Frederick Ashton and His Ballets* (London, 1977). The definitive and meticulously documented study of Britain's greatest choreographer.

WALKER, KATHRINE SORLEY, *Ninette de Valois: Idealist Without Illusions* (London, 1987). An account of the career of one of the most remarkable women of our time. With delightful and illuminating contributions from Dame Ninette herself.

WALKER, KATHRINE SORLEY, AND SARAH C. WOODCOCK, *The Royal Ballet: A Picture History* (London, 1981; revised edition, 1986). Originally a companion to Alexander Bland's history, but now updated and a delightful book in its own right.

WOODCOCK, SARAH C., *The Sadler's Wells Royal Ballet – Now the Birmingham Royal Ballet* (London, 1991). The history of the Royal Ballet's younger sister company, founded by Ninette de Valois when the Sadler's Wells Ballet moved to Covent Garden.

Chapter 8

AMBERG, GEORGE, *Ballet in America: The Emergence of an American Art* (New York, 1949; London, 1955). A general survey with a useful chronology and checklists.

BANES, SALLY, *Terpsichore in Sneakers: Post-Modern Dance* (Boston, 1980). An excellent survey of the pioneers of what came to be known as post-modern dance.

CHUJOY, ANATOLE, *The New York City Ballet* (New York, 1952). The full story of the Kirstein–Balanchine enterprise up to its first visits to London.

COHEN, SELMA JEANNE, *Doris Humphrey: an Artist First* (Middletown, Conn., 1972). An autobiography edited and completed by Selma Jeanne Cohen with an introduction by John Martin and foreword by Charles Humphrey Woodford. Contains a chronology of Humphrey's works. *The Modern Dance: Seven Statements of Belief* (Middleton, Conn., 1966). Seven major choreographers discuss their beliefs.

CROCE, ARLENE, *Afterimages* (New York, 1977). *Going to the Dance* (New York, 1982). *Sight Lines* (New York, 1987). Collected reviews by the most brilliant and influential dance critic of our time.

CUNNINGHAM, MERCE, *Merce Cunningham* (New York, 1975). James Klosty's superb photographs capture the essence of Cunningham choreography.

CUNNINGHAM, MERCE, AND JACQUELINE LESSCHAEVE, *Dancer and the Dance* (New York and London, 1985). Cunningham talks not only about his work and his dance pieces but also about his collaborations with musicians and painters, although he stresses they are three separate elements, 'each central to itself'. Contains a chronological list of his choreographies.

DENBY, EDWIN, *Dance Writings* (New York, 1986). Collected reviews from the 1930s onwards of the distinguished critic who was also a poet and revered by all who knew him.

KIRSTEIN, LINCOLN, *Three Pamphlets Collected* (New York, 1967). The three pamphlets are 'Blast at Ballet' (1937), 'Ballet Alphabet' (1939) and 'What Ballet is all About' (1959). They reflect Kirstein's personal opinions and his fight to establish an American school of classic dance. *Thirty Years: The New York City Ballet* (New York, 1978).

MAZO, JOSEPH, *Prime Movers: The Makers of Modern Dance in America* (New York, 1977).

MCDONAGH, DON, *The Rise and Fall and Rise of Modern Dance* (New York, 1970). *The Complete Guide to Modern Dance* (New York, 1976). The two books cover the period since the 1950s. *The Complete Guide* contains a chronology from 1862 to 1975.

PAYNE, CHARLES, *American Ballet Theatre* (New York, 1978). A lavish pictorial record with a commentary by the man who produced the company's souvenir programmes.

REYNOLDS, NANCY, *Repertory in Review: Forty Years of the New York City Ballet* (New York, 1977). A detailed account of the repertory, well illustrated and with critical assessments of the productions. Indispensable.

SEROFF, VICTOR, *The Real Isadora* (London, 1972). Written by the man who helped Isadora Duncan with her autobiography, *My Life*. To be read in conjunction with Ilya Ilyitch Schneider's book *Isadora Duncan: The Russian Years* (London, 1968; New York, 1969).

TAPER, BERNARD, *Balanchine* (New York, 1963; London, 1964; latest edition, 1984). The definitive biography, expanded from a brilliant profile written for the *New Yorker*.

Chapter 9

BELLEW, HELEN, *Ballet in Moscow Today* (London, 1956; New York, 1957). Written by the former dancer Hélène Kirsova to coincide with the first visit of the Bolshoy Ballet to the West, it describes the repertory at that time.

GRIGOROVICH, YURI, AND V. VANSLOV, *Bolshoi Ballet* (Neptune City, New Jersey, 1984). A lavish picture book with a short text and brief notes on the theatre and the repertory. Takes the story to *The Golden Age* and the Grigorovich production of *Raymonda* in 1984.

MANCHESTER, P. W., AND IRIS MORLEY, *The Rose and the Star: Ballet in England and Russia Compared* (London, 1949; New York, 1950). A discussion between two enthusiasts about the respective merits of British and Soviet ballet.

ROSLAVLEVA, NATALIA, *Era of the Russian Ballet* (London, 1966; New York, 1966). An excellent history, well illustrated, giving the Soviet view of what happened in the past and what ballet is trying to do today.

SLONIMSKY, YURI, *The Soviet Ballet* (New York, 1947, latest edition, 1970). A collection of essays by various authors on aspects of ballet and folk dance in the USSR.

SOURITZ, ELIZABETH, *Soviet Choreographers in the 1920s* (London, 1990). The distinguished ballet historian Elizabeth Souritz published this book in Russia in 1979 when various constraints were imposed, and she had no opportunity to update and revise her text for this translation. Nevertheless, it is an important book which provides much insight into Soviet thinking about key figures of the period.

SWIFT, MARY GRACE, *The Art of the Dance in the USSR* (Notre Dame, Indiana, 1968). A careful and well-documented analysis of how ballet survived under the Soviet regime and how it has been used there for political as well as artistic purposes.

Chapter 10

GADAN, FRANCIS, AND ROBERT MAILLARD (EDS.), *Dictionary of Modern Ballet* (New York, 1959; London, 1959). Not really a dictionary but a collection of entries arranged in alphabetical order. The illustrations, many in colour, are delightful and give a particularly good idea of the renaissance of French ballet after the Second World War.

GRUT, MARINA, *The History of the Ballet in South Africa* (Cape Town, Pretoria and Johannesburg, 1981). From the early years of the nineteenth century until today. Well illustrated and documented.

PERCIVAL, JOHN, *Modern Ballet* (London, 1970; New York, 1970). A picture book that illustrates the contemporary scene as it was in 1970. *Experimental Dance* (London, 1972; New York, 1971). Largely compiled from interviews with contemporary choreographers. It sets out their views on dance and is well illustrated. *Theatre in My Blood: a Biography of John Cranko* (New York, 1983; London, 1983). An excellent, sympathetic account of a career cut tragically short in 1973.

Index

Note: Where reference is to an illustration only, the page number (of the caption) is given in *italics*.